The Morality of Spending

New Studies in American Intellectual and Cultural History

Thomas Bender, Consulting Editor

The Morality of Spending

Attitudes toward the Consumer
Society in America, 1875–1940

Daniel Horowitz

The Johns Hopkins University Press
Baltimore and London

This book has been brought to publication with the
generous assistance of the Andrew W. Mellon Foundation.

The Johns Hopkins University Press, 701 West 40th Street,
Baltimore, Maryland 21211
The Johns Hopkins Press Ltd, London

The paper in this book is acid-free and meets the guidelines for permanence and
durability of the Committee on Production Guidelines for Book Longevity of the
Council on Library Resources.

Library of Congress Cataloging in Publication Data

Horowitz, Daniel.
    The morality of spending.

  (New studies in American intellectual and cultural history)
  Includes index.
    1. Consumption (Economics)—United States—History.
2. Consumers—United States—History.   3. Consumption
(Economics)—United States—Moral and ethical aspects—
History.   4. Intellectuals—United States—Attitudes—
History.   5. Social reformers—United States—Attitudes—
History.   I. Title.   II. Series.
HC110.C6H58   1985   339.4′7′0973   84-27851
ISBN 0-8018-2530-X (alk. paper)

With admiration and love to

Miriam and William Horowitz
and
Helen Lefkowitz Horowitz

Contents

Contents

List of Tables

Preface

In the early 1970s, when I began to think seriously about how Americans viewed questions raised by the standard of living, I started to read what late-nineteenth-century writers had to say about changing patterns of consumption. Before too long, I grew curious about what they meant when they spoke of profligacy and self-indulgence. So I turned to household budget studies. However, I found in these investigations the same attitudes toward the spending habits of workers and immigrants that appeared in sermons and advice literature. The parallels prompted me to think about the language Americans have used to discuss consumption, especially the persistence of a moral vision that emphasized the dangers of decadence, the loss of self-control, and the desirability of nonmaterialistic pursuits.

Although moralism is a central concern in this book, at the outset I should make clear that there is nothing per se wrong with moralism—moral outrage, judgmental positions, and an attempt to persuade others to follow one's own truth are essential components of a vital social critique of American society. Initially, I accepted without question much of the argument of what I have come to understand as the modern moralist position. Since then, I have hardly had a conversion experience. In fact, I consider this book a critique of a view of consumption that I still hold to a considerable extent. However, over time I came to see a number of things, including the parallels between a modern moralism and a more traditional one. Moralism itself, its changing animus and configurations, became the object of my inquiry. In one version or another, modern moralism is so commonly adopted by social critics and social scientists that we do not have a full understanding of its emergence in a specific cultural and historical setting. Moreover, several things came to trouble me about what I take to be the modern moralist position, including its contrast between an "authentic" culture of those unaffected by consumerism and a corrupted culture of the middle class.

Some people who read this book will doubtlessly see it as an apologia for materialism and extravagant consumption. However, this book does not advocate the blind acceptance of commercial goods and experiences, but it reminds us that throughout history people have responded to new goods in certain, now-predictable ways. I do not doubt that advertisers, social scientists, corporate executives, and the economic system to a very considerable degree have established the framework within which people, including consumers, have lived their lives. As consumers, however, ordinary people have not simply accepted what the economy offers on the terms that moralists, advertisers, psychologists, and industrialists have assumed. Consumer society did not obliterate an older America based on friendship, workplace, family, religion, ethnicity, region, and social class. People make meaning in their lives in a complex manner, bringing to their consumption of commercial goods and experiences the expectations and values that stem at least as much from their own lives and background as from what elites tell them to feel and do. Obviously, not all Americans have equal power—and relatively small numbers of people have been able to shape the world of the less powerful.

Thus consumer culture is not imposed by external forces, nor is it a spontaneous expression of the aspirations of ordinary people. Rather, a more reciprocal model best explains how consumption has achieved such a significant role in our lives. Consumer culture is a complicated phenomenon whose arrival and growth have involved a struggle in which some powerful people and institutions have tried to impose their vision of a good society. Recipients have responded by purchasing (or not purchasing) goods and experiences, to which they have given meaning derived to a considerable extent from their own personal, social, and cultural histories.

Since the late nineteenth century, many American intellectuals and social scientists have had difficulty seeing or acknowledging this point. Many still do. This inquiry, which is an intellectual history of attitudes toward consumption and not a social history of mass behavior, seeks to understand how American social thinkers have treated changes in the standard of living.

Acknowledgments

Nonmarket exchanges were among the items that most household budget studies did not adequately record. Had they wished to note the kinds of gifts an author receives, experts would have placed them under Miscellaneous. Though less essential than food, clothing, and shelter, assistance with a project like this is one of those higher and nobler endeavors so dear to the hearts of budget professionals. In writing this book, I have benefited from a great amount of such benevolence and this is the place where I can begin to repay in kind.

I did most of the research for this project at the libraries of the Claremont Colleges. I am especially indebted to Ruth Palmer, who arranged to have other libraries send what was not at hand. I also carried out significant portions of the research elsewhere and am grateful to the librarians at the University of California—Los Angeles, the Huntington Library, the University of Michigan, and the National Humanities Center. Among the others who helped with sources and questions are Robert H. Irrmann of Beloit College; J.R.K. Kantor of the University of California at Berkeley; Joanne Shafer of Alumnae House at Vassar College; Ruth Halloran of Alumni Affairs at the University of Chicago; Steven W. Gelston of the Center for the Study of the Consumer Movement; the librarians at the Manuscript Division of the Library of Congress, the Manuscript and Archives Division of the New York Public Library, the Archives at the University of Pennsylvania, and the State Historical Society of Wisconsin; Joseph Howerton at the National Archives; Martha Clark at the Archives of the Massachusetts State House; Edmond Dwyer at the Russell Sage Foundation; James E. Cyphers and Joseph W. Ernst at the Rockefeller Archive Center; Dennis Daellenbach at the Gerald R. Ford Presidential Library; Susan Gleason of the Sarah Lawrence College Library; and Judith A. Schiff at Manuscripts and Archives of Yale University.

The following people shared their work, read some of mine, or helped in other important ways: Robert H. Abzug, Naomi Aronson, Michael A. Bernstein, Alfred M. Bingham, Geraldine Clifford, Robert Dawidoff, Fay E. Dudden, Sarah Elbert, Anita C. Fellman, Michael Fellman, Marcus K. Felson, Daniel M. Fox, Richard W. Fox, Robert E. Gallman, Charles A. Goldsmid, Herbert Gutman, Morris B. Holbrook, Diane O. Hughes, Stuart B. Kaufman, David M. Kennedy, James Leiby, William Matthews, Char Miller, William T. Moye, Scott Nearing, Richard M. Ohmann, David Riesman, Ralph G. Ross, Steven J. Ross, Peter E. Samson, Ronald W. Schatz, Michael Schudson, Carole Shammas, David E. Shi, Norman I. Silber, Carl Siracusa, Robert Sklar, Judith Smith, David P. Thelen, Robert B. Westbrook, Rexford G. Tugwell, and Jeffrey G. Williamson.

I have used portions of this book in courses, and the students at the Claremont Colleges, Carleton College, and the University of Michigan responded with suggestions and questions. I am especially indebted to Kirk Jeffrey, Clifford E. Clark, Jr., Michael P. Zuckert, and Catherine Zuckert, who made my stay at Carleton College both pleasurable and productive, and to David and Joan Hollinger, who did likewise at the University of Michigan. Martin Burke and Christine Weideman listened to my lectures at the University of Michigan and offered important criticisms.

At various stages the following people read portions of what I had written and responded generously with criticism: Hal S. Barron, Daniel W. Howe, Kenneth S. Lynn, David W. Marcell, John Modell, Richard Rabinowitz, and Sarah Stage. I owe a special debt of gratitude to Cushing Strout who first sparked my interest in intellectual history. At a critical juncture Joyce Appleby's support and assistance were especially important. I came to know John P. Diggins when he led a National Endowment for the Humanities Summer Seminar in 1976 and he has continued to offer encouragement and advice. At a number of points, Richard D. Brown helped as only a person who is both a friend and a scholar can. Joseph Suarez made working with a computer seem simple. Susan Freeman transformed much of my prose in an early draft from paper to disk. William Horowitz and Elizabeth Lane helped check footnotes. As editor of the *Journal of American History*, Lewis Perry skilfully helped bring a version of chapter 3 into print.

A National Endowment for the Humanities Younger Humanist Fellowship for 1973 made it possible for me to begin work on this project; a faculty research grant from Scripps College supported duplication of material and travel to libraries; and a fellowship from the National Humanities Center provided an ideal setting for putting on the final touches.

I benefited from the hard work, tough questions, and generous help of the following people, who gave the manuscript exceptionally full, insightful, and critical readings: Roger D. Abrahams, Gordon Bjork, Thomas

Dublin, Ira Gang, Helen Lefkowitz Horowitz, Roy Rosenzweig, Dorothy R. Ross, Frank Stricker, John L. Thomas, Laurence R. Veysey, Maris A. Vinovskis, and Daniel J. Walkowitz. In copy-editing the manuscript, Ann E. Petty helped me clarify what I was trying to say. Thomas Bender and Henry Y. K. Tom helped me strengthen the manuscript and turn it into a book.

Support and encouragement from my family enabled me to sustain myself and my work. Miriam and William Horowitz continually demonstrated their pride in their son the historian. Sarah Esther Horowitz and Benjamin Horowitz helped me on the computer, provided comic relief, and reminded me that there were things in this world more important than completing the book. Finally, Helen Lefkowitz Horowitz not only shared food, clothing, and shelter but also made challenging and rewarding what some budget experts considered the other and less essential aspects of life.

Introduction

Is there a connection between a high standard of living and social illness? In *The Cultural Contradictions of Capitalism* (1976) the sociologist Daniel Bell warned of the consequences of the emergence of a consumer culture in the United States. "By the 1950s," he argued, American "culture was no longer concerned with how to work and achieve." Instead it "had become primarily hedonistic, concerned with play, fun, display, and pleasure—and, typical of things in America, in a compulsive way." For Bell, the tensions between an economy built on efficiency, a polity based on equality, and a culture that uses consumption to achieve "self-realization" or "self-gratification" threaten to tear apart the society. Similarly, in *The Culture of Narcissism* (1978) Christopher Lasch wrote of advertising's power to create "the consumer, perpetually unsatisfied, restless, anxious, and bored." Advertising "upholds consumption as the answer to the age-old discontents of loneliness, sickness, weariness, lack of sexual satisfaction; at the same time it creates new forms of discontent peculiar to the modern age." Though advertising "'educates' the masses into an unappeasable appetite not only for goods but for new experiences and personal fulfillment," ultimately it leaves people dissatisfied.[1]

The definition of consumption as a social problem is an old story and not an exclusively American one. Concern about the moral consequences of new patterns of consumption has persisted with remarkable tenacity from early in our history. From New England Puritans of the seventeenth century to contemporary social scientists, Americans have worried about the self-indulgence of consumers and the consequences of comfort, affluence, and luxury. Moralists have argued that a rising or changing standard of living endangered the health of America. Hostile to commercialism and supposedly corrupt kinds of leisure, they have advocated a combination of hard work, self-control, social concern, pursuit of Culture, and genuine forms of recreation. As the American economy grew and more people experienced affluence, censorious observers hoped that citizens would turn to "higher," nonmaterialistic goals.

Focusing primarily on the years from 1875 to 1940, this book traces the development of such misgivings. Drawing on the work of household budget experts and of a selected group of social critics and social scientists, it argues that from the nineteenth century to the present, different versions of moralism influenced the stance that many Americans have taken toward an improved standard of living.[2] Moralists have judged problematic the spending habits of their contemporaries. Again and again, commentators have worried about threats that profligacy, extravagance, materialism, and affluence pose to American society. Reflecting their own ethnic and class perspectives, writers have attacked the consumption patterns of others. They have seen changed patterns of living as a blessing and a curse: a blessing because greater wealth promised to improve the lot of millions of Americans; a curse because affluence threatened to infect and weaken the society.

Over time, a number of important changes occurred within this dominant moralistic vision. Although writers of the late nineteenth and early twentieth centuries persisted in fearing the moral consequences of new patterns of household spending, some of them saw an increasing level of comfort as a positive good. Changed economic conditions weakened, but never destroyed the moral vision used to judge the way people spent their money. For centuries, people have simultaneously welcomed and questioned the value of new consumer goods and services.

As concerns about the moral consequences of consumption persisted, among many budget professionals and social critics the primary focus of attention shifted from one kind of moralism to another. Throughout the nineteenth century and into the early twentieth century budget experts, reformers, and social thinkers remained fearful about the profligacy of workers and immigrants. For those who held this conservative or traditional moralist position, alcohol consumption and expressive ethnic traditions demonstrated a lack of self-control. In contrast stood the virtues of "respectable" people: hard work, plain living, and the belief in the uplifting power of Culture. Although the tone and content of conservative moralism changed over a long period, what persisted was a censorious attitude to the habits of workers and immigrants and a righteous belief in the superiority of the bourgeois way of life. Around World War I, modern or twentieth-century moralists drew up a new agenda that was both similar to and different from the older response. To them, mass commercialized consumption affected the entire society, but especially the middle class. Critics then argued that an expansive capitalist system produced movies, automobiles, and advertising that helped transform America into a nation of conforming, indulgent, and passive people. Those who maintained folk traditions, social critics believed, might successfully resist the deleterious impact of mass culture and sustain the vitality of their own distinctive way of life. In addition, writers honored intellectuals and artists who rejected mass culture and lived their lives based on a combination of sophistication and passion.

Even though conservative and modern moralism differed in fundamental ways, they shared certain similarities. Both feared that the lack of self-control would turn the nation toward materialism. Both responses were anticommercial, especially regarding recreation and leisure. Both believed that pleasures purchased in the marketplace were compensation for personal and cultural failures. Finally, both called for aspiration to goals higher than the pursuit of mundane and false pleasures. Indeed, the parallels are significant enough to suggest that the language used by generations of Americans to talk about the implications of consumer culture has shown considerable continuity. To a great extent, social critics have seen important elements of a higher standard of living as problematic, corrupting, and enervating.

To deepen an understanding of the ways observers have thought about changing consumption patterns, I examined several landmark household budget studies published between 1875 and the late 1930s. During this period investigators collected information on how millions of Americans reported spending their money. One of the unanticipated pleasures in researching this book was to discover and read published reports of how Americans spent their money in documents that reveal intimate details of people's lives. Some of the sources contained only numbers. In others, especially those published in middle-class magazines, consumers spoke directly to the readers and told of their successes and failures. Through household budgets one enters a world that is always fascinating, frequently tragic, and occasionally humorous. Though a work of intellectual history, this book brings together several topics whose treatment has usually remained separate: the social, economic, and intellectual aspects of consumption.[3] It insists on the benefit of exploring the interplay between the related stories of how Americans spent their money and how writers thought they should. The juxtaposition of data and advice enables us to see how changes in the standard of living prompted reconsiderations of the dilemmas of affluence, as well as how attitudes toward spending shaped the investigations.

There is a striking and important similarity between many of the assumptions behind these budget studies and the social criticism of consumption. My own approach is to use investigations of household expenditures in several ways but first of all as cultural artifacts that enable us to understand what was on the minds of those who made the reports. Thus what follows is not primarily a history of the standard of living or of the transformation of America into a consumer culture. Rather it is above all an exploration of the attitudes of writers to the dilemmas and opportunities of the phenomena they witnessed. Though I suggest some conclusions that emerge from changing expenditure patterns, more central to my story is the meaning that a variety of observers gave to what they believed was going on about them in stores, households, parks, and theaters. The household budget studies are rich reservoirs of information that historians are only now beginning to tap. Once more fully regained as sources, analysis of the data can sharpen the debate over when the United States became a consumer culture; help reveal the changing styles of life of different social and ethnic groups; enable us to chart more precisely the development of a market economy; make it possible enhance the examination of the contributions of husbands, wives, and children to the family economy; and shed light on the balance between defensive and acquisitive patterns of spending.

Though this book reaches back to the antebellum years, my main focus is on the period from 1875 to 1940. In four ways, this was an important time in the budget study tradition and in the response of American social critics. At the beginning of the last quarter of the nineteenth century Americans first systematically collected data on budgets of working-class households. In the early twentieth century, experts began to make available samples of expenditure patterns of middle-class families. Secondly, by the 1920s, even though by twentieth-century standards many Americans did not yet lead affluent and comfortable lives, the main outlines of modern consumer culture had taken shape. Thirdly, during the late nineteenth and early twentieth centuries, the implications and challenges of a consumer society became a major and sustained concern of American social critics. Finally, during the first thirty years of the new century the shift from traditional to modern moralism occurred.

The sources for a social and intellectual history of consumption in America are immense, and this study does not pretend to accomplish the seemingly impossible goals of comprehensiveness and representativeness. After extensive general reading, I chose to focus on writers for whom the issues discussed in this study were a major and sustained preoccupation. Moreover, I gravitated to people and issues I found puzzling, compelling, or fascinating. Moving as it does into new areas at a number of points, this book is more exploratory than definitive. But even though the material on which this study relies is hardly inclusive, I hope readers will find that the book has broad implications for some important aspects of how Americans have come to terms with consumer culture. Perhaps my work will stimulate others to take up where I have left off and write about the many people and issues I have not covered. Most importantly, we need to know more about the meaning consumption and spending had for workers and immigrants. I treat attitudes toward workers and immigrants, not the responses of these groups themselves. Moreover, I have not given the needed attention to a number of groups for whom struggling with or celebrating affluence was a major activity—psychologists, ministers, economists, industrialists, novelists, and politicians.

Similarly, with studies of household budgets published since 1875 I have selected key examples from the many reports on how families—mostly of the working class and lower middle class—spent their money. I have focused mainly on intact, urban, nuclear families with fully employed husbands between the ages of twenty and fifty-five because most studies collected data on households of this type and writers worried most about them. Yet even though budgets are important and often neglected sources, they can hardly tell us all we want to know about patterns of consumption. Obviously, census records, production statistics, advertisements, material artifacts, letters, diaries, and other sources can fill out the picture. Moreover, budgets containing only numbers do not easily tell us how spenders felt about what they bought and cannot measure many important dimensions of the quality of life in America.

As the following summary of scholarship demonstrates, the United States has become a nation of modern consumers through a complicated, uneven, and long-term process.[4] This transformation is part of a more general change, that from a traditional to a modern economy and culture. Some historians debate the value of the dichotomy between premodern and modern societies, and question (wrongly, I think) whether America ever was in any significant way a traditional society. Yet as ideal types these concepts remain useful. A traditional or preindustrial culture rests on religious, ethical, and communal values and institutions that restrain individualism and materialism. The commercial or market economy—and its accompanying mentality and acquisitiveness—remains subordinate. Traditional societies perceive history as static or circular, rather than progressive.

The transformation of Western culture from preindustrial to industrial was neither continuous nor uniform. Some of the first significant challenges to the traditional world view came at least as early as the seventeenth century. By the late 1600s in the Anglo-American world there emerged the ideological origins of an economic theory emphasizing the beneficial effects upon production of a free market, acquisitive instincts, and a rising standard of living. The critical shifts—from the sacred to the profane, from the communal and moral explanations for and sanctions of people's behavior to the individual and economic—were nonetheless far from complete in seventeenth-century England. In America, even on the eve of the Revolution, the market system and its related ideology had hardly triumphed.

Between 1800 and 1840 the balance between preindustrial and modern impulses shifted in the United States. Economic and cultural forces gathered enough strength to bring into play many of the elements critical in the formation of a modern society. There emerged a personality type built around ambition, a sense that time was money, and an appreciation of progress. Materialistic and individualistic ideologies found legitimization. Institutions arose that had the ability to mold disciplined workers and market-oriented consumers. Two related phenomena central to the transformation of traditional society and the full development of industrial capitalism appeared over a long period. First, industrialists, ministers, and reformers tried to persuade labor to accept industrial discipline. Secondly, advertisers, business representatives, and social scientists encouraged consumers to believe in mass-produced commodities and mass culture as the principal means of satisfaction outside work or substitutes for the pleasures of meaningful labor.

Industrial capitalism transformed the nature of work in the United States during the last two centuries. In preindustrial communities, natural rhythms to a considerable extent governed human effort. No sharp division separated work and leisure. People performed a wide range of nonspecialized tasks. Labor and family life were intertwined in an elaborate network of place, tasks, and time. Climate, season, and the pace and organization of economic activity combined to make labor an intense, sporadic experience. Obviously there were no good old days when life was easy. The daily round of activity lacked neither pains nor pleasures. In England during the eighteenth century and in the United States during the nineteenth, a number of forces began to change radically the nature of everyday life. Ministers, reformers, and industrialists, on occasion joined by representatives of elite groups of workers, sought to inculcate discipline in laborers. These groups saw preindustrial habits as wasteful, disorderly, and immoral and instead advocated a modern work ethic that emphasized sobriety, thrift, time-consciousness, and discipline. To these advocates, work could become a commodity, something measured in hours and dollars, thereby losing its justification as craft, creativity, religious exercise, or expression of familial and communal relations.[5]

Connected and equally important changes occurred in the nature of leisure pursuits. In preindustrial times most people enjoyed themselves in activities, such as festivals and celebrations, that were spirited, uninhibited, participatory, communal, and not bound by a sense of clock time. Not necessarily identifying happiness with an increase of material comforts, ordinary people did not seek satisfactions through marketable commodities. Much of this changed over the last two hundred years. The long transformation from preindustrial to industrial kinds of nonwork activities involved the weakening of opposition to the supposed extravagance of laborers and the strengthening of the expectation of continual material advance. Especially in the twentieth century, as psychological needs replaced more tangible ones and as time and money grew more important, leisure became something to be "spent," rather than a playful activity sporadically and intensely enjoyed. Nonwork endeavors took place, in turn, in saloons, parks, stadiums, and most recently in department stores and in front of television sets. Modern capitalism has tried to discipline people's labor and consumption. In contemporary society, with the shortening of the workweek and the expansion of living quarters, leisure and consumption have become both more commercial and more private. The family, once the center of production, in the late twentieth century is the center of consumption.

Influential representatives of the middle class and of the business community eventually realized the importance of matching mass production with mass consumption. In order to achieve this coordination, self-controlled savers and exhausted, disciplined workers had to become consumers. In part, advertising took on the task of creating the kind and level of consumption that provided a market for the commodities produced by industrial capitalism. Faced with excess productive capacity, industrialists and others realized that as consumers, workers should not be self-denying. More than that, modern mass culture became the instrument through which capitalism tried to control many aspects of people's lives, an effort that was not always fully successful. In the twentieth century, commodity consumption emerged as a way of life, a basic force that shaped American culture. People sought fulfillment through commercial goods and experiences. However, the kinds of satisfaction achievable through mass-produced commodities and commercialized leisure—though in some ways relying on a vision of the worker as extravagant consumer—hardly resembled those of preindustrial life. The lure of consumption threatened to obliterate public life and any possibility of radical social change. Disciplined workers enjoying truly free time and exhilarating nonwork experiences found they had to contend with pressures for increased productivity and regularized kinds of consumption. The cultural apparatus of mass media and commercial consumption, scholars have argued, urged people to spend "spare" time in mass (but not communal), passive, and ultimately unfulfilling nonwork pursuits.

Together the disciplining of the work force and the advent of mass consumption helped transform the economy of the United States from an agrarian and commercial one based on communal values and natural forces to one rooted in the world of modern capitalism and commercial consumption. Admittedly, the process was uneven, especially in the United States. With wave after wave of immigrants entering the country, the forces of industrialization impinged on a variety of groups at different times and in distinctive ways. Nonetheless, history transformed one world into another. Politics, religion, personality, family life, culture (in the anthropological and high Culture senses), and the forms and impact of economic institutions underwent fundamental changes in the process.

When did the United States become a consumer society? According to the new social history of the standard of living, in the Anglo-American world well before the nineteenth century there emerged a pattern of mass commodity consumption for the middle class and, in many instances, those below them. As early as the late sixteenth century but certainly from the late seventeenth century to the late eighteenth century, a substantial number of families in England and America began to buy mass-produced and commercially marketed consumer goods. Concerning the late sixteenth and the seventeenth centuries in England, one historian has written of the forces that "heralded the development of a consumer society that . . . included humble peasants, labourers, and servants," a world where manufacturers produced and consumers bought utensils for cooking and eating, sewing materials, clothes, and toys.[6] Referring to the years after 1670, J. H. Plumb has remarked on "the growth of a middle-class audience—not a mass audience by our standards"—for newspapers, books, theater, music, dancing, sport, and casual shopping.[7]

On the American side of the Atlantic, the most thorough exploration of these patterns points toward similar conclusions. Carole Shammas has discussed a wide range of commodities, mostly furniture and tableware, that encouraged domesticity and that by the middle of the eighteenth century "laboring class households readily purchased." As the wealth of colonial families grew, "the value of their consumer goods steadily increased proportionally."[8] Though stressing the inequality of wealth and the functional quality of most possessions, Alice H. Jones has written of the "substantial size and character of wealth in consumers' goods" among free colonists on the eve of the Revolution. "By the late 1750s," Lois G. Carr and Lorena S. Walsh have concluded, "items of comfort and convenience," such as furniture, tableware, and household utensils, "had ceased to be luxuries, being commonly found in middling as well as wealthy households, and increasingly at the bottom too." Indeed, they argued that among other factors "the kinds of possessions that people surrounded themselves with . . . were no longer part of 'the world we have lost,' but were well on the way to becoming something we can recognize."[9] In short, by the late eighteenth century, Western society had many markings of a modern consumer culture. People sought nonessential goods, entrepreneurs provided a profusion of new commodities, material possessions became a way of dramatizing social status, and the vision of an increased standard of living spread through most ranks of society.

The emergence of a consumer society continued in the Anglo-American world during the decades after 1760, albeit at an uneven pace. So fundamental were the changes that a group of British historians has argued that the period saw the "birth of a consumer society." Pointing to a "consumer revolution," Neil McKendrick has stated that "the later eighteenth century saw such a convulsion of getting and spending, such an eruption of new prosperity, and such an explosion of new production and marketing techniques, that a greater proportion of the population than in any previous society in human history was able to enjoy the pleasures of buying consumer goods." The "propensity to consume," he concluded, was "unprecedented in the depth to which it penetrated the lower reaches of society." Offering items such as tableware and linen goods, the new consumer economy reached below the middle class and went "as far as the skilled factory worker and the domestic servant class." Similarly, another British historian has written that in the same period in England there came "into being the first society dedicated to ever-expanding consumption based on industrial production."[10]

Roughly parallel patterns obtained for the United States, often at a later time. In the third of a century before the Civil War, members of the American middle class became more serious consumers. "The evidence of material culture," according to one historian, "demonstrates a great expansion of consumer goods aimed at a middle-class market in the decades after 1830—ever more elaborate fashions, furniture, decorative arts, carpeting, china, glassware, even 'collectibles,' manufactured in the expectation of selling not one but many nonessentials."[11] In the first half of the nineteenth century, the middle class faced a greatly expanded choice of consumer goods, many of them produced commercially for a mass market. In the same years, the wealthy in the United States were as extravagant as their European counterparts. The situation of the vast majority of Americans who lived between poverty and wealth—many farmers, artisans, and laborers—varied considerably. The most fortunate among them—those helped by such things as continuous employment, a good crop yield, good health, favorable wage rates, or the earnings of several members of the family—enjoyed some of the choices and comforts available to members of the middle class. The initial improvements came in food, clothing, home furnishings, and shelter. For others whose situation was not so favorable, life was harsh and consumer choices few.

By the Civil War, many ordinary Americans entered the commercial marketplace to purchase mass-produced clothing, furniture, and items for preparing and consuming food. Before the nineteenth century, millions of Anglo-Americans identified increased comfort and well-being with material possessions. Thus capitalism did not simply force commercial consumption and a higher standard of living on Americans. The birth of a consumer society came earlier than usually assumed and preceded (or was at least coincident with) the most intensive phase of modern industrialization. Thus to understand the well-springs of consumption, we have to look at Americans' desire for comfort, display, communication, and self-improvement, as well as at the economic, institutional, and cultural forces that worked from above.

The fact that most antebellum Americans participated in a consumer economy does not mean that, by our standards, they lived affluently and comfortably. Though the new social history of consumption has located the birth of consumer society in the late eighteenth century, its full elaboration came much later. If we remember a number of things about the standard of living of most Americans before 1860—poor diet, cramped quarters, child labor, lack of adequate sanitation—we realize that commodity consumption does not necessarily mean ease and a sense of material well-being. Technology and economic growth improved the objective conditions of millions of Americans. Yet often when people looked above them, they sensed a greater degree of relative deprivation. Older studies, the new labor history, and standard of living data from a later period remind us of the harsh circumstances of most families. The new consumer culture may have suffused the middle class and even touched the lives of skilled laborers, but perhaps it did not significantly affect the lives of unskilled laborers and their families. The majority of Americans, who spent most of their income on food, clothing, and shelter experienced choice and comfort only to a limited degree.

From 1880 through 1920 the shift from a producer to a consumer culture gained new momentum. As the workweek declined—for factory workers, from approximately sixty-six hours in 1850, to sixty by 1890, and then to fifty-five in 1914—millions of people found themselves with more time for leisure, something increasingly separated from work. Simultaneously, the sheer variety and amount of goods increased to an unprecedented extent. The role of advertising changed from providing unembellished information to surrounding products with more compelling qualities than they inherently had. Department stores and catalogues turned a series of local markets into integrated, national ones, a phenomenon connected with the development and proliferation of name brands. Institutions of commercial leisure—saloons, amusement parks, vaudeville, sports—overturned the expectation that leisure uplifted and refined. Entrepreneurs comprehended the potential of a market for mass culture, which the movie industry capitalized on in the early twentieth century.

Some of these changes in American life were not entirely new. However, they gained a new power around the turn of the century. In the late nineteenth century a shift started from self-control to self-realization, from the world of the producer, based on the values of self-denial and achievement, to a consumer culture that emphasized immediate satisfaction and the fulfillment of the self through gratification and indulgence. This change from the sanctions of religion to those of personality involved the increasing identification of happiness with pleasure.[12]

According to some scholars, "an emerging therapeutic ethos of self-realization," "the therapeutic sensibility," or "the triumph of the therapeutic" involved the substitution of "the image of the needy person, permanently engaged in the task of achieving a gorgeous variety of satisfactions" for traditionally moral and religious kinds of self-control.[13] What filled the void left by the weakening of religious and moral imperatives, they argue, was a pervasive sense of the unreality of the self and the attempt to achieve happiness through the false pleasure of consumer culture. The economic system, advertisers, psychologists, and even antimaterialistic elites thus promoted a way of life that was ultimately unsatisfactory. In a world where appearances and symbolism took on more weight than goods and experiences themselves, consumers became restless, anxious, and frenetic. Consumption thus became a substitution for compelling moral commitments, engaged political activity, or genuine selfhood.

In pushing back the origin of consumer society to the eighteenth century and its fuller development to the late nineteenth and early twentieth, historians have circumscribed the significance of the 1920s. Yet no one would deny the importance of the decade. Automobiles, movies, installment sales, and electric appliances, to varying extents available before World War I, in the decade following made the transition from exotic to ordinary for tens of millions of Americans. Even by the end of the 1920s, however, the triumph of new patterns of consumption was far from complete. A thorough examination of the evidence on wage rates, unemployment, household budgets, and the poverty line reveals that "for the majority of those below the median family income . . . in 1929, security rather than affluence or profligate expenditure lay at the core of the American dream."

Many Americans experienced new levels of comfort and wealth, but for many others, poverty and insecurity marked the 1920s.[14]

In other ways, the new consumer society had not fully arrived and triumphed in the interwar period.[15] Many people who experienced affluence sustained older patterns of thought and action. Despite the intention of capitalists and advertisers to control nearly everything, including consciousness, many Americans tried to use consumer goods on their own terms, in accord with their own cultural traditions and not simply on the terms capitalism offered. Though social critics worried about the triumph of mass culture and commercialism, Americans (including those with a high standard of living) attempted to create meaning in their lives in terms shaped by values that often conflicted with those of consumer culture.[16]

Thus the answer to the question of when America became a consumer society is complicated. In some ways it happened earlier than we have understood; in other ways, later; and in still other ways, never to the degree that some critics envision. Recent scholarship has convincingly demolished the notion of a sudden and late revolution that transformed America into a nation of consumers. The new social history of consumption has demonstrated the critical importance of the late eighteenth century. Then, greater and greater numbers of people (even many below the middle class) encountered goods and experiences in the marketplace; the frenzied pursuit of fashion emerged as a powerful force in the economy; and commercialization suffused many aspects of everyday life. Those American intellectual historians who emphasize the search for therapeutic self-fulfillment and define a culture of consumption in terms of a major shift in values and consciousness locate the beginnings of fundamental changes in the late nineteenth century. Those who have identified this shift in values range from the relatively specific to the vague when they describe whom the new ethos affected. One scholar has pointed to "a broad range of middle and upper class Americans."[17] At other times it seems as if the quest for therapeutic self-realization has come to pervade virtually all of American society.[18] Those who offer this kind of analysis are not always clear as to whether they are speaking of intention or achievement when they describe the power of elites and institutions to foster a consumer culture. Concentrating as they do on consciousness, they stake their claims for the power of consumer culture on what elites said and did, as well as what consumers bought. This view thus begs the critical and even more difficult question of what was on the minds of consumers. Capitalists, advertisers, and psychologists doubtlessly set the ground rules for the game of consumption. On the level of consciousness, to what extent consumers played by those rules is an issue on which there is less than abundant and hardly unanimous evidence. The relationship between seller and buyer may have been more reciprocal than we usually imagine.

In what follows, I do not undertake to reconcile the apparently divergent pictures of the timing and impact of a consumer culture. Rather, I suggest some added dimensions to the story. From the 1870s to the 1930s, budget study professionals and social critics had their own sense of how Americans did and should spend their money. They offered their own version of the good life, a vision that included moral, cultural, and social dimensions. Moreover, the data in the budgets themselves help raise questions about how many Americans spent what proportion of their incomes on acquiring new possessions and experiencing mass culture. Budgets do not allow us to judge expectations or consciousness, but they do help sharpen the argument about when a significant proportion of Americans could afford to become self-indulgent consumers.

The book begins in the 1830s and 1840s, when four observers—Daniel Webster, Francis Wayland, Henry David Thoreau, and Alexis de Tocqueville—articulated some of the principal ways in which early-nineteenth-century Americans wondered about the implications of increased levels of personal and national wealth (chapter 1). Wayland spoke for conservative moralists who worried about the self-indulgence of workers and immigrants and instead hoped people would seek to satisfy "higher" wants, especially benevolence and Culture. Thoreau offered a romantic alternative to refinement and self-control. Tocqueville pointed toward the influence of mass culture. Seeing no contradiction between virtue and materialism, Webster optimistically asserted that affluence solved all moral and social problems.

When these four men wrote, Americans did not have access to systematically collected family budget data. In 1875 Carroll D. Wright, head of the Massachusetts Bureau of Statistics of Labor (MBSL), published the first significant study of working-class household expenditures (chapter 2). His report revealed the importance the budget investigators attached to notions of character and morality. Consequently, the 1875 study tells us as much about how observers thought workers should spend their money as it does about actual patterns of spending. It shows how the MBSL surveyors sought evidence of respectability and worried about working-class and immigrant cultures that stood in opposition to the values of the American-born middle class.

In the late nineteenth and early twentieth centuries, Simon N. Patten, Thorstein Veblen, and George Gunton attempted to reshape conservative moralism to fit new circumstances (chapter 3). Patten sought to connect social reform and self-restraint. Veblen offered a radical alternative that criticized both the dominant tradition and the wealthy. In the course of his life, Gunton shifted from being a labor organizer who articulated a radical moralism to a celebrant of mass consumption and a rising standard of living. Yet even these three writers hoped that Americans might eventually choose something other than materialism. In different ways, Patten, Veblen, and Gunton remained captives of the ruling nineteenth-century moralist tradition.

Studies of household budgets carried out in the Progressive period provide a window through which we can see how authors of budget reports, in moving away from a search for profligate behavior and toward an acceptance of new levels of comfort, further weakened the tradition of conservative moralism (chapter 4). Though many of these studies criticized the working poor for not spending their money properly and only partially appreciated the culture of the lives they surveyed, compared with Carroll D. Wright's work, Progressive reports generally demonstrated a greater sense of the texture of working-class and immigrant life. Aware of their own increasing comforts, some middle-class observers wondered whether traditional moralism allowed them to draw an accurate picture of how the other half lived.

In the ten years beginning in 1906, an initially mild and somewhat sporadic inflation became the focus of middle-class worries (chapters 5 and 6). In the early twentieth century concern about inflation and changing patterns of consumption helped lead to the appearance of the first data on middle-class household expenditures. In the same years emerged two contrasting treatments of middle-class styles of life, neither focused primarily on consumption as therapeutic self-expression. In reasserting the claims of self-control and respectability, traditionalists like Ellen H. Richards articulated the values of the old middle class of farmers, townspeople, and independent entrepreneurs. In opposition, others, such as Martha B. Bruère, rejected excessive prudence and instead called for a mixture of comfort and refinement. Questioning too great an emphasis on self-restraint, advocates of comfort stressed the values usually associated with the new middle class of urbanites and suburbanites, professionals and bureaucratic employees. In moving toward a greater acceptance of new levels of comfort, people like Bruère helped further attenuate older, censorious ways of looking at household expenditures of workers, immigrants, and the middle class.

The inflation between 1917 and 1921, hardly mild when compared with that of the Progressive period, made for confusing debates over the meaning of savings, class relationships, and economic virtue (chapter 7). The attendant resurgence of traditional rhetoric often covered up emerging patterns of consumption. Dramatic price changes led to several budget investigations that in turn became a battleground for conflicting definitions of equity. As a crusade for virtue, the war intensified the commitment to traditional values. In its immediate aftermath, the old shibboleths of prudence and self-control lost their force, at least for many middle-class social thinkers.

During the 1920s and 1930s, a new twentieth-century moralism replaced an earlier conservative one (chapter 8). In these decades, but especially in the 1930s, the budget study tradition lost its critical edge. Changed economic conditions, a greater degree of relativism, recognition of the worker's importance as a consumer, and the Depression itself made budget professionals accept new spending patterns more wholeheartedly. Critics such as Helen M. Lynd, Robert S. Lynd, Stuart Chase, and Alfred M. Bingham turned their attention from workers to the whole society, especially the middle class. They argued that mass, commercial consumption threatened to dominate America. In their hands, the danger of conformity took the place of profligacy. Movies and automobiles succeeded saloons as the enemies of the good life. Where conservative moralists preferred refinement to immigrant and working-class culture, twentieth-century writers typically chose spontaneity and passionate, noncommercial self-expression.

Finally, the book explores the changes and continuities in the ways budget professionals and social critics have understood the dilemmas of a changing standard of living (epilogue). In the nineteenth and twentieth centuries, Americans have used a common but hardly unchanging language to talk about consumption, a language that speaks in terms of the dangers of self-indulgence and commercialism. Critics persisted in hoping that ordinary Americans would aspire to something higher than satisfactions achieved through a materialistic way of life.

The Morality of Spending

1 Consumption in Antebellum Life and Thought

As the economy of the United States developed in the decades before the Civil War, observers of the American scene wondered about the consequences of a changing standard of living. Four writers—Francis Wayland, Henry David Thoreau, Alexis de Tocqueville, and Daniel Webster—articulated positions that would compete for attention throughout the nineteenth and twentieth centuries. As many in the nation began to purchase new mass-produced goods, these four men greeted new patterns of consumption with mixed feelings. Wayland's conservative moralism, Thoreau's romanticism, Tocqueville's fear of mass society, and Webster's optimism would reverberate in future generations.

Francis Wayland (1796–1865) represents a New England tradition that significantly shaped how social thinkers of the nineteenth and twentieth centuries would respond to the arrival of a consumer society. A prominent moral philosopher and educator, Wayland spoke for many a Calvinist heir when he offered advice of unshakeable conventionality, matched only by its somber repetitiousness. For Wayland, individuals faced clear choices in which moral and economic elements were inseparable. Once people satisfied those wants essential to sustaining life and health, he believed, they had a number of alternatives. Self-indulgent individuals would gratify their lower senses by attending shows or eating things that satiated only physical appetites. Others could please their higher senses by tasting the pleasures of music and art, pursuits that resulted in cultivation and refinement. Only intellectual, social, and moral pleasures—exemplified by finer and higher endeavors like benevolence and the pursuit of Culture—satisfied the crucial test of costing little, yet contributing to the improvement of the individual and society.[1]

At every turn, however, temptation lurked, threatening to distract Americans from higher goals. "Thoughtless caprice," "sensual self-indulgence," and "reckless expense" were especially troublesome for those at either end of the social spectrum. By the exercise of industry and frugality,

1

Wayland felt, all able-bodied Americans could obtain basic subsistence and some comfort "without great difficulty." Yet he voiced the familiar refrain that laborers disliked hard work and sober living so much that they would become dependent on society. Fashion might snare laborers when conditions improved. Unrestrained habits of consumption would hurl them back toward poverty and dependence or forward toward a new immorality characterized by imitative extravagance. In either case, attendance at shows or the use of liquor was the best index of the inability to resist things "of which the only result is, the gratification of a physical appetite."[2]

The rich, especially the newly wealthy, had always received special censure from writers like Wayland. At least since the first settlers used sumptuary laws to mitigate the sartorial consequences of social mobility, many Americans have worried that affluence threatened the social order. Concern over the disruptive tendencies of wealth assumed a new urgency for the generation before the Civil War, partly because riches and democracy were increasing. Especially vexing was the possibility that, in a nation without rigid class divisions, the penchant of the wealthy for ostentation would excite the masses to disrupt society. "When the rich are hard-hearted and luxurious," Wayland warned in his exceedingly popular *The Elements of Political Economy* (1837), "the poor are disaffected, anti-social and destructive." Prosperity and democracy without moral leadership meant throwing cultural standards to the wind.[3]

The successful pursuit of wealth, once an outward sign of inward grace, had opened "new avenues to temptation." The exemplary life, marked by hard work and moderate living, threatened to turn Protestant virtues into dangerous vices by unavoidably increasing possibilities for materialism. American Calvinists since John Winthrop had tried to maintain a delicate equilibrium between effort and enjoyment. The balance tipped, Wayland feared, when people did to "excess what can be innocently done only within limits." Increased availability of possessions, however sanctified as private property, had disclosed "opportunities for accumulation clustering thickly just on the other side of the line of perfect rectitude." Once that line was crossed, the "insatiate striving for more" provided a roseate pathway to damnation. Virtue no longer automatically accompanied wealth; little stood in the way of the rampages of selfishness and materialism. Social mobility, hastened by economic development and democratic excesses, threatened to undermine traditional institutions and customs. History would repeat itself as runaway wealth led to the fall of a civilization.[4]

From another quarter of antebellum New England came a more incisive and romantic critique of the American desire for greater material comfort. "It would be some advantage," Henry David Thoreau (1817–62) remarked near the beginning of *Walden* (1854), "to live a primitive and frontier life, though in the midst of an outward civilization, if only to learn what are the gross necessaries of life and what methods have been taken to obtain them." The task he set for himself was clear. He took to the Concord woods to dramatize the advantages of a simple life, one free from the demands of convention. Not fashion and custom but necessity governed what food, clothing, and shelter he sought. His pursuit of an existence of "Spartan simplicity" involved using preindustrial methods to obtain subsistence. By turning away from comforts and commercial relations, he put toil into a small corner of his world, so that he could sample less materialistic pleasures. Although his tone was often mocking when he talked about the lives of ordinary Americans, he acknowledged the real and often insurmountable problems workers faced in trying to live good lives. For him, however, voluntary austerity meant being able to enjoy "true wealth." Simplifying the chores of living, Thoreau proved to his satisfaction "that to maintain one's self on this earth is not a hardship but a pastime."[5]

The standard of living he set for himself was hardly elevated enough to satisfy most of his contemporaries. That, however, was exactly his point. The pursuit of "more," choices of goods and experiences dictated by emulation and fashion, had forced Americans to labor unceasingly. Ironically, he argued, his fellow citizens lessened the quality of their lives by pursuing a higher standard of living. The result, Thoreau felt, was a situation worse than trying to accomplish the labors of Hercules. In order to earn the income necessary to live the way they wanted, most Americans had to perform tasks that provided little intrinsic satisfaction. Even most "games and amusements" concealed "unconscious despair." Nor was philanthropy a worthy endeavor. "Goodness must not be a partial and transitory act," Thoreau remarked, "but a constant superfluity, which costs . . . nothing and of which . . . [the individual] is unconscious." Although few Americans cared to consider it, there was at least one alternative to unending toil caused by a pursuit of greater comforts, false leisure, and benevolence: redefine the notion of necessities, avoid the "superfluities," simplify life, and begin living. In the first quarter of *Walden*, Thoreau looked at the items found in most household budgets and with considerable wit and penetration he demonstrated the relativity of contemporary notions of what was necessary for subsistence and comfort.[6]

The rest of his account described pleasures available to those who could break the hold of convention. His opposition to the accumulation of possessions, to the uncleanliness of commerce, to the accepted distinctions between necessities and luxuries, and to the crippling force of emulation provided a trenchant attack on the way Americans became "so occupied with the factitious cares and superfluously coarse labors of life that its finer fruits cannot be plucked." In contrast, Thoreau envisioned "a poetic or divine life" achieved through individual rebirth and purification. *Walden* described sensual but nonsexual pleasures. Reading, smelling, listening, walking, seeing, and playing provided ways to intensify the experience of wonder and to apprehend the meaning of the universe.[7]

On the surface, Thoreau and Wayland had much in common. They both assumed that it was possible to satisfy basic needs with some work and a great deal of care in spending. The lure of fashion and the desire for superfluous things distracted Americans from the goal of restrained consumption. Wayland argued for what Thoreau's experiment proved: that the "greatest expenses are for those objects, which yield no other utility than the mere gratification of the senses, or, which are rendered necessary, by command or fashion, or the love of ostentation." They both urged their contemporaries to pursue nonmaterialistic goals, to seek ennobling, inexpensive, and rewarding pleasures. For Thoreau and Wayland, the problem of materialism involved more than expense and luxury. It threatened to weaken individual and social vitality. It was corrupting and enervating.[8]

Beneath these common concerns, Thoreau and Wayland were worlds apart on many issues involving consumption. To begin with, they reacted quite differently to the tension between civilization and wealth. Wayland unintentionally straddled the fence. On the one hand, he saw inventions and increased production as central to "the movement of civilization." Unlike Thoreau, Wayland to a considerable extent linked increased consumption with greater individual happiness and national progress. On the other hand, for Wayland the sensual gratifications made possible by industrial growth served only to enervate the body and make thinking distasteful. An increase in the number of articles available for consumption might make people happier; too great an increase or too reckless an indulgence would help undermine an advanced culture. For Wayland, continual exercise of the virtues of hard work and thrift had resulted less in a reaffirmation of grace than in an unending series of temptations. Only the exercise of Christian benevolence or the embrace of Culture and refined consumption kept society from collapse and prevented Wayland from despairing over the outcome of the fight between puritan virtues, civilization, and materialism.[9] For Thoreau, on the other hand, mediating between savagery and civilization was a conscious, constructive strategy. He acknowledged that modern conditions represented an advancement—but only to those who realized that inventions were more than "improved means to an unimproved end." To lead a fulfilled life, civilized people had to appreciate the virtues of savagery.[10]

4

Wayland and Thoreau also differed about the kinds of work and consumption they opposed and the way of life they preferred. Like most nineteenth-century moral reformers, Wayland emphasized disciplined work and leisure. He disliked a group of premodern habits—an unwillingness to labor steadily and an eagerness to consume in what he saw as a licentious, sporadic manner. The temptations to be avoided were not so much the lures of materialism and commercialism as the stimulation of indulgences like alcohol and tobacco. Cultivation, hard work, selflessness—these were the goals of a life of self-restraint. Even Horace Bushnell, who broke new ground in his argument for play as impulsive and expressive, ultimately saw it as elevating and redemptive.[11] Though Thoreau, for reasons different from Wayland's, opposed luxuriousness and materialism, in some ways he was anything but puritanical. *Walden* rejected the Protestant virtues of hard work, steadfast habits, moderate comfort, and restrained feelings and opted instead for intense pleasures achieved not through material comforts but through transcendence. To put his position in more contemporary terms, Thoreau understood that there were two ways to try to achieve a rich life: by systematic restraint in consumption in order to have intense experiences or by the more familiar way of getting involved in an unbroken cycle of exhausting work and fleeting material pleasures that, when not always beyond one's grasp, were more troublesome than they were gratifying.

Few Americans acted on the advice either Thoreau or Wayland offered. The several hundred copies of *Walden* printed in its author's lifetime and the economic transformation of Concord suggest the limits of Thoreau's influence on people's behavior in the nineteenth century. Wayland spoke to but did not necessarily influence the lives of middle-class New Englanders. If neither Thoreau nor Wayland had the satisfaction of convincing substantial numbers of Americans to restrain their desires (an outcome the author of *Walden* denied he even wanted), then why are they important? Thoreau's impact on the imagination of successive generations of Americans was out of proportion to his ability to affect the decisions people made in the marketplace or in the corridors of power. His stance, if not always his direct influence, has remained an important aspect of America's reaction to the prospect of a higher standard of living. In later generations, Americans would follow in his footsteps by turning away from routinized work and commercial consumption, pursuing instead intense, personal pleasures. Ecologically minded citizens continually drew inspiration from Thoreau's example and from his poetic advocacy of respect for Nature.

The case for the importance of Wayland's position rests on somewhat different grounds. As a representative of the Protestant bourgeoisie, he articulated a particularly New England version of conservative moralism that dominated American responses to materialism for at least two centuries, beginning in the early 1700s. He was a moralist because he believed that all social and economic questions were ultimately moral ones, best resolved by having people accept a more righteous way of life. He was conservative because he thought that the way to attack troublesome problems was by exhortation, uplift, and reform aimed at strengthening the character of the poor, rather than by changes in the structure of the society and economy.

Throughout the nineteenth century, traditional moralists like Wayland shaped the framework that many Americans used to interpret changing patterns of consumption. At some point in the middle of the century, Wayland's successors stopped worrying about the profligacy of both the rich and poor and focused principally on immigrants and workers. Rich and poor proved somewhat impervious to their admonitions. However, through their control of publications, pulpits, and cultural institutions, conservative moralists spoke with an authority far greater than their numbers or direct influence might indicate. As ministers, college teachers, reformers, and editors, they had the ability to set the terms that dominated the public discourse on consumption throughout the nineteenth century and, in some cases, up to the present time. Character, corruption, hard work, profligacy, and self-restraint—this was the language that generations of social thinkers would use when they worried about the role of the consumer in American culture.

Somewhat earlier than Wayland and Thoreau, Alexis de Tocqueville (1805–59) provided an analysis of America's love of materialism that was similar to and different from the visions of Wayland and Thoreau. In an aristocracy, the French visitor argued, the wealthy did not fear losing their comforts and therefore could "display a haughty contempt" for worldly pleasures. Similarly, the poor, lacking any sense that their lot on earth might be different from what it was, dreamed of obtaining pleasures in another world. In contrast, Tocqueville argued, in a democracy the poor coveted what they lacked and the rich feared they would lose what they already possessed. Above all, the middle-class "passion for physical comforts" intensified the problem of materialism in the United States. An egalitarian society, by leveling taste and by easing class boundaries, had fostered in Americans "the love of well-being [that] has now become the predominant taste of the nation," sweeping "everything along in its course." Spreading upward and downward from the middle class, the preference "for physical gratification" made Americans "restless in the midst of abundance." Tocqueville pictured the American chasing after a standard of living that always remained just beyond his grasp. "He clutches everything, he holds nothing fast, but soon loosens his grasp to pursue fresh gratifications."[12]

6

Tocqueville returned again and again to the dangers of such a situation. It took a considerable psychological toll on individuals. "Always straining to pursue or to retain gratifications so delightful, so imperfect, so fugitive," people became restless, brooding, and anxious. More ominous were the threats of materialism to the social order. The loss "of self-restraint at the sight of the new possessions they are about to obtain" might make citizens of a democracy "lose sight of the close connection that exists between the private fortune of each and the prosperity of all." Materialism thus threatened to dissolve the social bonds and make more problematic the promotion of the common good. By and large, Tocqueville believed Americans could avoid the "perils" of an excessively materialistic society. If the rich in aristocratic nations might become corrupt or "debauched" by the pursuit of splendid vices, most people in a democracy, seeking "a moderate and tranquil course," would pursue a "virtuous materialism" that would "not corrupt, but enervate, the soul and noiselessly unbend its springs of action." Moreover, Americans still saw public life as instrumental in achieving public good. Finally, the strength of American religion, by turning people's minds to immaterial concerns, helped temper the force of materialism.[13]

In important ways, Tocqueville differs from Wayland and Thoreau. At first glance, he offers less a set of nineteenth-century moral prescriptions than a modern analysis that explains the impact of affluence on national character, religion, politics, and the social order. Unlike conservative moralists who worried about workers and their profligacy, Tocqueville focused on the middle class and mass consumption. Yet as his call for religion as the restraint upon materialism reminds us, Tocqueville was as interested as Wayland and Thoreau in the ways that comfort injured individuals and the society. Wayland, Thoureau, and Tocqueville saw excessive wealth leading to enervation and social illness. Just as Thoreau found trade unclean and Wayland saw the lack of self-control as a sign of individual and social disorder, so Tocqueville believed materialism was "a dangerous disease of the human mind." Especially in a democratic and skeptical nation, the Frenchman warned, the "moralist" had to teach that it is "only by resisting a thousand petty selfish passions of the hour that the general and unquenchable passion for happiness can be satisfied."[14]

Quite different from the concerns of Wayland, Thoreau, and Tocqueville were celebrations of the wonders of America's potential for achieving a high standard of living that came in thousands of speeches before Congress, Fourth of July audiences, and meetings of commercial, industrial, and civic groups. Daniel Webster (1782–1852) spoke for those who believed that economic growth and an abundance of consumer goods would solve the problems America faced. Asserting that "vastly increased comforts have come to be enjoyed by the industrious classes," Webster in 1836 answered several groups of doubters at once: farmers who held on to an agrarian dream, workers and the poor to whom the march of industrial capitalism seemed more hostile than beneficent, and moralists who believed that stimulation of the agricultural and commercial arts was "without some self-preserving moral power" and would therefore provide "fuel for the fire which is destined to consume us."[15] Mechanical improvements and capital investments, Webster argued, had equalized and diffused the national wealth, scattering "its advantages among the many" and giving "cheerfulness and animation to all classes of the social system." Here was a rhetorical formula, developed most fully by antebellum Whigs who represented manufacturers interested in a higher tariff, that unabashedly celebrated a higher standard of living. By uniting capitalism and democracy, as well as virtue and materialism, this position held out the dream of an abundant future for great numbers of Americans.[16] Work hard, respect the contributions of capitalists and inventors, Webster told his audiences, and the march of progress would ensure moral development and material comforts. Unlike Wayland and Thoreau, Webster asserted that civilization was inextricably related to material advancement. Unlike them, Webster recognized the centrality of mass-produced goods and of mass consumption. More importantly, he saw no contradiction between commercial and industrial development and moral elevation.

Webster completes the spectrum of opinions that have dominated much of the discussion in the United States on consumption and the standard of living from his day to ours. His optimism had its counterparts throughout the nineteenth and twentieth centuries in the writings of those whose facile reconciliation of virtue and materialism helped underwrite a celebration of a rising standard of living. Clearly fewer in number, those who followed Thoreau chose simplicity in material pleasures and passion in the experience of Nature. Wayland points toward others, influential especially in the nineteenth and early twentieth centuries, who have held steadfastly to the virtues of hard work, restrained consumption, and refined pleasures. The line of argument that Tocqueville pursued was especially attractive to social theorists of the twentieth century who sought to explain America's penchant for materialism and mass consumption by referring to the power of democracy and mass culture.

What can we say of the patterns of consumption and the standard of living of the contemporaries of Wayland, Thoreau, Tocqueville, and Webster? Do we know enough about the living standards of most Americans of the 1830s, 1840s, and 1850s to place in perspective what these four observers wrote? We can begin answering these questions by noting what these four writers singled out as evidence of prosperity, excess, materialism, or profligacy. When Wayland spoke of temptation and indulgence, liquor and tobacco were uppermost in his mind. What Thoreau wanted to eliminate in order to get at the meaning of life was excess food, clothing that followed fashion but did not provide warmth, larger homes, and the myriad possessions that filled the parlors of his fellow citizens, including some of those of modest means. Tocqueville did not worry about leisure. He mentioned a number of ways Americans would seek to satisfy their "taste for physical gratifications." They might undertake "to add a few yards of land to your field, to plant an orchard, to enlarge a dwelling, to be always making life more comfortable and convenient, to avoid trouble, and to satisfy the smallest wants without effort and almost without cost."[17] For Webster, mass-produced clothing was the best example of commodities diffused among the people. However, we must be careful to avoid reading into the writings of antebellum Americans our experience with abundance and a higher standard of living. Yet even if they had no inkling of the automobiles, appliances, and packaged goods that would surround people in the United States more than a century later, what is surprising is how Wayland, Thoreau, Tocqueville, and Webster agreed that most of their contemporaries could lead lives characterized by some modicum of comfort.

Though we would do well to be skeptical of Webster's judgment in this instance, what are we to make of the impression gained from reading Wayland that he was living in a society where gratification of desire through consumption was a dominant experience? In virtually every generation, some Americans have thought of themselves as living in an age of comfort, especially when compared with their ancestors who are thought to have lived when people endured great hardship. Thus while we see the antebellum period from the perspective of a greatly more affluent late twentieth century, Thoreau, Wayland, and Webster in turn looked over their shoulders at forebearers who painfully eked out a living from a rocky and resistant New England soil. This perspective makes more understandable the sense these writers had that they lived in a world where people were comfortable and could easily make discretionary expenditures.

Can we rely on their impressions for an accurate picture of the American standard of living in the antebellum period? Did most Americans live the way these four men assumed? What in fact do we know about spending patterns in the years Thoreau, Wayland, Tocqueville, and Webster were writing? In the scholarship of American consumption, the antebellum years are the neglected period, sandwiched in between the eighteenth century and the late nineteenth century, the two periods where most recent research has concentrated. Fortunately, work that Edgar W. Martin published in

1942 points toward the answers to questions about the American standard of living before the Civil War. Working from travelers' reports, government statistics, secondary sources, and a few household budgets, Martin noted several things that, he argued, by the middle of the nineteenth century had come to distinguish the American way of life from that of Western Europe. Americans felt their standard of living was the best in the world; compared with Europeans, they consumed food in greater quantity and variety, especially meat, bread, and fruit; their housing was more comfortable; they wore clothing that was more uniform and respectable, though hardly extravagant; and they exhibited a distinctive preference for gadgets and mass-produced goods. Perhaps of more importance than these differences, Martin wrote, "was that the Americans seemed to regard a high standard of living as their chief goal." Lacking an aristocracy, people in a democracy were "unquestionably . . . more materialistic." Thus "the possession of wealth was not only the way to creature comfort but to power and esteem."[18]

In using a Tocquevillean explanation, Martin unintentionally revealed how speculative was any conclusion about the American standard of living that relied so heavily on travelers' reports. In fact, when Martin stuck with evidence of how Americans actually lived and not of how Europeans thought they lived, his data put the claims of Webster and the concerns of Wayland and Thoreau into even clearer perspective. In the 1860s, the annual income of most industrial workers was between $250 and $400. Martin estimated that in New York City in the same period "only about 1 per cent of the population received incomes of $842 or more." "Expenditures for food, clothing, and shelter," he noted, "required almost the entire income of most American families." Perhaps, he continued, 5 percent of income remained for "all other" items. "This seems very small indeed," he noted, "when one remembers that the 'all other' includes medical care, local transportation, and education, as well as reading and recreation."[19] In the decades preceding the Civil War, middle-class Americans were able to purchase a greater variety and number of mass-produced goods, but very few Americans could live their lives with the degree of choice and comfort that Thoreau, Wayland, Tocqueville, and Webster believed possible.

How then do we evaluate the arguments of contemporary observers? Thoreau, Tocqueville, and Webster saw few differences across class lines. They tended to confuse comfort with commercial consumption. Though these three writers differed in how they evaluated what they observed, what struck them most was that the new consumer goods represented a commitment by millions of Americans to materialistic and commercially purchased standards of living. Whether what they witnessed was in fact new, they accurately judged middle-class participation in the expanding consumer economy.

Like that of conservative moralists throughout the century, Wayland's position is more complicated. Some people like Wayland gave sermons on the importance of self-restraint in consumption and yet spent freely, albeit on things they doubtlessly defined as refined. For example, Henry Ward Beecher's *Lectures to Young Men* (1853) warned that "satisfaction is not the product of excess, or of indolence, or of riches; but of industry, temperance, and usefulness." Yet Beecher himself in the 1850s habitually visited New York stores, spent more than he could afford on books and semiprecious stones, and then had to take to the lecture circuit to pay for his shopping sprees.[20] What operates here is parallel to the relationship between self-control and social control common in the antebellum period. Conservative moralists may have simultaneously worried about what they saw as the profligacy of others and their own penchant to spend beyond their means.[21]

The anxiety of advocates of self-restraint, though related to the effort to control their own impulses as consumers, transcended their personal concerns. With a special intensity, they righteously attacked consumption patterns that they believed threatened the virtuous Republic. They castigated the profligacy of the wealthy who indulged themselves in what they interpreted as a pattern of corrupt excess. By and large they did not censure the middle class. Though its increased comforts and consumption of mass-produced goods may have bothered them, these patterns escaped their attention or confounded their categories.

What especially irked people like Wayland was what they saw as the profligacy of workers, immigrants, and the poor, whose lives seemed so distinct from those of the middle class. In the antebellum period, many reformers opposed what they characterized as the wanton pleasures of laborers and immigrants on a number of grounds but not because they wished to turn workers into modern-day consumers. The evils were not so much modern forms of commodity consumption but sporadic premodern patterns of work and play. Saloons, street life, and communal celebrations represented a foreign and dangerous way of life that they hoped to replace with the "refined" middle-class culture of museums, books, and churches. People like Wayland and Bushnell also hoped that citizens who adopted disciplined and orderly habits might transcend selfishness and worldliness through spiritual means. In addition, many industrialists and conservative moralists felt that premodern habits interfered with the inculcation of discipline in work and consumption so necessary in turning ordinary people into workers and savers in a period of intense industrialization.

Time and economic forces were with New England moralists in their advocacy of disciplined work. In their call for refined consumption, however, they were fighting an uphill battle. Already by 1840 or 1850, they were living in a world they little understood. After the Civil War, there would be a widening gap between what they observed and what they believed. In the late nineteenth and early twentieth centuries, changes in American life and thought would further undermine the virtues of hard work, prudence, and refinement.

2 How Workers Spent Their Money and Should Have Led Their Lives: Carroll D. Wright and Late-Nineteenth-Century Labor Statistics

In the antebellum period, those who worried about the profligacy of ordinary Americans supported their views with moral sentiment and impressionistic evidence. After the Civil War, moralism persisted but data began to become available on working-class patterns of consumption. In 1875 the Massachusetts Bureau of Statistics of Labor (MBSL) provided the first set of systematically collected statistics that Americans could use to judge whether ordinary families in fact lived according to the dictates conservative moralists had established. Under the direction of Carroll D. Wright (1840–1909), the MBSL published the results of a path-breaking investigation of laborers' household budgets. This study shaped the ways that future generations would collect and examine data on working-class expenditures. Moreover, the 1875 survey makes it possible to see how several hundred families spent their money, or at least how a state labor bureau believed that they should have. The MBSL's report also revealed the clash of traditions: the often severe judgments of the investigators confronting long-established immigrant and working-class cultures. In the resulting report, Wright and his colleagues tried to determine whether workers were prudent, temperate, and thrifty. In the process, the MBSL representatives demonstrated how little they understood the lives they were studying. Though unreliable in some important respects, the information the bureau gathered is nonetheless the best available for the period. Only after understanding the context of their collection can we reconstruct and then cautiously use the data.

Wright, who headed the MBSL from 1873 until 1888 and served as the first U.S. commissioner of labor from 1885 to 1905, provided a simple solution to the problem of gathering evidence. He abandoned the bureau's prior reliance on voluntary responses to circulars and had his agents, supposedly armed "with no theory to maintain or demolish," personally interview workers who were both "typical" and ready to talk. The 1875 study resulted in the publication of information on 397 families, all headed by an

13

employed male. Wright's approach, formulated before the professionalization of the study of statistics in America but aided by European precedents,
was so successful that scholars have valued the detail and representativeness of the data.[1] The heart of the report was information on each family
(illustrated by table 1).

In terms of income, a fault line ran through the MBSL's sample. On one
side stood Scotch, American, and English families, with the father's average
yearly earnings ranging from $605.28 to $790.00. Clearly separated from
them were German, French-Canadian, French, and Irish households with
larger families and average incomes between $430.84 and $498.96. Not
unrelated was evidence of a clear connection between skill levels and the
father's earnings. At the top stood factory "overseers," with an average
annual income of $985. Then came high-income skilled workers in the
building, shop, and metal-working trades who brought in $724 to $795,
followed by skilled mill operatives and skilled boot, shoe, and leather workers who earned $561 to $568. Clearly below all of these groups were the
unskilled workers with incomes averaging between $392 and $459.[2]

A typical 1875 family used most of its income on food, clothing, and
shelter. In 1981, an urban family of four with an "intermediate" budget
spent slightly more than 50 percent of its income on food, clothing, and
shelter. In contrast, most of the MBSL's households spent 51 to 64 percent
of their funds on food alone and over nine out of every ten dollars on food,
clothing, and shelter.[3] The report stated that the families were "well fed,"
eating "in variety and quality" better than their European counterparts.
American workers were "well and comfortably clothed." Many of the families, especially those where the father was an unskilled worker or where
there were several child laborers, lived in "crowded" and "inferior" settings.
Most households, however, inhabited quarters "in good condition as
regards locality and needful sanitary provisions." Wright concluded that as
income rose, the "relative percentage" spent for subsistence decreased, for
Sundries increased, and for clothing and housing remained essentially stable.[4]

Given the small amount left for items other than food, clothing, and
shelter, the MBSL report concluded that "expenses on account of bad
habits or its twin evil of extravagance were kept at a very modest and
creditable minimum." The average amount put aside for savings was 3
percent of income, with slightly more than one-half of the families able to
save. Nor did much remain for nonessential items. After food, clothing,
and shelter, for many workers the most important expenditures were newspapers, organizational membership, and church contributions. Two-thirds
of the households at all income levels paid an average of $8.99 for books and

Table 1   Budget 223, MBSL, 1875

No. 223. Laborer in Mill	F. *Canadian*
Earnings of father	$385
son aged 12	145
son aged 10	120
	$650

Condition.—Family numbers 7, parents and 5 children from one to twelve years of age; one child goes to school all the time, and the other two who work, attend the half-time school. Occupy a tenement of 4 rooms in a good locality, with neat surroundings. The house is moderately well furnished, but no carpets. Family dresses poorly, and looks pale and unhealthy, but neat. Tries to keep out of debt, but the father has to work all the time, as well as the children. Lost six days through sickness last year, and had to go without necessary clothing.

Food.—Breakfast: Bread, butter, sometimes fish, or the remains of the day before, coffee.
 Dinner: Meat or fish, potatoes, bread, sometimes pie.
 Supper: Bread, butter, gingerbread, molasses, tea.

Cost of Living			$650
Rent	$84.00	Fish	$13.50
Fuel	38.75	Milk	14.80
Groceries	300.00	Boot and shoes	22.75
Meat	54.62	Clothing	79.00
Dry Goods	18.00	Sundries	24.58

Source: Massachusetts Bureau of Statistics of Labor, *Sixth Annual Report* (Boston: Wright and Potter, 1875), p. 295.

newspapers; one-third, an average of $14.60 for religious contributions; and one-third, an average of $8.60 for "societies." Only a few families paid money for taxes, recreation, travel to work, or health care. Five of the 397 families reported purchases of furniture and carpets during the year, 4 contributed to charity, 2 each noted expenses for illness and travel to work, and 1 each mentioned money spent for care of parents, care of house, "housegirl," and life insurance.[5]

Great variation existed in the amounts reported on items other than food, clothing, and shelter. On Sundries, families headed by unskilled workers spent an average of $31.72; those headed by skilled, $55.72; and those headed by overseers, $142.15. This category included furniture, books, religious and organizational contributions, and, though they were not specifically listed, liquor and tobacco. At one extreme was an Irish outdoor laborer whose family spent nothing on such items. At the other was a family with three income producers (an overseer and two children), with annual expenditures of $1820.00, savings of $275.80, and sundry expenses of $250.00, most of which went for a servant. To the MBSL, the tightness of the budgets not only proved the lack of "an excessive or disproportionate expenditure" for clothing "in obedience to fashion," but also the absence of "large sums of money [spent] extravagantly or for bad habits."[6]

Wright measured the results of the wage system against what he called a "natural and just" ideal. A man's labor, he stated, should provide enough money so that with "economy and prudence" he could "comfortably maintain" his family, educate his children, and be able to put aside enough "for his decent support when his laboring powers have failed."[7] With this as his yardstick, Wright asserted that his investigation disclosed important problems in the operation of the wage system. The families in his sample, with incomes ranging from $1820.00 to $331.00 a year and averaging $762.72, represented the situation of about 80 percent of the American population.[8] The conditions his survey uncovered contradicted the widely shared free-labor ideology of the nineteenth century that had prevented many Americans from recognizing the permanence of the wage system. For Wright the ability of the male head of the household to provide decent conditions for his family was the linchpin, since he objected to the employment of young children and opposed wives working for a wage outside the home, finding that alternative "baneful in its effects, and a false economy in the end."[9]

The report revealed that most families did not get along on the income of the principal wage earner. Wives provided little money income. Families consequently had to rely or were "forced to depend" on their children for between one-fourth to one-third of the household's income. Children under fifteen years of age brought in earnings that equaled approximately half of those fractions. Therefore, by their own efforts most heads of households could not earn enough to provide comfort and education for their families and still put aside savings for home ownership, emergencies, or retirement. "By paying no more for labor than the bare cost of existence of the body," the report stated, the wage system used people when they were strong and left "them to shift for themselves when they are sick, infirm or without employment." It forced children to work when, the MBSL thought, they should have been at school or play. In the case of the least fortunate tenth, it held out no hope of improvement and instead allowed them "to attribute their sufferings to the prevailing system of labor." Offering no alternative to the existing economic system, Wright hoped that some of its weaknesses could be reduced by the adoption of a minimum wage "for competent adult labor." Any remuneration below that level "should be discountenanced by public opinion, and, if persisted in, to the detriment of any, should be prevented by appropriate legislation, rigidly enforced."[10]

Conservative moralism remained the framework used to collect, categorize, present, and analyze information. The authors of the report were searching for prudent, hard-working, and refined citizens. Again and again the MBSL demonstrated how it could not accept the implications of its conclusions about the relation between the plight of the working class and the lure of extravagance and intemperance. Wright's predecessors at the MBSL, the enlightened factory manager Henry K. Oliver and the labor leader George E. McNeill, had articulated a radical version of New England moralism. They argued that brutish surroundings, the power of fashion, and the example of the extravagance of the wealthy had driven the poor, exhausted by toil, to seek release through drink and "vulgarizing allurement."[11] The 1875 study provided the first empirical test of the question of whether workers partook of what radicals and conservatives alike saw as wanton indulgence. At times, the household budgets seemed to Wright to provide an unequivocal answer. Given "the minuteness" of the investigation, it was hard to "think that the families visited copied costly fashions or are liable to a general charge of unthrift."[12] At moments like these, the report may have stressed the virtues of working-class families because the outgoing staff was still influential or, more likely, because Wright wished to protect the MBSL from criticism by union representatives. Yet again and again, the authors of the report demonstrated the strictness of their judgments of the lives of workers and immigrants.

One telltale issue was the report's attitude to consumption of liquor. The use of alcohol was central to the evaluation of righteous living and to immigrant and working-class life. For those sitting in judgment, drinking demonstrated a lack of self-control. For the judged, liquor was an integral part of the social life, work culture, and health care. The report's publication coincided with the passage of a Massachusetts law that ended a twenty-three-year dry era and began a gradual shift in the locale of drinking among workers from grog shops and barrooms to neighborhood saloons.[13] The MBSL did not collect direct evidence on expenditures for liquor. That was an issue, Wright felt, for which there was no justification for the state to invade the "sanctity" of the household.[14] More practically, it may have been the price that middle-class Anglo-Saxon investigators had to pay to gain the confidence of the working-class subjects of their study. The absence of data on this item casts serious doubts on the reliability of information they collected and calls into question the degree of trust established between those who asked questions and those who answered them.

Historians have documented the importance of liquor in working-class budgets, with estimates for Britain in the late nineteenth century ranging from less than 10 to considerably more than 25 percent of household expenditures. According to one American study, in 1875 the annual per capita consumption for those fifteen and older was almost three gallons of distilled spirits and slightly more than ten gallons of beer.[15] Yet, given the

17

small percentage of funds remaining for items other than food, clothing, and shelter, the MBSL was sure that workers did not consume much liquor. Even if all of the amount for which no account was obtained, the report remarked, went for expenses "for non-legitimate purposes," it was not enough to justify the apprehension of those who worried about the intemperance and thriftlessness of the poor.[16]

Despite the conviction with which the 1875 report spoke of the lack of the workers' extravagance, neither Wright nor his peers among late-nineteenth-century labor bureau officers moved completely beyond a concern for the self-discipline of American laborers. There were times when he continued to see the temperance and labor questions as "inseparable." In 1882, Wright called sobriety the "surest means to happiness." Temperance, he asserted, "induces frugal habits, and frugal habits prevent strikes." Even in the 1875 report, the investigators were unable to hide their censoriousness. The description of a machinist's family included the remark that "the father thanks the officers of the bureau for this investigation, and believes that the attendance at grog-shops would be less frequent if the homes of the operatives were made more attractive and comfortable." Three years later, a similar New Jersey report warned against the practice of spending money "with unconscious liberality and for improper purposes, until it becomes a fixed habit not easily subdued." Yet that report also offered abundant evidence of the tightness of the budgets. The Illinois study of 1884 also provided no way of reconciling the tension in the observation that the high earnings and steady work of one individual indicated "sobriety and industry, notwithstanding much of his leisure time is spent in beer gardens and like places of amusement."[17]

For the rest of his life, Wright in fact remained unconvinced by the thrust of his 1875 conclusions about the connection between poverty and intemperance. New England moralism remained the lens through which he viewed the relation between virtue and alcohol consumption. For example, his 1890 federal study noted that one table contained "some unhappy revelations of the amount of money that goes for intoxicating liquors." During a time of industrial violence, unemployment, and poverty, he spoke of licentiousness as the source of some of "the most gigantic evils which society has to deal with." Shortly after the turn of the century, a committee on which Wright was influential published *Substitutes for the Saloon*, which called for the establishment of social centers "where a man may enjoy the society of his fellows without being confronted with the evils of intoxication, of gambling, of social vice, and where he will not be tempted to squander his week's wages."[18]

Carroll D. Wright's reluctance to accept the conclusions toward which the 1875 MBSL study pointed reminds us that he was as much a product of a judgmental tradition as he was a pioneer in the development of scientific labor statistics. Involved in the professionalization of budget studies, Wright shared the values of an expertise that sought both to define emerging social problems and to assert its scientific neutrality. Yet his own studies belied his ideal of impartiality. He hoped to ensure the independence of government bureaus of labor statistics by keeping them out of partisan and ideological battles. "The point aimed at always in the collection of labor statistics is the truth," he wrote in 1888, "and the results must be fearlessly stated, without regard to the theories of the men who collect the information." As director of the MBSL, U.S. commissioner of labor, and head of the National Convention of Chiefs and Commissioners of State Bureaus of Statistics of Labor, Wright earned a commanding position in the field of labor statistics. Throughout his career, he tried to heed the advice of those who had encouraged him to make the bureaus "superior alike to partisan dictation and to the seductions of theory."[19] Such organizations, he argued beginning in the 1870s, rather than attempting to solve social problems, should simply provide the data that would aid legislators and the public in making decisions.

As we realize more fully than Wright's generation, the goal of value-free statistical studies is difficult to achieve. Economists and historians have begun to reexamine late-nineteenth-century budget figures but sometimes without enough recognition of the assumptions that governed their collection.[20] Indeed if we return to the data in the 1875 MBSL report, we can draw a fuller picture of how people lived, uncover a series of conclusions improperly drawn or not drawn at all, disclose evidence of the nature of the exchange between the families and the interviewers, and make explicit the assumptions built into the very categories the MBSL used.

The report contained striking evidence of divergent patterns of consuming and living. For the poorest (mostly unskilled, immigrant mill operatives and outdoor laborers whose children were too young to work), bread, butter, potatoes, tea, and coffee were the most common staples, with meat, vegetables, and fruits only occasionally providing more varied and balanced meals. Moreover, uncertainty dominated the households and dictated a defensive strategy that in turn shaped decisions about relationships among family members and the family's stance toward the world.[21] At worst, illness, old age, or unemployment made these lives desperate. Even in good times some people could not afford to dress neatly or live in healthy and uncrowded quarters. Money for something extra was simply out of the question. Most of these households continued patterns that had existed for more than a century: they accumulated few possessions, principally simple furniture and utensils for cooking and eating. There was virtually no evidence that they partook of commercial leisure. Indeed, given the very small amount of money they spent for participation in religious, labor, and fraternal organizations, many of those studied appeared to be "in" but not "of" American society.[22]

For the lives of the more prosperous (almost always skilled workers, usually of British ancestry, and frequently with three or more wage earners), extra income made a considerable difference. "Pleasant" and "healthy" neighborhoods (sometimes with a garden in the yard), larger quarters, carpets, a sewing machine, a piano, better furniture and more self-conscious decorative elements, stoves for cooking and heating, gaslights, running water, money in the savings bank, insurance, better clothes, organizational memberships, books, magazines, newspapers, and a more varied diet—these were the expenditures characteristic of those households most favorably situated. These families participated in American life through membership in local and communal institutions. In the late nineteenth century skilled workers were thus beginning to have some comforts and even some luxuries.

Although the households with the highest incomes, those headed by skilled laborers and often with children earning incomes, had comfort, luxuries, and choice, their lives were hardly self-indulgent. For the most part, it was rare for even these families to own a house, employ a servant, or make a careless expenditure. Only with great difficulty did they build an adequate fund for education, retirement, or loss of income through illness, death, or unemployment. Even these people spent almost all of their time in their neighborhood, having contact with the larger world mainly through the market and the printed word. Expenditures for commuting, excursions, or vacations almost never appeared as items in their budgets.[23] Such families entered the world outside the home and workplace principally through local, communal organizations, not by partaking of commercial leisure or participating in civic and cultural institutions.

It is unfair to expect the MBSL to have viewed these patterns as historians a century later have come to understand them. Yet the restrained and carefully balanced conclusions of the 1875 report missed what the data themselves highlighted: the drama in the lives of these families as they struggled against enormous odds to make ends meet. The comment sections, however brief and epigramatic, contained compelling and rich evidence of the challenges ordinary people faced. The bureau had collected the information in 1874, before an upswing in the economy had lessened the adverse effects of the economic crisis of 1873. In part this timing accounts for the dominance of struggle and uncertainty in their lives, with illness and unemployment (the latter only partially disguised with phrases like "dullness of trade") the principal specters that haunted people. A few respondents, at either end of the narrowed social scale, justified sending children to work instead of school because the family would not "curtail expenses," because it was in the children's "future interests to do so," or because the parents surmised that there was "no advantage" to be "gained from longer attendance." In one case, that of an Irish mill laborer, the MBSL reported that a father expressed the hope that children would stay in school so they would not have to work in the mill and live in company housing the rest of their lives.[24]

More typical was the story told of Irish, French, and English families headed by skilled and unskilled workers that had struggled heroically to pay off debt, save money, and live more comfortably.[25] Several fathers, all skilled and all of them English or "American" (a label the report apparently used to refer to white Anglo-Saxon Protestant families that had lived in the United States for several generations), expressed pride in a different kind of achievement: the father enjoyed spending "spare time" with his family, he provided a "neat and comfortable" home, and the household possessed symbols of respectability such as a "library," piano, or flowers.[26] Although it is not surprising such a study paid considerable attention to the home as the center of a social order, what is striking is how rarely the descriptions mentioned the world of work. The few such references usually emphasized the difficulty of industrial labor. "Weavers in Fall River," an English worker reportedly remarked, "run too many looms, which exhausts their strength, and leaves them without energy for anything else after the work is done."[27]

The most persistent refrain in the descriptions of the lives of the workers' families concerned debt and savings. This theme reflected the MBSL's assumption that deposits in a savings bank were a key to success in America and pointed to the respondents' struggles and more defensive strategies. Moreover, the patterns of saving confounded the bureau's expectations of a consistent relation between thrift and virtue. For a handful of cases, usually English or American skilled workers, the MBSL reported that some families unsuccessfully tried to save money, preferring instead "to expend it for home comforts," good food, magazines, clothes, an organ, or education.[28] A larger group successfully saved. The MBSL noted a number of different manifestations of virtuous heroism: the few, all American and skilled, who kept records and paid only with cash[29]; people whom only illness or unemployment prevented from saving[30]; families that could save only with great difficulty or by employment of children; householders who were "economical" but still incurred debts or at least could not save; or families that saved despite great odds.[31]

At times the report came up against evidence that families that saved despite great sacrifice in comfort did not necessarily conform to the authors' notions of virtue. In some instances, the report told of people "meanly dressed," living in neighborhoods and tenements that were filthy and filled with foul odors, eating meat that was "scarcely fit for food," but actually able to save money.[32] The extreme example of the commitment to save despite sacrifice of health and comfort was the unskilled Irish laborer who headed a family of seven and brought in less than half of the household's $655 in yearly income. The fact that the tenement was "scantily furnished," with "bare" floors and "dirty" surroundings, made it have "a general air of poverty throughout." The children, whose clothing was "ragged" and feet were bare, looked "untidy." The investigator judged the food "the poorest I have ever seen eaten." "What kind of living, or where the locality," the interviewer concluded, "is a matter of indifference, but the father is determined to save money if the family starve."[33]

The explicit interjection of the investigator's voice in this case suggests that the report reflected the expectations and perspectives of the MBSL representatives, who if not middle-class "Americans" themselves, certainly preferred bourgeois respectability. In most instances, it is difficult to separate what those interviewed actually said, what they thought the surveyor wanted them to say, and what the interviewers were interpreting or communicating. At several points, however, the voice of the MBSL spoke clearly. With a dozen households, most of them headed by unskilled Irish workers, the descriptions of living conditions conveyed a sense of revulsion or horror.[34] The report noted that one French family of six, with income of $396 and expenditures of $483.40, lived in a three-room tenement "situated in a very unhealthy locality, in the midst of filth and pollution." Outside, stagnant water caused "an offensive stench which can be smelled at a great distance." Nor was the inside much better. "Poorly furnished," it seemed the "abode of poverty." Doubtlessly without irony, at the end of the food section, the author noted that the family "cannot afford luxuries."[35]

In seven cases, all but one unskilled and almost all of them of ethnic origins other than American, the interviewer advised or chastised sometimes the landlords or city fathers but more frequently those families that seemed to be sacrificing their well-being because of what the MBSL saw as the false economy of low rents and unhealthy surroundings.[36] For example, a French-Canadian family of eight with income and expenditures of $836 lived in a "poorly furnished" but "neat" tenement "in a poor locality, with unclean and disagreeable surroundings." "It is strange," the report noted, "that people will live in such houses, when, for a few dollars more, they could be made comfortable; it is no saving, as it generally costs more for sickness, caused by living in such places, than extra rent would cost."[37]

The voice of the MBSL appeared as well in other more subtle but equally transparent ways. Words such as "refined," "tasteful," "order," "intelligence," and "respectable," showed up in more than thirty instances, characteristically in the descriptions of the lives of English, American, or German families, usually headed by skilled workers. Tasteful decoration, neatness, and books characterized these households. The MBSL gave only three families headed by unskilled, Irish workers such praise. Something special marked them: heroic efforts, aspirations for education, or a flower garden.[38] The highest praise the report could bestow was to say that a certain kind of attribute or behavior was exceptional for workers' families, a backhanded compliment that overlooked the integrity of working-class culture. Three households earned such recognition, all of them English or American and all but one (headed by a fisherman) skilled. Again, what set them off was evidence of what the interviewers doubtlessly saw as middle-class aspirations: possession of an organ, garden, or home; magazine subscriptions; or an environment the bureau characterized as tasteful, refined, and respectable.[39] The authors of the report used "respectability" as a way of drawing a line between a native labor aristocracy and immigrant, unskilled workers. The MBSL used life-style differences to separate the two groups, suggesting that only the upper working class had the aspirations and self-restraint necessary for development of middle-class values. The study thus ascribed to ethnicity and class the divergence in styles of living and consuming.

What are we to make of what the comment section of the 1875 report conveyed about the lives of the workers' families? Did English and American fathers really take more pride than Irish or French-Canadian ones in providing comfort and respectability for their families? Was one ethnic or occupational group more likely to spend and another to save even though putting money aside imperiled the family's well-being? Were families of English background more likely to be intelligent, neat, respectable, and aspiring? If these differences to some degree reflect the interviewers' judgments, then should we be suspicious of the numbers, which were, presumably, less likely to be distorted by the MBSL's influence?

Obviously, much of the evidence in the report reflected the views of the MBSL as much as it did the lives of the workers' families. Again and again the authors of the report demonstrated their class and ethnic bias. The interviewers doubtlessly provided much of the framework and language of the respondents' answers. Moreover, the process of asking questions may well have called forth answers in a patterned manner. American household budget surveys, pioneered by Carroll D. Wright in this study, relied on interviews, unlike European studies that used account books left with the household over time. In 1875, for a worker's family to have a representative of the state, of a different social and ethnic background, ask about personal details must have elicited an immensely complicated series of interchanges, especially from poverty-stricken immigrant families. From later, more closely controlled studies, we know of the variety of distortions such a process is apt to engender, especially in the direction of encouraging the understatement of expenditures for items like alcohol and exaggerating those for items such as life insurance, education, and necessities.[40] The interviewer and the interview process in 1875 doubtlessly encouraged similar responses, with the more assimilated families better able to offer evidence that the MBSL honored. Immigrants were more likely to be uncomfortable with the entire process. Indeed, at the very least it is clear that the interviewers paid particular attention to signs of respectability, or their opposite, preferring evidence of "intelligent," neat, economical, and optimistic households.

The representatives of the MBSL probably approached the households expecting to find congruent patterns of behavior among people who did or did not practice the virtues of clean living, hard work, thrift, and temperance. What the surveyors actually uncovered was more complicated and often defied assumed moral standards. There was no case reported of a family that could save but did not because of improvidence. There was no reference to a moral flaw in the description of the one family that, to avoid starvation, "received assistance." Its income of $331 came from the wife who went "out washing" and the husband who "worked but very little last year." In only three cases did the language of the report even hint that a family might have been responsible for its own misery.[41] Even in these instances there was evidence of what the bureau must have regarded as prudential or moral behavior: saving money, attending church, or hoping for an improvement in condition. In no case was self-indulgence, laziness, or drunkenness given as the cause of unemployment or difficulty. Similarly, the savers who preferred economy to comfort or decency provided evidence of the contradictory consequences of morally upright behavior.

If additional evidence of the MBSL's particular perspective is needed, it comes from other projects with which Wright was associated. In his writings, Wright often celebrated the virtues of thrift and temperance. As a young man he had absorbed an idyllic picture of industry from a teacher who had once worked in the Lowell mills and had contributed to the *Offering*. Though shaken by an event like the Pullman strike of 1894, throughout the late nineteenth century Wright nonetheless sustained an

24

optimism based on the hope that Christian ethics would temper the excesses of a laissez-faire economy.[42] For a man of his age and position, he was not especially conservative, but he consistently held a moralistic view of the "sober, industrious, and thrifty" worker who spurned "riotous living," "the display of enervating luxury," and "the insane attempt to keep up appearances which are not legitimate" and instead spent his money for things that were cultivating and elevating. He was never able to understand the lives, values, and aspirations of most industrial workers in America.[43]

Indeed we have one instance where a report Wright later supervised interpreted selectively the life of a working-class family by seeing struggle and poverty as heroic economizing. In 1890 a woman wrote Wright's office of how her family of seven got by on $576 a year. She described a household with few "bits of extravagance" and myriad economies, always haunted by the fear of the children getting sick or the father losing his job. She concluded that "in our efforts to make both ends meet we are like a kitten I once had who tried with all his little might to catch his tail. He kept twirling round and round, always with the end he so much wanted in view, but never quite catching it." In introducing this story, Wright (or his assistant) neglected the compelling lesson the woman drew and instead noted "the intelligent administration of a wife determined to get the most for the good of the family out of her husband's earnings."[44] The divergent conclusions drawn from this incident remind us that in the 1875 report and elsewhere Wright and the bureaus he directed did not let statistics speak for themselves. His ideology shaped the questions he asked and the answers he received. The 1875 study contained a good deal of evidence that the lack of character did not cause poverty. Yet the text of the report never pursued the consequences of such data. Instead, the MBSL denied that workers were extravagant at the same time that it found cause to chastise them for not being sufficiently virtuous. To Wright, the clash between native middle-class and immigrant working-class cultures never posed a problem of interpretation.

In explicit and implicit ways, the very categories of the 1875 study rested on fundamental assumptions about the way people should lead their lives. To begin with, the organization of the data on a household-by-household basis intensified the already dominant tendency to see the isolated and self-contained nuclear family as the principal economic and social unit. For analytic purposes, we can imagine alternative ways of organizing a study of how ordinary people lived. Extended families in different households or social networks based on neighborhood, occupational, or ethnic groups were focal points that would have fostered a fuller sense of the intergenerational and social aspects of people's lives.

In addition, without apparent reflection the MBSL accepted the notion that a year (rather than a month, a season, an entire life cycle, or the complete run of an industrial cycle) was the best time span for such a study. The uncertainties that such working-class families faced made it necessary for them to adopt a defensive income and expenditure strategy that had to work itself out over a period longer and more irregular than a year.[45] Working-class families in the late nineteenth century could not assume a steady or steadily rising income. Consequently, a study based on a year's budget not only reflected the distinctive employment and expense patterns of a particular and perhaps idiosyncratic year but also made it difficult to convey the ways that workers' families contended with the insecurities of their position. An annual perspective may thus have helped make working-class behavior seem erratic, irrational, or at least inexplicable. Moreover, from our perspective it is clear that the lack of attention to the relation between a family's position in the life cycle and its finances made it hard to see that many prosperous families had once suffered the hardships that the report documented for the less fortunate.

Also contributing to an incomplete picture was the fact that the household budget study included only income or expenditures that involved market transactions. Because there was no exchange of funds, goods given or received as gifts and food produced in a garden did not appear in the budget itself, a situation that some later studies remedied. Work not done for money was also absent from the budget. Occasionally the descriptive section mentioned unpaid labor. Children, especially in some very poor families, picked up pieces of wood that the family used for cooking or heating. And the condition section noted that wives and daughters (and occasionally husbands and sons) worked in and around the house. The report clearly sanctioned labor participation in the market and, therefore, men's work. The MBSL was quite explicit in its preference that men work outside the home and women inside, which may explain why it did not consistently record earnings of wives who did work for money and why it focused on intact families where the male usually brought in the most income.[46] By focusing on earned income, the report thus gave an inadequate sense of the nature of the family economy in which women played such a significant role.

In reporting on social life, the report similarly emphasized events that involved market exchanges. Free kinds of activities—participation in street life, an outing in a park, and attendance at religious, occupational, political, or ethnic gatherings—were more absent from the record of these lives than they were from the lives themselves. Thus, built into the study was a neglect of communal aspects of immigrant and working-class cultures, an implicit denial of their validity. The inattention to such phenomena helped reinforce the bureau's ethnic and class bias.

Indeed, the MBSL explicitly reflected a distinctive notion of the importance of various kinds of consumption. Despite an occasional disclaimer and abundant evidence to the contrary, the report conveyed the sense that people pursued or should pursue satisfactions in a certain order: first basics, then comforts and luxuries, and finally savings for education or a time when income slowed or stopped. The use of terms like "sundries," "miscellaneous," and "other," as well as statements in the report, conveyed the impression that items like organizational membership and excursions were somehow frivolous afterthoughts. In fact, as the evidence indicated, all aspects of a family's expenditures were inextricably linked and not pursued in the sequential manner the report assumed.[47] People sometimes sought to satisfy what the MBSL would have considered somewhat superfluous wants before they had met their supposedly more basic needs.

Moreover, in assuming that people would pursue "higher" goals, the MBSL used its own yardstick to measure "sundry expenses." Some miscellaneous expenditures were better than others. "The comforts or luxuries of life," the report commented, were "absolutely necessary for the development of the mind, of a love of beauty in the home, and of a man's social possibilities." Rich and poor alike, the MBSL asserted, sought the same things—books, newspapers, lectures, art, theater, celebration of holidays— all of which would add to "comfort, cheerfulness and beauty of home and the personal and social happiness of its occupants." The pursuit of a higher standard of living was thus a refining and ennobling process, often acted out in a social world but always with the benefit accruing to the individual household. Marginal expenditures on items other than food, clothing, and shelter were especially critical, because these extra purchases, the report assumed, signified the aspirations and qualities of a respectable life. Obviously some workers wanted to adopt a genteel and respectable way of life. However, Wright seemed to assume all workers should have such aspirations.[48]

Together all of these assumptions about income and expenditures tended to turn a budget into a normative statement. The report minimized the sense of a family's resourcefulness in finding satisfactions other than those that involved an exchange of money. It helped make the family appear as a ship cast adrift on a sea of financial turbulence. By so emphasizing the centrality of participation in a society through the market, the study tended to exaggerate the family's isolation from social institutions. By looking at working-class life from a middle-class perspective, the report gave an incomplete and distorted picture of the way of life (though not perhaps, in financial terms, the standard of living) of these 397 families.

The question of ethnicity and social class influenced the report in another critical way. Like most later studies, the 1875 effort concentrated on intact working-class families where the husband was not only regularly employed but also the principal wage earner. It thus avoided households at either end of the social spectrum. Political ideology and policy questions have always influenced household budget studies. Investigators have consistently avoided an examination of the expenditures of the rich and the question of the distribution of wealth in the society. That a bureau of labor statistics should concern itself primarily with the budgets of workers would not always be true, as later experiences proved. However, throughout the late nineteenth century, Wright and his successors searched for solutions to the labor problem by examining the condition of workers rather than the more extensive expenditures of the rich. The lack of evidence on the wealth and income of families at all levels of society made it impossible to study the distribution of wealth, an issue, Wright commented in 1899, that could not be pursued because "the government has never felt at liberty to make inquiry concerning the possessions of individuals."[49]

Such a statement revealed Wright's bias. In fact, the 1875 study had provided data on savings accounts, home ownership, and durable goods. The report noted that a few, "principally" skilled workers, "betrayed an indisposition to have their private lives inquired into."[50] Freedom from such intrusions was a class luxury: the budget of a worker was something moralists worried about; that of a member of the comfortable classes, because it involved more "proper" expenditures, something to be enjoyed.

The 1875 MBSL study was a landmark that inspired a host of similar reports. It provided the first representative selection of household budgets of ordinary Americans. At least until 1905 the investigations carried on by state and federal bureaus of labor statistics remained the most reliable source of information on how a substantial segment of the population spent its money.

Drawing on European examples, Wright established the main categories of subsequent American investigations. In the last quarter of the nineteenth century, Wright and other labor statisticians incorporated improvements. Later reports corrected the underrepresentation of large cities and the exclusively urban industrial nature of the sample. Yet the widespread anxiety that factories, cities, and immigrants threatened the social order made industrial workers the group most thoroughly examined during the late nineteenth century, except in times of agrarian distress. The exclusion of unemployed people and of fatherless households too easily gave a more optimistic picture of social conditions than reality justified. Separate reports somewhat redressed the imbalance of that selectivity. Other studies added information that deserves fuller examination by historians. In 1884, the Illinois bureau noted union membership and offered summary comments on the family's condition and outlook. The information provided in a Missouri study five years later was particularly descriptive, containing inventories of possessions and comments on the degree of contentment in the household.[51]

Bureaus of labor statistics increasingly avoided direct comment on policy issues and descriptive portrayals of the lives of their subjects and instead concentrated on presentation of massive amounts of statistical data. The necessity to collect, manage, and analyze a large amount of information was in part responsible for the shift. Also involved were the ways that bureaucratic, technical, and political interests of large corporations, social scientists, and policy makers reshaped moralistic concerns. An attempt at neutrality triumphed over advocacy—plain statistics over judgmental observations or policy recommendations. The tendency of government labor bureaus to let their beliefs remain more implicit and for men like Wright to confine their judgments to unofficial forums was a mixed blessing.[52] Though it doubtlessly enabled surveyors to minimize political interference, it made the reports considerably less informative about the texture of working-class life and about the investigators' responses to what they found.

With all their imperfections, the state and federal labor bureau reports of the late nineteenth century remain one of the richest sources of information on the household budgets and living patterns of working-class Americans. In subtle and not so subtle ways, the assumptions Wright and his colleagues brought to the study shaped the information gathered. Conservative moralism influenced the questions labor bureaus asked and the analysis they offered. At least in the 1875 study, ideology stood fast against evidence that did not easily confirm the picture of how people should have spent their money and lived their lives. Toward the end of the century, a number of economists would reconsider traditional moralism and attempt to bring it into line with changing patterns of consumption.

3 Rethinking Conservative Moralism: Simon N. Patten, Thorstein Veblen, and George Gunton

By the late nineteenth century, a number of changes in American life began to pose ever more serious threats to the arguments of traditional moralists. Factories, machines, and corporations made it increasingly difficult to speak convincingly of the nobility of physical labor. With the questioning of the work ethic as the primary source of values, social thinkers looked for ways to make leisure a fulcrum for uplift. Influential observers shifted their attention from production to consumption, with Edward Bellamy, for example, drawing a picture of a world where affluence arrived effortlessly and abundantly.[1] Burgeoning cities attracted greater numbers of people whose habits seemed unrestrained. The newly rich ostentatiously displayed their wealth. To some observers, it appeared that self-indulgent extravagance too easily tempted the poor, especially immigrants. Around the turn of the century the signs of an emerging consumer society were visible in a shorter workweek, more elaborate advertising campaigns, the display of goods in department stores, and proliferation of institutions of commercial leisure such as the amusement park. In many ways, the shift from a producer to a consumer economy and culture accelerated during the last two decades of the old century and the first two of the new.

More than any other writers of their generation, Simon N. Patten, Thorstein Veblen, and George Gunton attempted to comprehend these changes. They struggled with the ideas conservative moralists had offered and tried to rework the inherited categories into new syntheses. Patten shaped a social reform substitute. Veblen devised a radical alternative to old-fashioned censoriousness. Over the course of his lifetime, Gunton shifted from a radical moralism to a celebration of mass consumption society. Although they rethought familiar approaches, in varying ways they all remained captives of the tradition they were challenging.

Beginning in the mid-1880s, these three writers concentrated on the persistent problem of the relation between affluence, morality, and the social order. They deserve consideration together because these issues were so central to their work and because their varied resolutions shed light on some important ways that Americans came to terms with a rising standard of living. Patten and Veblen offered provocative analyses that transformed the meaning of well-worn concepts. Both were as concerned with the problems of affluence as they were with its promise. It remained for George Gunton, heir to the labor movement's arguments for an eight-hour day, to break more completely with the dominant nineteenth-century vision and advocate an unending succession of pleasures for consumers. The continuing hold of conservative moralism on their thinking limited their understanding of the forces changing America. Yet Patten, Veblen, and Gunton contributed to the weakening of that tradition and offered valuable insights into the meaning of the emerging consumer economy.

Simon N. Patten (1852–1922) struggled to recast conservative moralism in a social reform mold. Focusing on workers and immigrants, he rethought the relationship between self-discipline and pleasure. In the end, he remained beholden to the inheritance he questioned. His life resembled that of many in the first generation of social scientists in the United States.[2] From the energetic, prosperous, and upstanding Presbyterian families among whom he grew up in Illinois, young Patten learned of the importance of restraints, of the adherence to the Protestant ethic of hard work and temperate living. In 1876, he began his formal education in economics with three years of study in Germany. After he returned to America, Patten faced a decade of considerable personal frustration and career uncertainty. Despite his participation in the founding of the American Economic Association and the publication, at his own expense, of his first book in 1885, not until the 1890s did Patten's future as a writer and a professor seem reasonably secure. Teaching at the Wharton School of the University of Pennsylvania from 1885 until 1917 and publishing books and articles from 1885 until the end of his life, he focused on the prospect and problems of an affluent society. With considerable justification, Patten has earned a place, as his student Rexford G. Tugwell wrote, as "a prophet of prosperity and progress." However, to see Patten as someone who embraced affluence and minimized the importance of restraints, the way historians have often interpreted his contribution, is to neglect precisely the concern that he shared with those he challenged: the dilemma materialism posed to the values of hard work, saving, and self-discipline.[3]

Patten shared with conservative moralists the realization that the arrival of a pleasure economy presented Americans with both problems and opportunities. Like his predecessors, he tried to distinguish between beneficial and destructive needs, to prescribe clear rules governing the behavior of consumers, and to argue for moral and intellectual pleasures that were both elevating and inexpensive. Similarly, Patten echoed the emphasis that earlier writers had placed on restraints as a way of preventing materialistic excess and transforming private and selfish wants into public and nonexclusive ones.[4] However, Patten also searched for new terms to sustain puritanical judgments. Where his predecessors appealed to traditional ethics and theology as a basis for restraints, he looked for more "scientific" grounds. At various points beginning in the 1880s, he found in history, psychology, culture, and scientific nutrition the means of guaranteeing that more wants would mean higher ones, that as the nation grew richer it would spend more of its resources on education, culture, and philanthropy. More than anyone in his generation, he pondered the important question of how to ensure restrained consumption in an increasingly abundant economy.

However, Patten was more than a moralist in the clothing of a social scientist. He struggled with a problem that earlier thinkers had faced but left unresolved: the reconciliation of the Protestant ethic with an economic growth based on increasing consumer demands. The tension between more and better, once minimized by the connection between ethics and economics and by the very real limits to the increase of wealth, in the late nineteenth century was no longer so easily resolved. With some success, Patten struggled to find a way out of this dilemma, to see how restraint, rather than limiting growth, might promote wholesome national development. By making the variety and quality of desires more important than their brute force and quantity, he was able to argue that control over baser passions resulted in improvements in society that were both materialistic and ennobling.[5]

Of much greater importance was Patten's ability to put self-restraint into the service of progressive social change. Other reformers—Richard T. Ely, Edward Bellamy, Ignatius Donnelly, and Laurence Gronlund—had tried to make this shift but with less success than Patten.[6] Initially, he was more interested in excluding the poor because he feared that they would displace skilled workers.[7] Slowly and hesitatingly, he tempered his fears with hope and sought methods of reform that would lift the downtrodden so that they would not threaten the social order. Society could raise people from poverty, he had come to argue shortly after the turn of the century, by using surplus funds for cultural and educational purposes. Such an approach would begin to modify the habits and inherited traits of the poor and eventually lead to permanent conditions of social improvement. Yet in the late nineteenth and early twentieth centuries, Patten was treading a thin line. He was still advocating self-control in consumption, but more and more he balanced this position with an argument that restraints and character served to bind people together, to make society altruistic and cohesive.[8]

However incomplete and uncertain, these shifts were important, but their direction became fully clear only in 1907 with the publication of *The New Basis of Civilization*, Patten's most influential book. He elaborated and clarified the changes he had struggled to make for more than twenty years: from the exclusion of the poor to their inclusion in an abundant society; from an emphasis on individual character to concentration on the social and environmental causes of poverty; and from individual salvation by restraint to social salvation through public use of the economic surplus. Addressing the fears that worldliness created a situation where "prosperity lulled spiritual alarms to a dangerous moral peace" and "degeneration follows a prolonged period of material success," Patten refused to accept the common parallel between ancient Rome and Victorian America. He argued instead that affluence was creating a new basis of civilization that would prove historical precedents invalid.[9]

The new environment of abundance, Patten argued, at last made it possible to raise the masses to a plane above uncertainty in order to improve permanently their heredity and character. Patten depicted poor, immigrant workers as heroic people whose aspirations and impulses demonstrated the possiblity of a new basis of civilization. Society would elevate them by a number of methods, including labor unions and a tax on prosperity, but especially by fostering new attitudes among social workers. Stop trying to "suppress vices," he told members of that profession, when you should be attempting to "release virtues." "The new morality," he argued, "does not consist in saving, but in expanding consumption. . . . We lack . . . courage to live joyous lives, not remorse, sacrifice, and renunciation."[10]

The attack on excessive self-denial and the call for passionate self-expression made *New Basis of Civilization* an important document. Recognizing the brutal nature of labor under modern industrial conditions, Patten was among the first social scientists of his generation to turn away from the world of work as the source of pleasure. More than most Progressive social reformers, he recognized the authenticity of immigrant culture. He argued that commercial and noncommercial public amusements and recreations—carnivals, picnics, and ethnic festivals and theater—would use the laborer's latent vitality and primitive instincts as a fulcrum for uplift. Consequently, he could see an infusion of elemental passions as an aid to higher aspirations, not as a cause of decline or a sign of weak character. That was as far as Patten could go in 1907 in rethinking the relation between desire and restraint. Once passions had uplifted the poor, he argued, the motive of abstinence would emerge and the nation would advance into a period of restrained living. Citizens of an abundant society would eventually pursue respectability and culture, not self-indulgence and materialism. A complete day, one that balanced good work and wholesome leisure, would subject impulses to control. Raised above grinding necessity, immigrants and the poor would become willing puritans.[11] Patten had initially accepted primitive passions but a reassertion of the hierarchy of cultural values had kept him from going farther in his attack on restraints.

A series of events in Patten's life gave a greater urgency to his reconsideration of the relation between passion and self-control. In 1903, he married a wealthy and vivacious woman twenty years his junior. In 1907, the year *New Basis of Civilization* appeared, his wife, perhaps rebuffed by Patten's self-restraint, began an affair with a younger member of her husband's department. Divorce proceedings, initiated the following year, concluded in 1909. At the same time, Patten produced *Product and Climax*, his least puritanical book. In the long run, the issues raised in the divorce meant that sustained belief in restraint was essential to the preservation of Patten's self-esteem. In the short run, however, the divorce, for reasons that will probably remain unclear, coincided with a fuller acceptance of the passions in economic life.[12]

In *Product and Climax*, a short and incomplete essay, Patten offered his most suggestive and powerful challenge to a censorious approach. He argued that those who labored under conditions set by industrialism had become exhausted by the quest for material goods. The urge to work harder and consume more thus had to be opposed because, Patten argued, "more good things will not elevate in the same way that fewer bad things relieve." To remove production from its false position as the foremost goal of national welfare, it was necessary to have "climaxes enjoyed together," the "reward of recreation . . . [that workers] rush toward after the stupefying day at toil, that means nothing to them but bread." As society's "prohibitory moral agencies," institutions of high culture, such as universities and libraries, had failed to promote social health. Workers left the factories, Patten remarked, "bearing marks of degradation which no preacher of thrift and sobriety has yet undertaken to frame into a text upon the ennobling influences of labor." Only nonwork pursuits, "the eager demand for climaxes of satisfactions that renews men," could lift the shroud of degradation.[13]

Even more than in *New Basis of Civilization*, Patten in *Product and Climax* located the source of regeneration in cultural institutions of workers and immigrants that moralists had denounced: nickelodeons, street life, ethnic theater, sports, social clubs, and activities that would "gratify men's thwarted necessities for vital excitement." Like many Progressives involved in the settlement house movement, Patten saw the potential for uplift in organized play and social gatherings. Participation in these endeavors, he argued, would strengthen democracy and help emphasize the social nature of pleasures. Once regenerated through primitive passions, people would arrive at a higher level of civilization. Only then would they experience morality, religion, and Culture. However, the institutions incorporating these higher experiences would have been purged of their censoriousness.[14]

Product and Climax is Patten's most provocative book on the consequences of a nation's entry into an age of abundance. To be sure, a number of important issues were unresolved. Patten failed to explain how institutions of high culture could encourage expressiveness. In addition, he remained equivocal in his view of popular culture, at times arguing that especially if commercialized, it provided debased experiences. "In their lowest form," he wrote of some elements of commercial leisure, "they destroy as do the saloon and other resorts frankly depending for private gain upon debasing appeals to pent up passions." Nonetheless, the argument was distinctive in important ways. Where *New Basis of Civilization* attacked the back-to-nature movement as a retrograde solution to the problems the poor faced, *Product and Climax* proposed a version of primitivism less individualistic in thrust than Henry David Thoreau's *Walden*, a way of life that Scott Nearing, Patten's student, was later to pursue.[15]

Product and Climax opened with an evocation of the joys of a summer spent on a lake in the woods, albeit with a group of people. Patten portrayed a world where no repressive moral agency was necessary as a check upon desires, where product (catching a fish) and climax (eating it for dinner) were closely tied. He then explored how street life and recreation made it possible to infuse into urban living the pleasures of a summer in the woods. He wrote of city dwellers enjoying "warm evenings of free movement, country holidays, boat excursions, Sunday picnics." Patten had also changed his attitude toward industrial work. In his earlier book, he argued that the zest of young workers "for amusement urges them to submit to the discipline of work, and the habits formed for the sake of gratifying their tastes make the regular life necessary in industry easier and more pleasant."[16] In *Product and Climax*, on the other hand, he did not argue for revitalizing the energies of the poor so that they could return to debilitating industrial work. Rather, he wanted society to reject overproduction, thereby lessening the burden of workers.

Thus *Product and Climax* represents important but subtle shifts in Patten's view of alternatives to work. *New Basis of Civilization* envisioned using the culture of the poor so they would eventually become consumers guided by restraint and an appreciation of high culture. Though *Product and Climax* appeared to acknowledge a hierarchy of low (recreation) and high (elevation) culture, Patten espoused more firmly the virtues of the life of "country folks and working people" and hoped to use its vitality to repair the damage done by industrial work, to avoid the pitfalls of a repressive high culture, and to protect against the calls of debased elements of commercialized consumption.[17] Patten thus showed his appreciation of the fact that the urban working class, in its enjoyment of group pursuits, might build a base from which it could try to resist the ministerings of moralistic reform, as well as the pressures of commercialism.

In *Product and Climax*, Patten fully recognized the difficulty of obtaining satisfaction from industrial work and turned instead to find rewards that were not connected with moral prohibitions. By celebrating noncommercial leisure, Patten questioned the worth of the emerging forms of mass culture. He presented an alternative to nineteenth-century moralism, industrial work, and commercial consumption, an alternative that involved community celebrations, albeit often organized by social workers. By opposing possessions but not passions, Patten could stand against materialism without continuing to emphasize self-control. Citizens of an abundant society would thus be seekers of passionate experience rather than avaricious consumers. Strong passions could be felt and acted upon, at the same time that an extravagant consumption of goods could be checked.

What made *Product and Climax* so important was that Patten, however tentatively, was moving toward a fresh consideration of familiar attitudes to work and consumption. Most New England moralists and even most social scientists of Patten's generation, having recognized the difficulty of deriving a sense of meaning from industrial labor, tried to discover ways to make leisure the character-building activity they once hoped work would be, an effort in which Patten often participated. Fearful of the consequences of undisciplined use of free time and yet more accepting of recreation, reformers tried to mold the leisure pursuits of the working class. What made Patten's responses urgent, somewhat tentative, and not altogether precise was that he was responding to swift and important changes in the development of mass, commercial culture in the United States. In the 1880s, the saloon had emerged as an institution that provided workers and immigrants with commercial leisure. Yet these groups managed to shape the saloon to their own ends, a place that sustained their culture and stood in opposition to respectable values. Then around the turn of the century, two new institutions heralded even more dramatic changes in American life: amusement parks and movie theaters. They both threatened middle-class mores and promised release, not uplift. Initially, they remained beyond the control of custodians of culture and Progressive reformers. Movies and amusement parks allowed workers and immigrants to enjoy their own culture and participate in American society as well. Patten worked to understand the implications of these changes. Indeed, the publication of *New Basis of Civilization* and *Product and Climax* in 1907 and 1909 coincided with the years when movie-going grew dramatically among working-class families, causing considerable alarm among middle-class observers.

The resolution of the tension between restraints and desires that Patten struggled to achieve was incomplete—in part because it was not fully worked out, in part because the divorce ultimately pointed away from a passionate life, and in part because Patten could not wholly turn his back on the judgmental tradition.[18] What makes Patten so important a bellwether is that as a transitional figure he vacillated on the question of whether censoriousness could be used to discipline people's desires.

In fact, by the end of the first decade of the twentieth century, it was clear that the United States was less and less likely to pursue the future that Patten outlined in *Product and Climax*. Mass production and consumption, middle-class patterns of work and leisure, problems of standardization of culture—these were the issues to which Patten turned in the dozen years before his death in 1922. Again he tried to find a position between desire and restraint, at one moment celebrating "extravagance as a virtue" and at another recognizing the limits to consumption imposed by the constraints of middle-class budgets in a period of inflation, the importance of self-control, and the advisability of repressing primitive instincts. Patten thus moved away from earlier concerns with the poor and workers and from the task of considering the full range of possibilities in a world increasingly dominated by routine industrial work and commercialized consumption. His interest in problems of standardization and budgets pointed away from celebration of socialized, noncommercial recreation and expressions of passionate desires within a communal setting. Even so, to the end of his life, Patten remained concerned with the central issues that had always commanded his best energies: the consequences for the social order of the eternal battle between "new wants" and "old restraints."[19]

If Patten advocated social reforms that would improve working-class patterns of consumption, Thorstein Veblen (1857–1929) launched a fundamental criticism of the habits of consumption of the wealthy and the ideology of conservative moralists. In much of what he wrote for thirty years beginning in 1891, Veblen combined economic radicalism with an emphasis on restraints to produce a penetrating analysis of the wasteful and extravagant consumption of the leisure class. In the process he raised basic questions about the direction of the modern economy and the importance of a rising standard of living. Veblen's ironic tone and radical thrust arose from his rhetorical ability to parody his predecessors, accepting their terminology but radicalizing its meaning. As a final irony, Veblen's attack on conservatives and the leisure class rested on his espousal of restraints not unlike those that moralists had long embraced.[20]

Veblen's treatment of profligacy demonstrates how he transformed the terms of discourse. Many reformers had considerable difficulty in developing a consistent position on extravagance. Not wanting to associate themselves with attacks against the wealthy, some of Veblen's predecessors used a double standard that made them less likely to criticize the profligacy of the rich than the extravagance of the poor. Veblen, however, used a single standard, whose application made the wealthy the recipients of the brunt of his attack.[21] He found "a substantial ground of truth in the indictment" of workers as "improvident and apparently incompetent to take care of the pecuniary details of their own life." However, what Calvinist heirs ascribed to weak character, Veblen saw as a virtue. The "trouble," he wrote in 1900, ran "deeper than exhortation" about "thrift and self-help" could reach. Workers, engaged in industrial rather than pecuniary employments, were not governed by "the intellectual discipline of pecuniary management." This condition indeed made them improvident, but, more importantly, Veblen concluded with a final twist of the argument at the expense of conservatives, it encouraged a "growing lack of deference and affection for" "the institution of property" and "other conventional features of social structure." In contrast, the wealthy consumed conspicuously because their insulation from industrial realities allowed them to maintain leisure-class conventions and indulge in essentially archaic, barbarian habits.[22]

Veblen shared with traditionalists a sense of tension between imitation as a welcome spur to development and as an unfortunate destroyer of restraints. He broke fresh ground in converting the familiar concern for the way that emulation undermined restraints into an unequivocal attack on the leisure class for slowing the pace of economic development and causing the immiserization of the poor. The extravagance of the wealthy, by stalling industrial innovation and lowering the energy of the poor, encouraged a chase after "conspicuous decency" rather than satisfaction of "physical comfort and fullness of life."[23]

More than a witty parody of the rich in America, Veblen's writing involved a fundamental reexamination of the ways that generations of Americans had thought about consumption and a rising standard of living. Nowhere was this clearer than in his questioning of the central and usually unexamined notion that with increased wealth people would choose moral, elevating, and socializing objectives, an assumption that Patten usually accepted. Veblen thus broke with a central tenet of nineteenth-century moralism. For him, the consumer's "so-called higher wants—spiritual, aesthetic, intellectual, or what not" merely represented a "badge or insignia of honour that will serve as a conventionally accepted mark of exploit." Where Patten hoped that affluence would promote communal experiences, Veblen saw it leading to an "exclusiveness," a "habit of privacy and reserve." The finer things of life were thus artificial tokens of "pecuniary reputability," a proof that the individual, excused from productive work, remained in touch with an archaic, barbarian way of life. No distinction obtained between private and government expenses, since both could be "wasteful." Similarly philanthropy, for traditionalists the principal bulwark against temptations of riches, was for Veblen an endeavor suffused with invidious habits, perhaps even a means of saving pecuniary interests from the imperatives of technology. In short, what others had "euphemistically spoken of as a rising standard of living," Veblen interpreted as part of the "cumulative growth of wasteful expenditures."[24]

Veblen's denial of the equation of more with better posed a problem with which he continually wrestled.[25] If economic development did not foster the emergence of higher wants, then what was the end of economic activity? In struggling to answer this question, Veblen faced the conflict between arduous effort and the excessive enjoyment of the resulting comforts, between the celebration of economic progress and the necessity for restraints. Patten's way out involved the use of restraints as the handmaiden of both growth and reform. For Veblen, modern societies found themselves trapped by a conflict between his own version of the work ethic and the emulation of the pecuniary habits of the leisure class. The instinct of workmanship, the elemental drive that made men prefer "effective work" or industrial "serviceability" to unproductive or "futile effort," constantly forced people to realize that fruitful activity was a primary and abiding good. However, ends of dubious value always threatened to contaminate the instinct of workmanship. In fact, Veblen argued, the successful exercise of this drive was self-destructive. Resulting as it did in technological advances and abundant production, hard work led to a victory of pecuniary habits and "threw the fortunes of the industrial community into the hands of the owners of accumulated wealth."[26]

Veblen thus shared with the ideology he attacked a preference for purposeful work (something Patten doubted was possible under modern industrial conditions) and an abhorrence of wasteful consumption. He differed in defining the desired ends of productive effort. Veblen's own choice was maximum production to satisfy noninvidious desires. This reflected his love of workmanship, as well as his embrace of technology and mass production.

Given the existing social system and cultural dispositions, he argued, there was no resolution of the tension between good production and bad consumption. "The need of conspicuous waste," he wrote, "stands ready to absorb any increase in the community's industrial efficiency or output of goods, after the most elementary physical wants would have been provided for." Modern industrial societies, he remarked in 1921, work at about half of their full capacity and "something like one-half of the actual output is consumed in wasteful superfluities."[27]

Nonetheless, it was not always clear how an alternative system would take up the considerable slack such an estimate implied. Satisfaction of physical needs, "full and reasonably proportioned" use of men and equipment, and "an equitable and sufficient supply of goods and services to consumers" were clearly desirable. Veblen suggested that something more was worthwhile. He sprinkled his writings with references to goals such as industrial serviceability, the enhancement of life, and "other, perhaps nobler and socially more serviceable, activities."[28] Unfortunately, Veblen never went beyond such vague hints about what these "nobler" efforts involved. He eliminated the most obvious alternatives—leisure, cultural activities, philanthropy, public welfare. For him, most familiar forms of expenditure above subsistence were wasteful and tinged by invidious considerations. Like Patten, Veblen was a transitional figure. In his inability to elaborate alternatives Veblen seemed trapped between his love of production and technology and his predisposition toward restrained consumption.

On one level, he shared that dead end with his predecessors. Yet Veblen was also willing to consider a possibility some of them felt an unknowing ambivalence toward—that economic growth (under existing or perhaps any circumstances) was not necessarily good, that a simple life should triumph over the future that technology opened up. Nowhere was this clearer than in Veblen's occasional embrace of the notion that excessive consumption and the breakdown of restraints would bring the demise of civilization. For nineteenth-century moralists, this was a possibility worth avoiding. Patten had toyed with and then moved away from the notion of invigorating civilization with "uncivilized" passions. In view of Veblen's belief in the primacy of the "savage," prebarbarian traits of peacefulness and productivity, the likelihood of a lapse from civilization was logically necessary and preferable. His predictions of an eventual undermining of the leisure-class, barbarian civilization were sometimes vague and contradictory. The process did, however, involve a disintegration of pecuniary culture and a resurgence of admirable savage qualities. This made Veblen seem like a latter-day

Thoreau. They shared an ability to penetrate the conventions of a consumer society. However, Veblen's indecisive evaluation of the back-to-nature movement reminds us that though he and Thoreau rejected leisure-class "civilization," Veblen embraced some important aspects of machine production.[29]

Veblen remained distinctive for his ability to combine an appreciation of machinery and mass production with an emphasis on restraints. Moreover, he then used both to question the existing economic system. How much he shared with his predecessors is quite striking, as are the ways he modified the meaning of their position. Veblen's exposure to orthodox economics as an undergraduate (an experience that Patten did not have) gave him something clear and firm to absorb and transform. Patten's youth on a successful farm reassured him that restraints paid off with bourgeois pleasures, a lesson that Veblen could not learn from his less comfortable upbringing. Patten's grappling with his own drive for self-restraint more or less paralleled larger intellectual concerns. Veblen's involvement with issues of constraint resulted in some puritanism in his thought and in his patterns of consumption but not in his sexual life.[30] Consequently, a number of factors dovetailed to produce Veblen's emphasis on restraints. As successfully as almost any American of the period, he sensed the dynamics of mass production and a rising standard of living but broke the connection between the introduction of machinery and the spread of commercial goods by criticizing the influence of conspicuous consumption in a democratic society. His disinclination to break with puritanism makes it necessary to look elsewhere for someone who welcomed mass consumption and a rising standard of living, someone who would attack the dominant nineteenth-century ideology from a somewhat distinctive perspective.

George Gunton (1845–1919) recast the tradition in ways quite different from Patten or Veblen. He started with a radical version of moralism and ended with a celebration of consumption that evidenced few traces of any commitment to puritanical self-discipline. He offered one of the most systematic and sympathetic appraisals of many elements of the modern consumer economy. In contrast to Patten's "excellent ideas [sunk] in a bewildering metaphysical marsh" and his "system of suggested ratiocination," Gunton preferred the simple argument that the increase of wealth involved trouble-free growth. Perhaps Veblen "reads and ponders too much," Gunton quipped in 1891, "and thinks of mankind too often as a possible race of professors instead of a race of burly as well as highly-developed citizens."[31] By the turn of the century, Gunton, who lacked the stature and influence of Veblen or Patten, had emerged as the least puritanical of the major theorists of consumption, an effective critic of the excessive emphasis on prudential virtues, and one of America's strongest advocates of leisure, extravagance, and unlimited comforts.

Gunton came from the ranks of those who supported the eight-hour day. In the late nineteenth century workers demanded more time when they could pursue leisure activities that employers, in their drive for rationalization, had eliminated from the workplace. By the 1860s, Ira Steward (1831–83), Gunton's mentor and the leading advocate of a legislative reduction of the workday, had used a radical version of moralism to pose a fundamental challenge to conservatives who worried about the perils of unrestrained consumption. Poverty, not weak personal character, made men intemperate and extravagant, Steward had argued. Consequently, "the morality that is taught to poor people means, an attempt to make them virtuous, by leaving them *empty!*" "Those who now live in palaces, dress in silk and broad-cloth, take the most journeys and own the best private libraries," Steward continued, should not be listened to when they warned workers against excessive consumption.[32] Steward taught Gunton that workers would improve their condition not by saving but by spending. Steward sought to prevent a deterioration in the labor aristocracy's standard of living by improving the lot of all workers. In the process, he developed an argument for the importance of mass consumption in economic development. The death of his wife in 1878 and his own death five years later made it impossible for him to turn scattered statements into a sustained formulation.

In 1874, Gunton migrated to Fall River, Massachusetts, a city that in the late nineteenth century experienced fierce struggles between capital and labor over wages, hours, and working conditions. Though we know little of Gunton's life in England, we do know that in the 1870s many workers, blacklisted for activities in the Lancashire textile unions, came to the Massachusetts mill town, making it the locus of laborers committed to union organizing and class consciousness.[33] With the help of Steward and other union organizers, Gunton emerged as an important labor radical. His leadership of a strike in 1875 caused the factory owners to blacklist him, though that hardly prevented him from continuing to participate in union activities. In 1879 he led another strike, the failure of which helped undermine the union's strength.

Then in the mid-1880s came a major turning point in his life. In 1883, he stopped work as a labor journalist and organizer, divorced his first wife, and assumed the responsibility for using Steward's papers to develop an ordered, theoretical justification of the eight-hour movement. He moved to New York City in 1885 and married a second time a year later. In New York, there were labor radicals whom Gunton had known earlier and toward whom he could have gravitated. Instead he accepted support and encouragement from others, including the reform-minded clergyman R. Heber Newton, the influential Columbia University economist Edwin R. A. Seligman, and, at a later point, John D. Rockefeller.[34] One of Gunton's earliest and most timely patrons was Parke Godwin, a leading New York editor and genteel reformer, who retained from his antebellum experiences a desire to support programs that would transform the society without revolutionary or radical action. Godwin saw in Gunton an ideal foil for Henry George, whose candidacy for mayor of New York on the Single Tax platform went too far in threatening the established order. In a time of tremendous labor agitation and social unrest, Godwin doubtlessly recognized how useful it was to have Gunton, a former union leader, argue that along with progress came wealth, not poverty. Gunton accepted Godwin's assistance and with it came pressure to turn away from Steward's radicalism.[35]

In the late 1880s, Gunton thus found support and audiences outside the labor movement and faced the possibility of changing the ideology he had inherited from Steward. Gunton was sensitive to charges that patronage caused him to shift his position. He once commented that he did not feel himself "as under the slightest obligation to change my view or policy by receiving aid from anybody."[36] The relation between patron and client was more subtle and complicated than Gunton acknowledged. In fact, modifications in his analysis accompanied new sources of support and improved social position. The rise of George Gunton meant the declining influence of the ideas inherited from Steward. From 1885 on, Gunton executed a shift from a labor radicalism that foretold a cooperative commonwealth to an acceptance of the capitalist system, albeit with a continuing emphasis on the consumer and the rising standard of living.

Gathering the loose strands of Steward's argument into a tightly woven fabric in his two most important books, *Wealth and Progress* (1887) and *Principles of Social Economics* (1891), Gunton asserted that a legislative reduction of the hours of labor would provide more leisure. Such added time would stimulate consumption, raise the standard of living, and foster elevating desires among the workers. The starting point of Gunton's elaborate argument reflected his debt to his mentor: the growth of wants, habits, and opportunities—especially those of the workers—was the basis of increased consumption. The standard of living—the customary level and style of social relations—was the mechanism that translated wants into a powerful economic force. Gunton made the process dynamic by asserting that the most expensive families—those containing rebellious, dynamic, or cultivated workers—chafed against habitual patterns of living. Following Steward, Gunton asserted that increased wants ultimately led to high wages, which in turn created a mass market. The rise in the standard of living thus made improved technology necessary by forcing labor costs up and made its use possible by creating mass demand.[37]

The ambitious English immigrant unabashedly envisioned an unending progression of escalating desires and a continually rising standard of living. He spent little time worrying about the possibility of wasteful consumption by the rich or poor. He could thus confidently and naively assume that leisure, wealth, and social opportunity, by providing experiences with new tastes and thereby promoting greater desires, would be both socializing and elevating. He argued that new wants would make more frequent and varied social intercourse necessary, since he believed that shopping in a department store, reading books, going to a concert or a museum provided people with ennobling, public experiences. Nonnecessities were tantamount to social wants because he accepted no distinction between enjoyment of public experiences and private goods. Habit and abstinence, not unbridled expenditure, threatened the onward movement of society. Only the immigrant worker who saved rather than spent could unhitch Gunton's wagon and prevent it from reaching a consumer's paradise. As late as 1889, however, Gunton remained certain that a shorter day would help raise the most unassimilated immigrants to the native's level.[38]

Gunton remained optimistic about the future. Unlike Patten and Veblen, he equated increased consumption with civilization. "Exclusive egoism," he wrote, was to be "transformed into all inclusive altruism, and savagery" would be "converted into civilization." Increased consumption would benefit workers and capitalists alike. Under the wage system modern society advanced with the growth of desires. Individualism survived because the "individualization" the worker gained through greater comforts was not threatened by the "socialization" caused by the concentration of production.[39] The enactment of eight-hour legislation would bring heaven to earth by improving but not overturning the existing economic system. Gunton denied rather than resolved the tensions that traditionalists and Patten felt between work and pleasure, restraint and enjoyment.

In developing his argument, Gunton had relied quite heavily on what Steward had taught him and on what he himself had written before 1883, when he was a labor radical. Especially in his earlier writings, Gunton articulated a vision of free labor and elevated consumption. In the late 1880s, when Gunton was still somewhat identified with organized labor, he began to complete his attack on restraints and his advocacy of a consumer society. Steward had launched an elaborate and penetrating attack on the dominant nineteenth-century ideology, yet he had hardly called for the elimination of all restraints on consumption, even all morally based ones.[40] Gunton, whose early writings had cautioned against profligacy, had removed virtually all traces of restraint by 1891. In the late 1880s, Gunton had changed higher wages and shorter hours, for Steward a means to a utopian end, into goals that were important in themselves and supportive of capitalism. Neither practical considerations nor concerns about the pace of enrichment remained. That more desires meant higher ones was the only brake on acquisitiveness he envisioned, and, as we shall see, this was one of the most vulnerable parts of his argument. In a sense, Gunton continued a process his mentor had begun, the removal of all puritanical restraints on consumption.

In the dozen years after the publication of *Principles of Social Economics* in 1891, Gunton and his spokesmen departed even more dramatically from a theory of consumption that placed the aspiring worker in a central position. Gunton's reaction to the opening of Biltmore, George Washington Vanderbilt's 250-room, 125,000-acre estate, in 1895 showed how his theory of consumption might easily move from praise of ambitious workers to the kind of justification of lavish expenditures of the very rich that Veblen had mocked. Gunton hailed Biltmore as "leading the way to a new direction of devoting American wealth to the uplifting of [the] American standard of taste and social cultivation." By treating a private and secluded estate as if it were an accessible public park, Gunton had made great wealth almost solely responsible for stimulating desires and elevating tastes. The wealthy not only replaced the most ambitious workers as the leaders in the rise of the standard of living but also edged aside the masses as the creators of effective demand. The opening of Vanderbilt's estate inspired him to believe that the United States was "just entering upon the threshold of the leisured phase of its societary development." He now hailed a civilization that would avoid a relapse into barbarism by excluding puritanical immigrants and by allowing rich and poor to let their desires have full rein.[41]

In 1904, Gunton abruptly ended his public career. He married once again, this time to a wealthy widow, and retired to Virginia. His third marriage failed and Gunton died in 1919. One obituary ironically distorted an incident in his life. Gunton had worked in the mills of Fall River in the 1870s, a newspaper reported, "it was said, merely to study conditions, and not from necessity."[42]

What explains Gunton's change from an ambitious labor leader who argued for the betterment of the working class into an aspiring entrepreneur who eventually justified colossal wealth? Perhaps when he left England in 1874, he was already hoping for a life of greater comfort and leisure.[43]

During his years as a labor leader, he had shown a flamboyance in his personal style and an appreciation of the comforts of life in his writings. As a British emigrant and as an American labor leader, he was hardly alone in his embrace of the temptations American society offered.[44] We will probably never know whether, when he moved to New York, he had already decided to seek new audiences and temper his radicalism. Aid from patrons was thus but one of the factors that explain why he changed. It is likely that only slowly did he see the possibility of rising above the middle class and turning so strongly against radicalism. There did come a point in the 1890s when gradual modifications in his ideology turned into a clear break with much of his past.

In a very real sense, however, there was considerable continuity in Gunton's position from the 1870s until the 1890s, leading one to ask about the relation between Gunton's experience as a laborer and his celebration of comforts. Members of the working class unhappy with their position in the nineteenth century had at least two options. On the one hand, they could avoid acquisitive individualism, foster their sense of class solidarity, try to liquidate great wealth (which they often saw as a moral anathema to a disciplined and cultivated life), and thereby improve their position collectively. On the other hand, on an individual or group basis they could struggle to escape from their origins. To solidify the working class and to rise above it were two tendencies often held in tension. Ira Steward chose to emphasize class allegiance; over time Gunton came to deny it.

Changes in working-class culture facilitated this acceptance of a rising standard of living. Many laborers in the nineteenth century persisted in pursuing preindustrial habits of work and consumption characterized by spontaneity and a lack of division between work and play. Yet within the antebellum Protestant working class a small number of people emerged who accepted the new industrial discipline in order to seek satisfaction outside work.[45] In addition, because laborers did not always act on the advice about self-denial, they were freer to see the positive implications of greater pleasure in consumption. Gunton recognized the ill effects of long hours of industrial work. He knew that many types of work were unrewarding in and of themselves. In arguing for a reduction in hours without suggesting any more fundamental modifications in the nature of production, he was asking that laborers separate work and leisure, that they accept industrial discipline as a given and time as a commodity that could be bargained for. Then they could seek rewards elsewhere, in consumption rather than production.[46]

Gunton was thus calling for a major reorientation of labor's aspirations. Traditionally, labor leaders had asserted the primacy of the worker as producer, one outcome of which was the dream of mobility into the ranks of entrepreneurs. Whereas trade unions responded to the recognition of the difficulty of achieving such a goal by political action, Gunton chose the path of improvement through a higher standard of living. Though conservatives would eventually discover the usefulness of fostering loyalty to the social order by replacing the artisan with the consumer, by the 1880s Gunton was already paving the way.[47] Earlier than many other writers, he suggested breaking labor's allegiance to class and work and called for a reorientation around the dreams of affluence and leisure. As a labor radical and more fully as an apologist for industrial capitalism, he offered a broad attack on the preference for self-control.

Yet the consumption toward which he was pointing is curiously different from that of the late twentieth century. Gunton felt that genuine needs for comfort and aspirations for a cultured life, rather than advertising and materialism, would shape the future. He was trying to lessen the hours of labor so workers would have more time to enjoy a higher standard of living, especially the leisure to experience music, literature, and art. Thus Gunton continued to share at least one thing with traditional moralists: the hope that with a growth of desires would come a decision to choose "higher" wants. Reflecting his past as a labor aristocrat, here Gunton's theory was at loggerheads with itself. Though he spoke of "material comforts and social refinement" as if they were the same, he clearly pointed down the road that led not to mass consumption but to an embrace of cultivation and refinement. His theory rested on the assumption that economic growth stemmed from the wide acceptance of material goods, not from attendance at cultural institutions, like symphonies and museums, whose connection with mass production remained obscure. Consequently, Gunton's advocacy of restrained and refined notions of enjoyment, which bespoke his debt to middle-class reformers and his own aspirations (and perhaps those of some members of the labor aristocracy), curiously undercut his larger argument. Gunton failed to understand the force of advertising and the characteristic buying behavior of a mass society. He saw no contradiction between mass consumption and individualism. Americans in the twentieth century would not so easily accept the argument that mass-produced goods, like enjoyment of culture at a concert or in travel, could provide moral uplift for consumers.[48]

These problems, though significant, should not negate his importance as one who challenged the dominant New England tradition and celebrated the transformation of an American society increasingly shaped by the culture of consumption. Though with little apparent influence on others, Gunton was reasonably accurate in predicting the direction in which America was headed.[49] His writings make clear that important elements of

47

an emerging consumer society and ideology existed well before the 1920s. If Gunton were correct, then many Americans, including some workers, had a desire to consume comforts and luxuries well before modern advertising shaped their consciousness. The striving for a higher standard of living came from a number of sources, including genuine needs for comfort and emulation of social superiors.

Patten, Veblen, and Gunton were transitional figures who struggled to reshape conservative moralism. With the benefit of hindsight, we can see how their writings were problematic in several ways. By emphasizing that the drive for a higher standard of living came largely from psychological sources, only in rare moments could the three writers speculate on or appreciate the implications of a world where the signals for economic behavior came from institutions as well. Partly because their experience with a world of commercialism and mass consumption was relatively limited, only indirectly or occasionally could they provide ways of understanding lives influenced by advertising, disposable consumer goods, and instant, artificial experiences.[50] Moreover, they did not always comprehend the emergence of the United States as a nation significantly shaped by a middle-class consumer culture. Finally, all three could not think beyond the idea that more economic development would prompt people to seek higher, more refined wants. Even Veblen, who poked fun at such strivings, did not clearly and consistently articulate an alternative to a restrained way of life. The framework and assumptions of the beliefs they were attacking left their mark on the ideas of Patten, Gunton, and Veblen.

All of this should not prevent us from realizing that better than almost any other members of their generation, Patten, Veblen, and Gunton comprehended the direction in which the United States was moving. Veblen helped his own and later eras understand the cultural and psychological dynamics of consumption, conspicuous and otherwise. His was among the most important voices calling for a reconsideration of the assumption that a higher standard of living necessarily meant a more refined one. Patten turned moralism away from its conservative origins and toward social reform. He was among the most perceptive social scientists of his generation in his appreciation of the differences between working-class culture, the culture of libraries and museums, and the new mass, commercial culture. Veblen and Patten worried about restraints as their contemporaries entered an age of abundance. All three recognized that the answers of their predecessors were not satisfactory and helped considerably in shifting the nature of the debate to new issues or at least new formulations of old ones.

In the quarter-century after 1885, Patten, Veblen, and Gunton had moved considerably beyond Carroll D. Wright's much more ambiguous stance. As inheritors of a tradition more than a century old, they looked back on a world where restraint had long been an economic necessity and an ethical imperative. As people who looked forward to a new age of affluence, they understood some of the forces transforming America into a nation of consumers. Their intellectual journeys demonstrated that New England moralism had not died as the nineteenth century ended and the twentieth began, but events and ideas had weakened it. Along with economic and social forces that technology and industrial capitalism unleashed, Patten, Veblen, and Gunton helped undermine what they were reformulating. In the first twenty years of the new century, inflation, the changing nature of class relations, a world war, as well as new patterns of consumption, would prompt further questioning of the assumptions behind nineteenth-century attitudes toward virtue.

4 Progressives, Morality, and Reality

Shortly after the beginning of the twentieth century, when Gunton had retired from public life but Veblen and Patten were still developing their interpretations of the challenges of affluence, Progressive social reformers carried out a series of investigations of the standard of living of families of urban immigrants and workers. At a time when middle-class households were experiencing new comforts and a new sense of choice, these investigations revealed that working-class households made their discretionary expenditures in ways that reflected old patterns more than they foretold new ones. The reports also show how the authors of budget studies, in moving away from a search for profligate behavior and toward an acceptance of new levels of comfort, weakened the tradition of conservative moralism. Like Patten, Veblen, and Gunton, Progressive household investigators to a considerable extent still worked within the framework they were trying to reshape. Though concerned about the plight of those whose lives they examined, the Progressives only partially appreciated working-class and immigrant culture. By opposing the way of life of the poor, preferring middle-class aspirations, and yet welcoming some new patterns of consumption, household budget investigators continued in but modified the judgmental tradition. By shifting from character to conditions as the explanation of the plight of the poor, Progressive moralists became less conservative and censorious than their nineteenth-century counterparts. However, the preference for self-control and refinement demonstrated that early-twentieth-century writers continued to emphasize bourgeois virtues of hard work, respectability, and self-restraint.

By the 1890s, state and national bureaus of labor statistics, in compiling plain and impersonal data, had lost the ability to dramatize the lives of immigrants and workers. The initial attempts to understand ordinary people anew came in studies like Jacob A. Riis, *How the Other Half Lives* (1890); Helen S. Campbell, *Prisoners of Poverty* (1887) and *Women Wage Earners* (1893); Walter A. Wyckoff, *The Workers* (1897–98); and Bessie and Marie

Van Vorst, *The Woman Who Toils* (1903). Struck by the deplorable conditions that existed in American cities and factories, these writers gathered information through firsthand observation, produced vivid narratives, and dramatized the struggles of the poor to survive when faced with harsh living and working situations. Though these books did not contain systematic examinations of budgets, they nonetheless helped awaken interest in how the other half lived.

Shortly after the turn of the century and under the influence of English examples, reformers and social workers undertook scores of investigations of an adequate standard of living for small samples of poor, working-class, and lower middle-class urban families. These studies were part of the social scientists' emerging interest in systematically studying the world about them and of the Progressive reformers' commitment to understanding poverty and social reality. The examination of the way people spent their money made it possible for observers to explore the nature of America as a consumer nation at precisely the time when work had lost so much of its meaning for many middle-class writers. In addition to revealing the nature of household expenditures during these years, these reports provided a way the middle class considered its own changing patterns of consumption. Such investigations also served as instruments that observers used to try to influence the behavior of their subjects. In their focus on a minimally acceptable standard, in their effort to help families budget more carefully, and in their use of categories foreign to the experience they were describing, these studies were as much didactic as they were descriptive. The judgmental tradition encouraged the investigators' suspicion of the workers' participation in events that had an expressive and communal dimension. Yet, especially compared with Carroll D. Wright's 1875 work, those of the Progressive period diminished but hardly eliminated the censoriousness with which the middle class had long approached the expenditures of workers and immigrants.

Though it was neither the first nor the most comprehensive such study, Robert C. Chapin's *The Standard of Living among Workingmen's Families in New York City* (1909) was a widely respected one that as well as any other illustrates the nature of the Progressive generation's examination of the standard of living. Chapin's father, Aaron L. Chapin (1817–92), was a Congregational minister, a founder and the first president of Beloit College, and a moral philosopher who brought out editions of Francis Wayland's textbook in economics. The son both modified and retained the tradition that his father had helped shape.[1] Under the auspices of the New York State Conference on Charities and Correction, Robert C. Chapin (1863–1913) began to gather data for his Columbia Ph.D. thesis while he was on a leave of absence from his professorship at Beloit College. When reliance on volunteers produced only a few completed questionnaires, the Russell Sage Foundation underwrote the payment of interviewers—charity and social workers, union members, and teachers, "persons who either possessed a personal acquaintance with families suitable for the purposes of the inquiry, or who had experience in similar social work." These assistants obtained 391 completed family budgets, mostly from households "of normal composition and of moderate size, that is, having both parents living and from 2 to 4 children under 16 years of age," with primary focus on families that had an income between five hundred and a thousand dollars a year. In half of the cases, the interviewers already knew the family and Chapin assumed that the selection of households capable of giving detailed information tipped the sample toward those "showing better management and a higher standard than that which prevails among the mass of families having corresponding incomes."[2]

Of the 391 families, 318 (the central group) reported incomes between $600 and $1100, with 25 below $600 and 48 above $1100. The central group thus had incomes roughly comparable to $6540 to $11990 in 1984. In Chapin's study, as in Carroll D. Wright's, there was a clear relation between earnings and occupation. Earning high incomes were professional and white-collar people—most of the fathers employed in "professional service" and several of those who worked as "agents, clerks, salesmen" and "merchants and dealers." At the lower end were laborers in the textile and building trades. In terms of total family earnings, those with the highest incomes (above $1500) were also professionals and white-collar workers: families headed by clergymen, dentists, barbershop proprietors, railroad inspectors, and telegraphers. Those with the lowest family income (with medians clearly below $800) were manual and service workers: journalists, barbershop employees, cooks, office cleaners, watchmen, porters, waiters, casual laborers, clerks, pedlars, merchants, dealers, teamsters, and many of those in "manufacturing and mechanical trades." Compared with the 1875 study, the relationship between ethnicity and income was somewhat less uniform, probably reflecting the Americanization of family, consumption, and occupational patterns.[3]

The report revealed that the higher the income, the greater the funds brought in by lodgers, wives, and children—indeed an income above $700 or $800 was "obtainable as a rule only by taking lodgers or by putting mother and children to work." Fifty-eight of the mothers of this central group worked outside the home, about half of them in "janitor service, in many cases in the tenement buildings in which they live" and usually in exchange for rent. Especially when the father's income was low, children went to work as soon as legally possible, so that the family could maintain its standard of living when growing children required more food and more costly clothing.[4]

For rent, the higher the family income, the smaller the percentage spent—from 27 percent for the poorest to 18 percent for those earning between $1000 and $1100. What this translated into was hardly comfortable: 53 percent of all of the families had at least one room that lacked direct access to outside air or light; within the apartment, only 20 percent had bathrooms and only 41 percent had toilets; and 48 percent had more than 1.5 persons per room, a degree of density that Chapin considered overcrowded. Most families reported spending money for transportation to work, with no significant increase for those with larger incomes. Expenditure for fuel and light decreased as income rose—from 5.8 percent for those at the $600 to $700 level to 3.8 percent between $1100 and $1200. Food thus took the lion's share of household expenses, going under 44.3 percent only for families with incomes less than $400 and above $1300. Working with a nutritionist, Chapin established a figure of $0.22 per grown man per day as necessary "to maintain physical efficiency." Using this standard, the report concluded that the proportion of underfed families fell from 76 percent at the $400 to $600 level to zero above $1100. Spending on clothing increased steadily with income, from 12.9 percent in the $600 to $700 range to 15.5 percent at the $1000 to $1100 level. With an estimate of $100 a year as necessary to clothe a family of five adequately, Chapin found that 40 percent of the families with an income between $600 and $1100 were underclothed.[5]

Expenditures on food, clothing, and shelter left relatively little for other items, especially for the poorest families. For all families, the amount for medical care fluctuated between 1.5 percent and 7.4 percent of annual income. An income below $800 did not permit "expenditures sufficient to care properly for the health of the family." Families purchased a variety of insurance policies. Slightly less than half had property insurance. The most common kind of protection provided money for burial costs: most of the families in the central group took out enough to cover funeral costs, causing Chapin to conclude that money for "the last sickness and burial constitutes an essential part of the American standard of living, and that most families will go without many comforts in order to" make payments. Provision for unemployment due to illness was much rarer, with Russians and Austrians especially relying on membership in fraternal organizations to provide such benefits.[6]

Chapin included everything else under Sundry Minor Items. For furniture and furnishings, an inventory was obviously a better measure than one year's expenditures. So the study placed the families' possessions into three categories: "meagre," with "nothing beyond the barest supply of indispensable articles—beds and bedding, chairs, table"; "fairly comfortable," for families that had "some additional articles—rugs or oilcloth, mirrors, easy chairs"; and "ample," where there was "an abundant supply both of necessary articles and of accessories," with a piano a typical accessory. On this scale, the standard rose evenly with income, though there were significant differences among ethnic groups, with Russians spending "most liberally" and blacks least so. Very few families used an installment plan to finance purchases. Expenditures for Taxes, Dues, and Contributions were infrequent: almost 20 percent of the central group, the poorest especially, reported no outlay for any of these items, taxes were reported only for the six families who owned homes, and "gifts of friendship and charity" were "few and far between." Of those who made contributions to organizations, 68 percent gave to religious ones, 49 percent to lodges and similiar organizations, and 32 percent to unions.[7]

To Chapin, it was "very plainly" clear that poverty limited expenditures for recreation and amusement, with the average climbing from $3.79 for the families at the $600 level to $22.29 above $1100. Thirty-two families, most of them in the lowest income groups, reported no such expenses. Instead they told the interviewers that they would go to a park, visit relatives, sit in front of the house, and, in one case, "display . . . their furniture" as their "only recreation." Most families spent money on carfare to visit parks and friends and about one of every three families went to the theater, with those having higher incomes partaking of these activities to the greatest extent. There was also a relation between nationality and expenditure, with the greatest propensity to spend on recreation being characteristic of Italians and those groups, American and "Teutonic," "that have adopted most completely the American standard." Nonetheless, Chapin felt, individual patterns were so varied that numbers alone could not convey how people pursued recreation. Some families "occasionally" went to "'the five-cent theater' or moving-picture exhibition" or purchased phonograph records. Though very rarely did the father report paying for a vacation, one mother did take the children to visit her sister "in the country" for three months. A day trip to an amusement park during the summer was "not infrequently mentioned." The most common recreation was through membership in "voluntary societies," which often provided the occasion for "social gatherings, picnics and excursions."[8]

Chapin noted that public schools and libraries provided much of the education and reading material. Families spent very small additional amounts on these items, $5.56 at the $600 level and $8.54 at $1000. Daily newspapers accounted for almost all of such funds. Nationality appeared to affect these expenditures more than income, with English-speaking people spending the most, Italians the least.[9]

Under the umbrella category of Sundry Minor Items, Miscellaneous Expenditures was the catchall that included tobacco, alcohol consumed outside the home, shaves and haircuts, funerals, moving, and spending money. Expenditures on these items, which Chapin considered "an index of the character and experience of members of the family," showed "a marked increase with increase of income." They started at $25.47 at the $600 level and rose to $63.31 at $1100, with nationalities showing "little difference" within an income group. Chapin noted several interesting patterns. Spending money, for which the mother often acted as "cashier," regularly went to husbands for "car-fare, lunches, tobacco, and what not" and more irregularly to children for "luxuries" such as candy, ice cream, and soda. The purchase of tobacco was so widespread that Chapin felt it "must be included as forming part of the established standard of living."[10]

With more consistent and complete evidence, Chapin might well have drawn the same conclusion for the consumption of alcohol outside the home. When he considered drinking within the home under the food category, Chapin had a "fairly complete report . . . inasmuch as the families regarded this item as a matter of course, and felt no more reticence about it than about any other detail." But "what was drunk away from home," he concluded, "was considered as a more personal matter, and the information was not as readily secured," partly because it was hard for the interviewer (and often the wife) to know what was "hidden under 'spending money' or 'meals away from home,' or in one or two obvious instances omitted entirely, leaving an apparent surplus quite irreconcilable with the meagre provision reported for the necessities of life." Indeed there were a few cases that Chapin felt would provide "illustrations for the temperance lecturer . . . in the report of one woman that she bought heavy cups so the drunken husband might not break them, and in the entry under 'playthings for children' that the only expenditure was on one occasion when the father was drunk and bought a 5-cent toy for each child."[11] Information on such extremes was possible to uncover but day-by-day social drinking was apparently impossible to document. In fact, the word *saloon* never appeared in the report. To those who studied household budgets, liquor consumption was an important issue. However, they could not gather the information needed because pressing for answers would have jeopardized their relationships with their subjects and adversely affected the quality of the data they obtained.

For Chapin, sundry minor items, including furniture, dues, recreation,

reading, tobacco, alcohol outside the home, funerals, moving, and spending money, went for satisfaction "of the desire for intellectual, social and
aesthetic gratifications" as well as those "physical" ones, such as tobacco
and soda water, which "are not indispensable to life." Most of the expenditures under this heading were for "that which makes life worth living." As
incomes rose, spending on these items "constantly" increased in amount
and percentage, from $47.55 and 7.3 percent for those with earnings
between $600 and $700 to $114.59 and 11.4 percent at the $1000 to $1100
level. Such a rise prompted Chapin to conclude that the "desires for such
satisfactions . . . always tend to push ahead of the means available for
satisfying them." It was important to remember, Chapin cautioned his
readers, that "much that satisfies the extra-physical wants" was free: public
schools, parks, playgrounds, as well as visits with friends and family. Nonetheless, he concluded, these free things aside, expenditures for sundry
minor items were indications of the "standard of culture attained, and of the
opportunities for raising it."[12]

When he turned to the issue of how many families made ends meet in a
given year, Chapin cautioned that a balanced budget was not in and of itself
a good sign. The level at which ends met might be so low that "the physique
and morale of the family must deteriorate." Nonetheless, a comparison of
income with outgo did indicate whether households could keep up the
standard of living its expenditures represented. Of the 318 in the central
group, 116 came out about even, the same number reported a surplus, and
86 had spent more than they earned. The balance within these three categories did not change dramatically or consistently at different income levels,
leading Chapin to conclude "that there are extravagant families and economical families on whatever income." Nationality, more than income,
appeared the crucial difference and here Chapin believed that the data
pointed to two distinct groups: immigrants from southern and eastern
Europe (Italians, Russians, Austrians, and Bohemians), who were likely to
balance their budgets or achieve a surplus, and Americans, "Teutonic,"
Irish, or "Colored," who were more likely to end the year with a deficit. The
first group had a "lower standard of expenditures." They began to save
above $700 to $800, with incomes above that level not bringing a propor-
tionate increase in expenditures. With northern and western Europeans,
"the point where saving is preferred to immediate satisfaction is scarcely
reached at $1100." In addition, families that relied exclusively on the
father's income were more likely to run a deficit. Those that sent their
children to work early or took in lodgers did so in order to "lay up money,
rather than to maintain a given standard of living."[13]

Indeed, the struggle to make ends meet was considerable, especially at the lower income levels. Poorer families had the best record of keeping expenses within income but they achieved this by "a lowering of the standard of living below the normal demands of health, working efficiency, and social decency." For Chapin, an income of $800 seemed the dividing line. About 70 percent of those in the central group who were underfed, underclothed, and overcrowded had incomes under $800 and most of those who were below par in two of these categories earned less than $800. With an income between $900 and $1000, a family could "get food enough to keep soul and body together, and clothing and shelter enough to meet the most urgent demands of decency." Such a household did not have to rely on charity for medical care, could purchase and maintain "fairly comfortable" furnishings, participate in labor, religious, and fraternal organizations, and still have "some margin . . . available for the pursuit of amusements and recreation, the purchase of books and papers, and the indulgence of personal tastes outside of the indispensable necessities of existence."[14]

Chapin concluded that social conditions, not individual character, set the limits within which families achieved a standard of living. "Improvidence, extravagance, and vice" did not "explain why so many families make so poor a showing" at the lower income levels. To be sure, he admitted, "the personal factor" always operated. In some cases, "excessive expenditures for indulgences" such as drink and tobacco led to lower earnings or curtailment of "expenditures of more fundamental importance." However, the number of such cases was not enough to make "over-indulgence . . . a comprehensive explanation." In most instances, he had to conclude, there were limits to what a family could do by trying to earn more or spend less. "The exceptional woman" could reduce spending by hunting for bargains, preparing meals with perfect economy, and making and mending clothes for an entire family. It was wrong, he argued, to make the exceptional the "measure of what the average woman may be expected to do." The "ordinary" wife had to use the housekeeping methods "that are traditional in her environment and apply them as skillfully and intelligently as her native and acquired powers of mind and body permit." Only with the diffusion of "education in a better economy," he concluded, "will it be possible to maintain the existing standards of physique and character on a lower absolute income."[15]

When Chapin first attempted to gather data for his study in 1907, he encountered a problem that helps us understand the assumptions behind the Progressive period's effort to measure the standard of living. He distributed more than four hundred schedules to volunteer interviewers but it soon became evident that the return would be small. In fact, he received only fifty-seven completed forms and it was then that the Russell Sage Foundation agreed to underwrite the data gathering. Chapin believed that the difficulty lay in "the fulness of the schedule and the pressure of many duties upon" the interviewers, an assessment that the experience with paid survey-takers seemed to bear out.[16] As other studies made clear, however, there were considerable problems in gathering information on household budgets, not the least being the reluctance of the subjects to comply.

The experience George E. Bevans had in collecting data for his 1913 study, *How Workingmen Spend Their Spare Time*, was more revealing. Failing to learn from his predecessors' mistakes, Bevans distributed four thousand schedules and received only slightly more than one hundred completed ones. When he appeared at a labor union meeting held to explain the form, he reported, "pointed questions were frequently asked as to, 'Who is back of the study?' 'What capitalist scheme is this?' 'Why not investigate the employers and see how they spend their spare time?'" In reply, Bevans rejected the workers' views and argued instead that keeping a record of expenses "was a Benjamin Franklin idea of a daily diary." The difficulty in obtaining information, he concluded, lay in the workingman's "indifference, forgetfulness, ignorance, misunderstanding, or suspicion."[17]

The questions raised in "fiery speeches" of "radical" union members deserved fuller answers than the academics, reformers, clergymen, foundation executives, and businessmen who supported budget surveys were willing to offer.[18] Those who carried out the budget studies did not understand the self-interest of their supporters from the business community nor did they even recognize the validity of the question of why reformers did not study the wealthy as much as they did the poor. Moreover, report after report failed to realize that families, randomly selected and lacking a commitment to scientific investigations and middle-class reforms, would not produce detailed, problematic, and intimate information on impersonal forms that tried to impose meaning on experience. As Bevans' reference to Benjamin Franklin revealed, the people who supervised these studies, but probably not many of their subjects, believed that daily expenditure records were instruments of self-examination and self-improvement. Because the early-twentieth-century investigations did not usually contain comments on individual households, the degree of the bias is not as clear as it was in the case of the MBSL's 1875 study. Although it is hard to gauge to what extent the Progressives' approach casts doubt on the data collected, there is reason enough to question the assumptions people like Chapin brought to the efforts.

At the heart of the Progressive standard of living investigations was the attempt, by force of law and public opinion, to make informed citizens and "thoughtless employers" realize that poverty undermined the general welfare. These studies reflected Progressive commitments in several ways: they sought to know "reality," to use publicity and professional expertise to ameliorate social conditions, and to avoid threatening existing economic relationships. The solution was a "decent livelihood," enough, Father John Ryan wrote in *A Living Wage* (1906), so that a man would be able to support himself, his wife, and his young children "in a condition of reasonable comfort." Experts tried to determine "the minimum amount of goods and opportunities" necessary to ensure "the power to exercise one's primary faculties, supply one's essential needs, and develop one's personality." Historically, in real dollar terms, the estimate of the minimum level has risen, reflecting changes in society's definition of poverty. In judging the adequacy of income to meet expenditures, the reports did not often discuss the world of work. They usually focused on income levels and ethnicity, not skills, thus often missing the critical correlation between achieving a high standard of living and having a skilled job.[19]

Concern thus focused on the role of these families as consumers. Specifically, the Progressive studies concentrated on subsistence, the border between poverty and adequacy but not, given the interest in establishing minimum levels, that between adequacy and whatever was above comfort. The lack of a larger context was striking in another way. The most common reference to the spending habits of the wealthy appeared in studies of working women. In their 1911 study, Sue A. Clark and Edith Wyatt expressed no surprise that female store employees unwisely adopted "the New York show-window-display ideal of life manifested everywhere around them."[20] Cross-class comparison thus emphasized the dangers of working-class emulation of the rich without criticizing the spending habits of the wealthy.

The lack of a comparative framework (other than poverty) and the insistence on discovering the minimum necessary often limited the surveys' expectations for workers' incomes. Indeed in some instances, notably Robert Hunter's influential *Poverty* (1904), writers advocated a basic level of earnings to ensure the existence of efficient producers, a concern that Chapin shared. "It is precisely the same standard that a man would demand for his horses or slaves," Hunter wrote in reference to life "above the poverty line" and in an appeal to the self-interest and paternalism of employers. Concentration on the minimum acceptable income appeared in other ways. For example, though Chapin could develop specific ways to measure if a family were underfed, underclothed, or overcrowded, when he came to categories like recreation and amusement, he could offer no standard, not even a floor. More clearly than the MBSL's 1875 study, those of the early twentieth century set quantifiable guidelines and minimums for most categories. Yet in many respects, the notion of a fair standard articulated in the first decade of the twentieth century was not decisively different from what had reigned during the last quarter of the nineteenth century, something one contemporary noticed when she criticized Chapin for interpreting "present-day ideals of normal living in static rather than dynamic terms."[21]

Instead of exploring the benefits of income levels above a minimum, some Progressive studies tended to focus on the lowest acceptable step. The implication was that the situation of most working-class families was not degraded but pinched, ethically unjust without being horrible. Researchers in the early twentieth century thus sought to identify clusters of expenditures appropriate for specific social groups. This was understandable, given the investigators' antipathy to luxury and extravagance, as well as their concern for the effects of poverty. Nonetheless, the emphasis on a minimum often made the sense of adequacy not very generous and seemed to rest on an assumption that different classes and ethnic groups deserved different levels of living. Moreover, in focusing on a fair standard for families, most studies neglected to explore what percentage of various income groups attained the established level and how the economy distributed income. This class segregation enabled middle-class investigators to skirt questions of equity that would have touched upon the moral dimension of their own social position and that of their supporters in the business community.[22]

A serious problem also appeared in the implications these studies had for wives, children, the sick, and the elderly. At the end of his book, Chapin held out the hope that better education in household management would make it possible to maintain existing standards on lower incomes. With such a large percentage of budgets spent on food, reformers saw scientific nutrition as a means of raising working-class standards of living without altering existing social relationships. The burden of such economizing efforts would fall on the wife, something that one of the authors of the Pittsburgh Survey recognized in 1913 when she criticized Chapin for creating an economic woman "who without waste or extravagance, can on 22 cents per man per day" feed a family. In addition, despite contemporary warnings, many of the standard of living studies neglected the implications of a tight budget for education of children, as well as for the comfort of the unemployed, the ill, and the elderly.[23]

Chapin's hope that the poor, especially women, might eventually learn to manage their spending more effectively reminds us that the moralism of Progressive reformers and the interests of wealthy supporters helped shape budget studies of the early twentieth century. These investigations offered immigrants and workers lessons in moral education and money budgeting. To begin with, the categories used to pigeonhole data imposed a framework on the lives of the subjects that was in many ways foreign to their experi-

ences. For example, Chapin included contributions to volunteer organizations under insurance, as well as recreation, even though he recognized that
"expenditure for recreation is sometimes not differentiated from dress and
payments to the society." Children living in cramped tenements during the
summer's heat may well have disagreed with his labeling candy, soda water,
and ice cream as luxuries. Similarly, he included alcohol consumed at home
under food, even though it often had medicinal and recreational uses.[24]

As we know from other studies, Progressives hardly confined their advice
to vehicles as indirect and subtle as the categories and language they used.
An extreme instance of the use of household expenditures to advise people
how to spend their money came in Louise B. More's *Wage-Earners' Budgets:
A Study of the Standards and Cost of Living in New York City* (1907). As she
reviewed the material on individual households, in effect she read a morality play to her middle-class readers and her working-class subjects. More
mentioned one "pretty, bright, and ambitious" wife who was "entirely
untrained and without system in her work," leaving "piles of clean clothes
. . . everywhere" and "unwashed dishes . . . on the table." She criticized the
family for burning gas "extravagantly" and not making sufficient plans for
the future. She chastised another family for its "improvidence and shiftless-
ness," apparently insensitive not only to the reality it faced (feeding eight
people on an income of $895, the death of the oldest child during the year,
the father's loss of eight weeks of work because of illness) but also to the
strengths of the mother, who was generous with help for her neighbors and
their children. Perhaps what most bothered More was the untidiness, the
$31.50 spent during the year on drink, and the fact that the wife, when
asked what she would do when she could no longer borrow money, "merely
smiled and said she didn't know!" Unaware of how different was her own
sense of time, More concluded about the mother that "the thought of the
future didn't seem to trouble her in the least."[25]

Louise B. More was hardly the only person who used these studies to
suggest appropriate behavior. One commentator hoped that the provision
of separate bedrooms for children would help instill notions of private
property. Reflecting the middle-class notion that thrift was central to success in America, another writer argued that saving money helped inculcate
a future orientation in laborers.[26] Study after study criticized the families of
workers for supposedly unwise spending habits: mothers for their poor
training in shopping for and cooking food; fathers for throwing away
money on liquor at saloons; families for spending "freely on festive occasions" like weddings and not being frugal with their spending, especially on
sundries; and young women for buying clothing extravagantly as they
chased after cheap fashion.[27] In numerous unexamined ways, the budget

studies attacked immigrant and working-class culture, hoping to replace it with the bourgeois emphasis on self-help and personal discipline. Moreover, concentrating as they often did on how families could improve their lives within the constraints of limited income, long hours, and terrible working conditions, some of the standard of living studies did not sufficiently emphasize the possibility that improvements would come through better working conditions, a shorter workweek, and a more generous pay scale.

The studies of the standard of living often reflected a middle-class lack of appreciation for the texture of working-class and immigrant life. The most symbolic expression of this attitude was the continued use of terms like *miscellaneous* and *sundry* to cover what food, clothing, and shelter did not include. Despite their own unease with these phrases and even some efforts to find substitutes, the authors of the Progressive studies thus acknowledged that they considered "nonnecessities" as leftovers that reflected no particular direction in the lives of people whose expenditures they were recording.[28] This attitude explicitly reflected several elements of nineteenth-century moralism—hostility to the social life of the poor, opposition to commercial entertainment, preference for the pursuit of Culture, and insistence on monetary expenditures as the best way of measuring the standard of living.

To a considerable extent, the Progressive period studies were suspicious of the workers' participation in events that had an expressive and communal dimension because, the investigators felt, festivals and street life were not elevating. The reports fell far short of including in their definition of adequacy the importance of group participation in formal and informal activities. They were somewhat equivocal about giving full recognition to forms of recreation—pageants, plays, celebrations—where no money changed hands. The difficulty lay in the surveyors' insensitivity to the characteristics of immigrant and working-class culture. They regarded street life as the nemesis of their subjects' lives. As Clark and Wyatt had written of the youthful working girl without a place in a home to entertain a man, she turned "to trolley rides and walks and various kinds of excursions,—literally to the streets,—for hospitality" when she received a male visitor. Young people seemed peculiarly vulnerable to what observers saw as lack of worthwhile facilities for recreation. Minimizing the richness of folk traditions and neglecting how children created their own sports, the caption under a picture of some youths playing a street game lamented that the city elders had made no provision for the "simplest recreational needs." Consequently, Progressives emphasized the link between physical culture and personal development. Reformers called for parks and sports facilities that would build character and inculcate discipline and thus turn the children of their day into industrious and moral citizen-workers of the future.[29]

The saloon, dance hall, and other forms of commercial recreation called forth the strongest criticism. Progressives often saw participation in such institutions as unwholesome in large part because they felt that working-class drinking and the proprietors' profit motive encouraged excessively reckless behavior. One author argued that outside of "the library, the free concert, the park," the families of poor urban workers "are living without any of the forms of amusement that make for the natural enlargement of life." The more exhausting a man's work, she wrote, "the more recreation will sink to the sensual and the exciting." Saloons and dance halls were the greatest lure for those who, depleted by work, craved "stimulants." Though "innocent and delightful" in themselves and not without social functions, they were "often debased to the most vicious uses." Especially troublesome was "the element of abandon, of relief from the absolute deadness that comes from overwork that can find pleasure only in the most highly stimulating forms of amusement." Vaudeville, amusement parks, skating rinks, pool halls—these were the places where thrills were purchased but life was not enhanced, places "run for profit and not for the sake of clean recreation such as the community should provide."[30]

The response of budget investigators to movies is particularly instructive. Although the years between 1905 and 1910 witnessed a sudden increase in attendance by working-class families, the early-twentieth-century budget studies did not often mention this change. Moreover, Progressive moralists used the same language of degradation and uplift to attack a wide range of immigrant and working-class recreations, from old ones like saloons and street life to newer ones like amusement parks and movies. One observer found movies "sinking from a true kind of recreation to a mere titillation of the senses."[31] Thus to some Progressives, mass commercial consumption was tainted by its association with immigrants and workers.[32]

The budget studies of the early twentieth century constantly reiterated the notion that with physical necessities taken care of, ordinary people would strive for "higher" things. Rarely did the surveys assume that workers with a minimal sufficiency would pursue an unending succession of material pleasures purchased in the marketplace. Progressives hoped that if hours were shorter and wages higher, people would have the "surplus vitality" needed for "proper enjoyment of . . . evening privileges" like lectures, concerts, and social events at settlement houses. This expectation reflected the influence of New England moralism and provided justification for settlement houses that supported many of the studies. Besides parks and playgrounds, authors of standard of living studies hoped that the community and civic-minded citzens would "provide more night schools, social centers, men's clubs, public lectures and concerts for the improved use of leisure hours."[33] "Constructive diversion . . . of lasting value to the body and spirit," satisfaction of "higher wants," "wants arising out of the desire for intellectual, social and aesthetic gratifications," wholesome pleasure—these were the aspirations the studies pointed to again and again. "The ideal standard of living," Frank A. Streightoff wrote in 1911, demands the satisfaction of "reasonable wants of both body and intellect, and includes an ambition to improve," best seen in the continuous uncovering of "wholesome" desires. With amusements tending "strongly to the sensual," the actual situation was far from ideal. Like others he placed great hope in a future when people would seek "social and literary functions similiar to those so much enjoyed in the settlements."[34]

It is important to put in historical perspective the emphasis these studies placed on social control, the finer things of life, and the dangers of communal and expressive aspects of the culture of workers' families. Especially in comparison with the 1875 MBSL report, what marked the investigations produced in the years before World War I was an appreciation, albeit partial, of the social life of their subjects. Chapin had expressed well the ambiguous quality of this recognition when he wrote that "the ever-varying pageant of street life, sordid though it often is, gives constant novelty and diversion." Along similar lines, in her 1910 study of Homestead, Margaret F. Byington wrote with verve and sympathy of people gathering "around the stove gossiping of home days, playing cards, drinking, and playing musical instruments," of women talking "around the pump or at the butcher's," and of families going to festivities like weddings and funerals where "joy and grief and religious ceremony are alike forgotten in a riotous good time." Yet she also exaggerated the Slavs' eagerness to assimilate to an American way of life, perhaps because she saw them defensively clinging "to the few festivities their limited opportunities make possible" since they were "cut off from what little normal amusement Homestead offers."[35]

Mary K. Simkhovitch produced one of the more complicated appreciations of immigrant cultural opportunities. In The City Worker's World in America (1917), Simkhovitch acknowledged at the outset that it would be impossible to expect exhausted workers to engage in "purposive creative play." Consequently, they turned to institutions like saloons that offered "the stupefying pleasures of dissipation [that] have in them nothing that rejuvenates." Simkhovitch, long active in settlement house work, recognized the pleasures of street life, amusement parks, and family celebrations but always with the lingering hope that such experiences were acceptable especially if they led to "something more worth while," more "purposive" or involved "sustained" effort. Ethnic theater was good, but it too required "no concentration or sustained interest." Similarly, a trip to Coney Island offered "the pleasure of sensation with no arousing of the creative faculty."[36]

The leverage for truly worthwhile improvement was elsewhere. The pleasures of association through unions, clubs, lodges, and the "informal unorganised groups that centre about cafés or saloons" provided "release... from the lower forms of recreation." It was impossible to expect "shipwrecked" people, living below the "security line," "to be bothered with books, interests, ideals." Rather, associational life would enable people "to develop forms of recreation that have in them the promise of unlimited development." Helped by the abolition of poverty, these groups would foster qualities like regularity, steadiness, "mutual forebearance, a common understanding,—all those elements that make for a constructive society."[37]

Though the Progressive studies often criticized the lives of their subjects, they nonetheless attacked some important elements of the older moralist tradition, which had so berated workers for their profligacy. To begin with, several of the investigations were realistic on the question of saving. Louise B. More, though critical of the habits of those she studied, pointed out that immigrant families were more thrifty than nonimmigrant ones, "a condition," she argued, "which must be rather startling to those pessimists who bewail the phenomenal growth of our foreign population." Scott Nearing, having noted that most households did not have enough income to provide a decent standard of living, argued that "no one need discourse at length on the theme of the spendthrift laborer." Others went farther, stating that the failure to save, rather than proving the "unfitness of the family to meet its problems," was a result of legitimate difficulties and agonizing choices. Indeed, as a reviewer of Chapin's book remarked, once it was clear that the number of those judged to be underfed, illclothed, and overcrowded tended to have higher surpluses at the end of the year, it was possible to "wonder whether saving is always an economic virtue."[38]

The question of the extravagance of the families of workers also came under careful scrutiny. The fullest attack on this aspect of moralism came in a study of young working women, the group most often accused of giving in to fashion and excess. In The Living Wage of Women Workers (1911), Louise M. Bosworth argued that her average subject, "while she may sacrifice comfort to appearance occasionally, has not so many comforts that she can easily dispense with any of them." Young working women spent money on clothing, she noted, in order to be able to obtain and keep a good job. Though at times critical of their not saving more, Bosworth nonetheless concluded that these women were neither selfish nor extravagant. By giving money to her family after she had spent "a reasonable amount" on herself, she devoted "a much larger sum to the welfare of others."[39]

One of the most significant contrasts with the 1875 study was in the tone that Progressive moralists used in the examination of working-class households. The twentieth-century reports conveyed less shock and more urgency than did the MBSL's path-breaking study. With conservative moralism diminished but not dead, there was an important shift of sympathies. Hauteur, even when present, was less stark and dominant. The form of the studies, which with few exceptions did not present the data on a household-by-household basis, was more impersonal and less intrusive. The later studies demonstrated a greater concern for the objectivity and for privacy of the subjects. The authors also made fewer patronizing or critical comments on the spending habits of individual families. Of course, the causes and implications of the decreased censoriousness involved more than questions of form. Though Progressives had only the beginning of an appreciation of immigrant and working-class culture, to a considerable degree they were aware of the very real problems their subjects faced. A sense of expertise caused investigators both to distance themselves from and wish to improve the lives of their clients. The heightened understanding of the situation of ordinary people paralleled the erosion of the dominant nineteenth-century outlook. In the early twentieth century, increases in consumer prices and changes in middle-class standards of living would further undermine the judgmental intepretation of the workers' struggle to make ends meet. When the Progressives wrote about the spending habits of the families of workers and immigrants, they were also wondering about changing patterns of consumption among the middle class.[40]

5 Frugality, Inflation, and the Middle Class: The Resurgence of Traditional Attitudes, 1900–1916

At the same time that social workers and reformers offered a less censorious look at working-class household expenditures, a major shift occurred in the treatment of middle-class consumption. From Carroll D. Wright's 1875 study until the early twentieth century, budget experts paid remarkably little systematic attention to how people other than workers and their families spent their money. This situation changed in the decade and a half before American entry into World War I. The emergence of university-based academic disciplines, economics and sociology especially, helped enhance intellectual curiosity about social conditions. Experts in home economics set out to educate middle-class women in the proper running of a household. Inflation and new patterns of consumption, class relationships, and family life prompted increased interest in the way middle-class people made budgetary choices.

Escalating prices shaped the conditions under which Americans learned how the middle class spent its money. During the early twentieth century, Americans experienced the first sustained escalation of prices since the Civil War. In 1910, the inimitable Mr. Dooley, realizing that inflation was causing his expenditures to rise faster than his earnings, remarked that he "wudden't be surprised anny time to pick up a pa-aper an' read: Darin' burglary! Last night burglars broke into th' joolry store iv Soakem an' Co., blew open the safe an' carried off th' entire contints, consistin' iv a pound iv butter an' a scuttle iv coal."[1]

The impact of a rising cost of living depended on a number of factors, including occupation, income, age, gender, and psychological expectations. For most adults, historical memory intensified inflation's impact. The generation coming of age after the turn of the century, having grown up during a period of declining prices, might naturally have expected deflation to continue. With 100 as an index figure for 1860, prices rose to 196 in 1865 and then fell—to 132 in 1875, to 116 in 1885, and then to their low point of 100 in the last three years of the nineteenth century. From that point on they

67

rose—to 106 in 1905, 114 in 1910, and 121 in 1915. The increase was slow but steady: in the sixteen years beginning in 1901, prices went down in three years, stayed even in one, and went up in twelve. Events in the first decade of the new century upset American expectations in another way. In the late nineteenth century, a significant downward adjustment of prices had followed every industrial crisis. No such major price break occurred after the 1907 recession.[2] It is difficult to judge whether contemporaries were responding to changes in their economic situation, in their status, or in their aspirations. The picture for specific middle-class occupations is complicated, with the earnings of many, but hardly all, keeping pace with inflation.[3] However, even if people were not actually losing out in the struggle to keep up with inflation, many in the middle class felt they were fighting a losing battle. Moreover, unexpected price changes were fundamentally disorienting, for they called into question what was real about money.

The onset of inflation coincided with a number of other changes in the standard of living and in American society. In the first decades of the twentieth century, motion pictures, automobiles, department stores, expanded forms of advertising, and increased comforts offered more and more Americans new experiences as consumers. Inflation, along with changes in shopping patterns and in family life, caused people to worry about the implications of woman's position as the household's consumer. Observers argued about the causes of inflation, with some blaming middle-class acceptance of a higher standard of living. Above all, rising prices intensified the struggle between adherence to a moralist tradition and a fuller acceptance of new comforts and patterns of consumption. Inflation made some cling even more tenaciously to traditional values. Price changes also brought to the surface shifts in middle-class styles of living. Inflation thus intensified the battle between an old pattern of consumption, based on a hostility to extravagance and a resolute clinging to thrift and restraint, and a new one that more fully reflected the acceptance of new goods and experiences.

Changes in the nature of American middle-class life complicated the response to inflation. Here and elsewhere in the book I use the word *class* in a cultural sense, relying on occupational patterns, on how contemporaries saw social differences, and on the importance of real and perceived group traditions and ways of living.[4] *Middle class* is a problematic concept, partly because the groups it covered hardly remained constant. In the years between 1890 and 1920, the composition of the middle class became even more diverse than previously. Those committed to prudence and self-restraint—frequently but not always the old middle class of farmers and small entrepreneurs—became less numerous and powerful. At the same time there emerged a new middle class, composed of salaried professionals, managers, salespeople, and office workers employed in bureaucratic organizations. Many members of the new middle class tended to have less than total allegiance to traditional moralism. Of course, the lines between these two groups remained irregular. Nor was there a simple and direct connection between group identity and a distinctive style of life. Factors other than class—gender, ethnicity, age, and place of origin—frequently cut across differences between the old and new middle class. Nonetheless, writers for middle-class audiences articulated two distinct but frequently overlapping styles of life, represented by the contrasting values of frugality and comfort. Writers from a variety of backgrounds argued for combinations of prudence and pleasure but most of them felt that what was at stake was the soul of the middle class, especially its urban and professional members.

Middle-class patterns of living were changing in significant ways. With the exodus of millions of Americans from farms and the rise of large national corporations, many writers questioned whether work was still the moral center of an independent and virtuous life. As labor lost some of its potential for providing satisfaction and as the line between work and leisure became more distinct, questions about how people spent their time and money became more critical. Also involved was the shift from farms and small towns, where a considerable degree of household self-sufficiency had seemed possible, to cities and suburbs, where families were more dependent on participation in a commercial marketplace. Middle-class families faced an increasing choice of goods and services. New meanings of cultural and class relationships further complicated the situation. The emergence of mass culture threatened the dominance and health of a crumbling genteel culture that had stood as a bulwark of Victorian bourgeois life. Ostentatious patterns of leisure and consumption of the wealthy and greater awareness of the expressive quality of immigrant and working-class culture made many middle-class observers intent on more clearly defining the borders with those above and below them.

Moreover, changes in family life and gender relationships—new sexual mores, the entrance of women into professional and service occupations, and the increased independence of women—intensified the strain within middle-class households. The inflationary pressures of the early twentieth century were inextricably connected with changes in American family life. To many observers, rising prices were bringing about momentous social upheaval. Observers believed inflation was among the forces undermining the traditional family in which the man worked in the world and the woman in the home. Though in fact relatively few middle-class married women worked outside the home, to many contemporaries the emergence of the "New Woman" threatened to undermine the traditional household.[5] Inflation seemed to undermine family life in other ways. Tension between spouses, sometimes leading to divorce, often resulted from fights over family budgets thrown out of kilter by escalating prices and a wider range of economic choices.[6] Above all, inflation seemed to increase the danger of race suicide, the lowering birth rate of middle-class white Protestants.[7]

Dominating the discussion of middle-class household budgets was the belief that, with the removal of productive activities from the home, the woman's most important contribution was as consumer, not producer. To many observers, women seemed ill prepared for the roles in which history had cast them, a condition that rising prices made even more critical.[8] In the fight against inflation, writers now echoed what the home economics movement had long argued: the responsibility for making ends meet rested on the shoulders of the individual housewife. Careful spending, efficient household management, meticulous record keeping, energetic housekeeping—these were the keys to economic independence for those who believed that the problem was extravagance. To people who argued that basic social conditions had changed, victory in the battle against rising prices necessitated cooperative and political efforts that went against the grain of housewifely individualism.[9] Consequently, in the discussion of the impact of inflation on family budgets, issues often became confused. Much of what people explained by referring to inflation or extravagance in fact stemmed from new patterns of family life or consumption.

All of these changes—in inflation, class composition, gender relationships, and consumer goods—made the study of middle-class budgets urgent. As people began to view work more instrumentally, consumption patterns became the ground on which they struggled to reconcile economics and morality, individual choice and social good. The attempt to define distinctively middle-class patterns underlined the importance of discovering and shaping emergent styles of living. Middle-class writers attempted to delineate a way of life at precisely the moment when that class itself was changing and when cross-cultural borrowings were blurring the borders with other social and ethnic groups, a process that the emergence of mass culture was accelerating. Thus as economic and social changes were eroding the basis for nineteenth-century moralism, it became necessary to come to terms with the prospect of living with a lessened degree of self-restraint.

For the first time in American history, a considerable number of middle-class people discussed their household budgets in print, something that inflation made topical and even urgent. Budget studies, no longer confined to examinations of working-class expenditures by social workers, reformers, and government agencies, broadened to include popularized treatments of middle-class spending. Indeed the flurry of studies of working-class and middle-class patterns of consumption in the years around 1906 served to help educated people explore the morality of new styles of life. If inflation made discussions of middle-class budgets timely, changes in journalism made them profitable and widespread. In the dozen years before American entry into World War I, *Woman's Home Companion*, *Ladies' Home Journal*, *World's Work*, *Literary Digest*, *Harper's Weekly*, *Harper's Bazar*, and *Good Housekeeping* carried a flood of articles in which readers described their household expenditures and authors made judgments. With a respectable and educated middle-class audience, these magazines offered suggestions through their advertisements, advice columns, and articles on how to navigate the uncharted waters of a rapidly changing consumer society.

Part of the revolution in publishing, the popularized form of budget presentation was unprecedented in the United States. Throughout the nineteenth century, from antebellum reformers like Catharine Beecher to late-nineteenth-century home economists like Ellen Richards, writers had offered advice on expenditures in popular homemaking books. What happened in the early twentieth century was different. Though writers and editors offered their judgments, ordinary people were now telling their own stories to large audiences. It was a decidedly confessional mode, the forum especially attracting families proud that they were able to economize and make ends meet, including those who confessed their redemption from a previous failure to do so.

Studies of middle-class budgets differed in a number of ways from those of workers and immigrants. The middle-class reports were more concerned with inflation than the working-class investigations that had rarely contained a hint of the impact of rising prices. Contemporaries considered inflation a middle-class problem. They were probably wrong, however, in their assumption that white-collar households suffered most. Between 1986 and 1914, with income inequality growing, it appears likely that the relative position of skilled laborers, professionals, and the wealthy improved, while that of unskilled workers deteriorated.[10] Inflation was more prominent in working-class lives than in working-class studies. The format of labor studies necessitated a more static treatment of household expenditures, however, making consideration of longer-term price changes harder to convey or dramatize.

Middle-class budget studies were also more personal than those of the working class. If social workers, government officials, reformers, and even the workers themselves felt there were boundaries of privacy that they were unwilling to cross, the publication of middle-class budgets in popular magazines appeared to overcome such scruples, albeit with some self-consciousness. "I often feel," a man wrote in *Good Housekeeping* in 1910, "that I would like to sit down in a semi-confidential way with some of these neighbors of mine and compare notes on the cost of living, but it seems to be a tabooed subject."[11] By printing letters whose authors were not usually identifiable, popular magazines became a place where it was possible to discuss private issues with both candor and anonymity. Those who wrote in the magazines shared their budgets and at the same time they recognized that they were breaking a taboo. As one woman exclaimed in a letter that revealed her family's choices and habits, "Do you know it's very saucy to inquire into people's private affairs like this!"[12]

At first few Americans realized that inflation was creeping up, partly because statistics were not reliable or widely publicized. In one of the first budget stories in the magazines, a Mrs. P. of Detroit in 1904 wrote confidently "How We Live on $1000 a Year or Less."[13] The situation changed suddenly by 1906, when stories that emphasized the difficulty of making ends meet came in response to requests for readers' budgetary experiences. A *Harper's Bazar* series entitled "The Increase in Household Expenses," that ran from August 1906 to September 1907, marked the beginning of what quickly became a torrent of articles on the topic. "Thousands of homes in America to-day are suffering from a decided rise in the price of household necessities," the editor wrote in August 1906. What started out as a "gratifying response" quickly became "an almost startling" one. "So many articles are pouring in by every mail," the editors commented in October, "that the task of properly examining them is a serious and lengthy one." Originally intending to run the series for only a few months, the magazine continued it for a year.[14] Other magazines followed suit and it was not long before they established regular household budget departments, including columns that contained letters where families explained how they coped with inflation.

What emerged from the discussions of inflation in magazines was the claim that rising prices threatened the survival of the middle class. As early as 1902, one writer offered what would become standard rhetoric in the years before American entry into World War I. Referring to urbanites with an annual family income between $600 and $5000, the author remarked that "this great body of the really best people this country possesses is left to be ground between" the rich and the poor, "the upper and nether millstones."[15] Inflation augmented the number of such complaints. Contemporary observers produced a chorus of shouts about the survival of the middle class, especially those on salaries. A woman in 1910 wrote that inflation was killing "the trunk of our very verdant tree," "the small-salaried man, the clerk, the shop-girl." Simon N. Patten echoed this sentiment when he wrote that immigrants from below and those with incomes greater than $5000 from above were squeezing the urban middle class, "once the city's pride," now swiftly becoming "a homeless class" with its independence eroded.[16] One observer remarked that rising prices, often a boon to farmers and wage earners, were a "bitter pinch," especially for professionals on fixed salaries.[17]

In seeking to explain the onset and growth of inflation, contemporaries found little on which they could agree. Some of the most perceptive observers noted two things: no single factor explained rising prices and the phenomenon was international in scope.[18] For many, however, the culprit was one or another of the nation's economic policies—the tariff, paying for past wars or preparing for future ones, and changes in the monetary situation. Calls for government action were relatively rare and the responses somewhat scattered, mostly involving resolutions to study the subject.[19]

A number of writers argued that the complex organizations of a modern capitalist economy were responsible for inflation and for limiting opportunities for social mobility. Frederic Howe in 1917 claimed that the United States was not the "land of overflowing abundance" it could be, because "parasitical agencies," especially monopolistic corporations, interfered with the laws of supply and demand and artificially raised prices, especially for food. Some placed the blame at the feet of middlemen, who stood in increasing number and force between the producer and consumer. Many who spoke for the middle class thus saw giving full rein to the laws of supply and demand as the individualistic solution to the consequences of an increasingly centralized economy. Others wanted to combat the system or organizations they felt were hurting them. As the young Greenwich Village resident Hutchins Hapgood wrote, the salaried middle class, "the real underdog," had to organize and fight for its survival.[20]

The debate over inflation and family life made clear that at issue were two competing sets of values. The rest of this chapter focuses on how rising prices provided some writers with a timely opportunity to reassert the validity of conservative moralism. To them, issues of work, thrift, and desire were central. They tended to equate new goods and ways of doing things with extravagance. As chapter 6 demonstrates, inflation made others realize how greatly middle-class styles of living had changed, how important new comforts had become, and consequently how workers and immigrants were not so extravagant after all.

The debate over the causes of inflation provided a platform for the party of prudence and self-restraint. Contemporaries argued that inflation stemmed from people's desires for new standards of living. Many observers castigated specific groups for what they saw as wanton extravagance. Some contemporaries blamed advertisers for having created unnecessary costs and for having caused people to wish to consume more. In defense, a University of Pennsylvania professor of advertising and salesmanship asked if it were "wrong" for advertising to "force every one into a greater appreciation of this 'thing realm?' "[21] Some economists, women, and businessmen argued that the extravagant consumer was at fault. The American wage earner, commented the mining tycoon S. R. Guggenheim, "is more extravagant in proportion to his earnings than the multi-millionaire." For others it was the wealthy who had made "the spirit of extravagance" contagious. Having recognized that Americans, "to keep up in the procession with the successful rich," wanted more and more, the economist J. Laurence Laughlin wondered about the possibility of creating "a new aristocracy of the simple life." Still others believed the spendthrift housewife was responsible. If most men ran their businesses as carelessly as most women ran their households, remarked the president of the Housewives League in 1913, "the country's bankruptcy courts would be running day and night."[22]

For many observers what endangered the middle class was not simply a rise in prices but an increasing and extravagant standard of living. Many argued that the root of inflation lay deeper than the discussion of responsibility of any one group suggested. The cry that high prices stemmed from pursuit of a higher standard of living was more likely to come from men than women and from professional commentators indebted to a moralist tradition rather than from people writing about their budgets who hoped they could afford new goods and experiences. Those who saw rising prices as a trial for the prudential worried that the new middle class of professionals and employees did not have the toughness of the more independent old middle class. At issue, a contemporary writer suggested, was "the pinch of extravagance, due to habits of luxury and expenditure." The problem, wrote a contributor to *Woman's Home Companion* in 1911, was not only the high cost of living but also "the cost of high living," a "*serious* . . . [and] *dangerous . . . menace to American home life.*" The culprits were new consumer items and practices: marketing by the phone, using "prepared or ready-to-serve food," thoughtless chasing after supposed bargains, purchasing ready-made clothes, and entertaining as "part of the profitless game of keeping up appearances." These were the supposedly wasteful expenses that had taken their toll on families with annual incomes between $1200 and $3600, people who knew "neither the pinching dread of poverty nor the recklessness of great wealth."[23]

Nor was this an isolated accusation. In response to the railroad magnate James J. Hill's statement that the cost of high living caused inflation, several commentators in 1912 agreed that America had become "a nation of facile spenders" infected by a "national vice of extravagance." The United States, remarked George K. Holmes of the National Bureau of Standards, was engaged in "unproductive consumption" with its expenditures on automobiles, telephones, amusement parks, Sunday and holiday excursions, summer vacations, club dues, and card parties.[24]

Fabian Franklin's explanation of these changes reflected the hold of a traditional moralism. A Hungarian-born university professor turned newspaper editor, in 1915 Franklin distinguished between increased costs of living that originated in higher prices and in a higher standard of living. Society had long known the process of a "subtle but steady growth of the list of things which, in any given walk of life, comes to be regarded as necessary to 'living.'" For example, equating the new and the extravagant, he argued that middle-class standards of living had insidiously and inconspicuously changed with new expenditures such as home delivery of food, gas and electricity, bathrooms, smooth pavements, modern sewers, and street lights. Americans had often turned "economic advances into advances in standard of living." However, the "chorus of complaint over the difficulty of maintaining the standard" came from something new: rising prices due to changes in the money supply and in the business and credit system. Stemming from price changes, most of the increased cost of living was difficult for the individual to control. It was possible to decrease the cost of living by restricting desires. "Doubtless a great many of us would be happier if we spent less," Franklin remarked judgmentally. Since much of the spending aimed at keeping up appearances "rather than for the gratification of any genuine personal taste," pursuing a simpler life would help solve the problem of the cost of living. However, Franklin concluded, there was no evidence that Americans would choose that alternative.[25]

Simon N. Patten similarly drew on the old moralism in his discussion of whether the squeeze on the middle class came from rising prices or from some fundmanetal economic and social changes. Backing off from the commitment to passionate experiences made in *Product and Climax* (1909), he soon turned his attention to the effect of the cost of high living on the salaried middle class. In the process, he redressed the balance between pleasure and self-control. The problem of household survival, he wrote in 1910, resulted from the "perfectly normal tendency for the standard of living in a rich, dynamic nation to advance with rapid strides." The fact that "wants in a progressive society grow more rapidly than the means of satisfying them" thus inevitably created "in family budgets a state of chronic deficit." The desires for better "health, leisure, recreation, education, shelter, food, clothing and social service" were evidence of both "social progress" and the pressure of a more uniform pattern of consumption. By 1910, he wrote, a number of "luxuries denied to kings in the Middle Ages" were becoming increasingly common in households of skilled laborers and the middle class: more commodious homes, hot and cold running water, steam heat, more varied diet, ready-made clothing, a more nearly universal education, finer public buildings, theaters, amusement parks, nickelodeons, and resorts.

In "The Standardization of Family Life" (1913), Patten briefly struggled to integrate notions of mass culture into his theory of a consumer economy. He wrote of the imposition of standardized budgetary patterns, mentioned how women took their clues from advertisements, and alluded to the way that food, furniture, and ornaments obtained "a similarity that is deadening viewed as a mass." In the end, however, he was more concerned with the battle between restraint and desire than with explaining the power of new forms of mass affluence.

Patten offered several explanations of why the economic system did not automatically correct the seemingly inevitable rise in prices by generating forces that would provide downward pressures. Following familiar lines of argument, he asserted that capital had become scarcer because the middle class struggled to keep pace with "the new standard of liberality" the wealthy were setting and because there had occurred "a decay of the moral instruction emphasizing the benefits of frugality and saving." In addition, the urbanization of the American population led to higher prices because many people no longer lived near food supplies and a lack of planning helped increase rents. Thirdly, the proliferation of middlemen made the distribution system "cumbersome" and therefore costly. Finally, the new status of women had inflationary effects related to the removal of the production of food and clothing from the home and the adoption of an "increased standard of elaborate dressing."[26]

Solutions to the problem of higher prices, Patten argued, would come partly through changes in family life, principally through the exercise of greater self-control. For the individual household, several strategies were available. Having women work outside the home and having housework done commercially would help, as would the "shifting of consumption from costly articles to those less expensive." Patten preached other economies for the middle class. Checks to expenditures would follow from a greater exercise of restraint, including delaying marriage, producing fewer children, purchasing fewer luxuries and less liquor, and expressing a "love of economy for its own sake." Even Patten's opposition to saving for retirement rested on a commitment to self-control rather than self-expression. It was possible to achieve "budgetary equilibrium" not by lowering expenditures but by "elevating the family to a higher social status where more efficiency produces" the necessary additional income.[27]

This was not, Patten argued, a question of simply increasing family income in one generation, for that only subjected the household to pressures to spend according to the higher standard of its new income class. In his mind, social mobility rested on a more complicated basis. Were one generation to reduce its savings in order to keep its children from early employment and educate them instead, Patten argued, their offspring would achieve higher social status and, being educated, would be less subject to pressures to adopt a purely monetary standard of living. Like moralists before him, Patten thus asserted that refinement, not materialism, was the path to individual and social advancement. Thus even when he urged young women to spend freely on fashionable clothes, he hailed the end result as "a new womanhood with higher morality and more beauty. Dressing is thus more than an economy: it is the essence of moral progress."[28]

In the end, Patten applied to middle-class extravagance the same nostrum he had recommended for workers' profligacy. The prospect of replacing primitive urges by cultivated ones made him confident that the middle class could deal effectively with inflation and a rising standard of living. Beyond the pain economy, "in which fear and suffering drive man to his daily tasks," and a pleasure economy, "in which the motive of action is the pleasure derived from the goods enjoyed," Patten now envisioned a third stage, "a creative economy," where "budgetary concepts" would come to govern the family's activity. By standardizing taste and economizing patterns of living, advertising would eventually encourage middle-class women to accept new concepts of beauty and morality. "In the endeavor to bring the family budget to an equilibrium," Patten wrote in 1912, "activity is increased and consumption is put on a cultural basis by increasing the intensity of new wants." With newer, higher wants replacing older, primitive ones, there would be "a self-repression which is the essence of character building." "A higher culture will result," Patten concluded with characteristic vagueness, and "there will be a new type of men forced into a common mode of living by their culture, education and activity." For Patten, new social policies would also help lessen the pressures on increasing prices. Focusing on the salaried middle class, he sought ways to encourage greater savings, thereby increasing capital investment. This and other elements of a "comprehensive social policy," he said in 1910, made it possible for the middle class to save and live comfortably.[29] In short, inflation and a higher standard of living prompted Patten to see the study of middle-class budgets as a way to teach people to dampen wanton ambitions and live within their means.

People like Patten, who honored the value of self-control, faced rising costs as well as rising standards of living with some trepidation. Others who advocated prudence doubted that more goods and services, above a certain level, made people happier. They rejected striving after an elusive higher standard of living, counseling "let them climb and die" to families that needed more than a very moderate income. The solution, as William Jennings Bryan remarked in 1907, was to find a mean between being a spendthrift and being a miser. Avoid debt, spend carefully, and live modestly— these were the rules of proper living. "There has never been a time when the people of America so much needed to have their conscience directed to the merits of the simple life as now," remarked one observer. "Break away from the thraldrom [sic] of fashion," he advised, and live "without regard to the people next door."[30]

Thrift and self-denial stood as the central issues for those who shared such concerns. The foibles of individual character, not the power of social and economic structures, was the critical issue in the development of living styles. The pressures of inflation and the recognition of the benefits of a higher standard of living caused a number of people to worry about the possibility that thrift was "becoming a relatively rare virtue in America," even among the middle class.[31] Several studies revealed how salaried and professional families were no longer saving or were saving relatively little, something disquieting to advocates of traditional virtues.[32] Some members of the business community worried that because people sought pleasure in consumption rather than work and savings, the nation had "mortgaged the future so recklessly."[33]

More than the question of capital formation, what mattered was the implication that members of the middle class rejected thrift because they lacked personal character under the pressure of inflation. That the average American was spending rather than saving threatened the vision of a virtuous middle class that practiced self-denial. John M. Osikson spoke of a generation "educated in prodigality" and possessing an "exaggerated taste for self-indulgence." People with moderate incomes, someone else remarked, are "plunging into luxury and extravagance at a rate never before equaled, perhaps in the history of the nation." To this observer, the "most sinister" example of the new recklessness was mortgaging the home "for the purchase of luxuries [such as automobiles] that are themselves of a flimsy and not at all permanent character."[34]

Ellen H. Richards (1842–1911) offered the sharpest attack on extravagance and the most urgent advocacy of frugality, self-denial, and hard work. "Softer beds and comfortable chairs may be agencies to better living," she cautioned in 1910, "but not if they tend to laziness and sloth." With thrift "out of fashion" and "personal exertion . . . distasteful," it was now necessary to prevent "degeneracy and social ruin" by resisting temptation, distinguishing between needs and wants, avoiding waste, and turning away from "stimulation by suggestion of the correct thing."[35] Richards, whose *The Cost of Living as Modified by Sanitary Science* went through several editions in the late nineteenth and early twentieth centuries, represented an end point of the traditional advice literature. Basing her writing on how she thought people should spend their money, not how they actually did, she emphasized the virtues of parsimony, respectability, and self-control, now cloaked in scientific as well as moral terms.

Richards tried to persuade the new middle class to stick to patterns of consumption usually associated with the old middle class. A graduate of Vassar and Massachusetts Institute of Technology, Richards sustained a lifelong interest in popular and professional scientific education for women. An instructor of sanitary chemistry at MIT from 1884 until her death and the nation's leading home economist, in the early 1890s she had failed in her attempt to interest immigrant women in the scientific preparation of nutritious Yankee dishes.[36] As she turned to a different audience, she was in many ways attempting to bring up to date the work of Catharine Beecher (1800–78), whose *Treatise on Domestic Economy* (1841) and *The American Woman's Home* (1869) were landmarks in nineteenth-century domestic advice literature. Beecher gave women a vital role in creating a moral home. Richards' focus on the middle class differed from Beecher's desire to cut across class lines, an effort even Beecher found increasingly difficult. In most ways Beecher marked out positions her successor would follow: drawing a sharp division between sexes that made the woman powerful in the home, integrating national and personal goals, emphasizing the importance of orderliness and self-sufficiency, standing in opposition to commercial and acquisitive values, and preferring instead the virtue of self-denial.[37]

Richards wrote for educated, American-born women, who, she felt, had an important responsibility now that the home had changed from being the center of production to the center of consumption. She worried about the loss of skills that children had learned on farms similar to the one where she lived as a child.[38] What Carroll D. Wright in 1875 had tried to impress on working-class families, Richards hoped the middle class would embrace: respectability in leisure and self-restraint in consumption. In the face of rich and poor who seemed to have adopted more flamboyant styles of living, she advised the middle class to maintain its commitment to self-control. To Richards, woman's work in the home was central in the endeavor to keep family life self-contained and respectable. As a consumer and scientific manager, the housewife was to sustain the home as a moral universe. Faced with declining birth rates among American-born, middle-class women, Richards worried about the society's future. By combating "race suicide," a proper way of living would produce a new generation of virtuous citizens.

Though containing some actual family budgets, *The Cost of Living* was largely prescriptive. Her book, Richards wrote, involved "a study of all that physical and mental environment which leads to the highest utilization of man's powers for the progress of civilzation." She recognized that there were plenty of studies of how the poor spent their money. "But," she cautioned, "the real test is with the class which corresponds to the plastic middle layer, the fermentable mass of humanity, out of which rises the cream of society or from which sinks the dregs." More specifically, she directed her advice to "the majority of the most intelligent American families, students, professors, business men, and professional men" who "are obliged to do the best they can do on from two thousand to five thousand dollars a year."[39] Her definition of her audience, as intelligent, mobile, and malleable, reveals her concern about how vulnerable "proper" people were to new forces at work in the society. Her mention of "intelligence" and "civilization" reminds us that her audience was the "respectable" white, Anglo-Saxon Protestants of moderate and comfortable means who were living in or near cities.

Her advice was especially important in 1910, she argued, because costs were "rising like the incoming tide on the shore until the small household is in danger of being overwhelmed." Richards set out to show how economies would enable the besieged middle class to sustain the quality of its life in a period of inflationary pressures. People who complain about high prices, she warned with a reminder of the importance of self-control in face of new temptations, "do not stop to think that the ever-increasing *standards of style of living* (not necessarily right standards of life)" were augmenting the demands for products like breakfast steaks, fresh fruits, vegetables, and dairy products. "Temptation to buy beyond one's needs is found on every hand," she cautioned, and middle-class families should not stray from restrained patterns of consumption. Consequently "better satisfaction" would result from "conscious *regulation* of the expenditure according to the right ideals and standards of human efficiency."[40]

Richards thus gave the housewife the pivotal task of saving civilization by strengthening the home against the forces undermining the nuclear family. The household, she argued, had sunk into "the slough of despond." It was the locus "of so much wrangle, worry, and disorder as the house-roofs cover but do not hide." Without its "unity of purpose," it had become a "collection of individuals under one roof," resembling "a boarding-house in which each member feels at liberty to complain of every other and to exact service of every other without giving in return." Richards argued that "all interesting occupations" had gone from the home to the world outside. Therefore, it was time for housewives to become business managers and spiritual leaders of the family.[41] The educated woman had to take as her career "the elevation of the home into its place in American life." The "ideal" of the home as "that place of *moral* education where the *mother* is" would "preserve the Anglo-Saxon superiority if anything is able to do it."[42]

Household expenditures based on both scientific and moral principles provided the means to accomplish this grandiose task. Educated people with family earnings between $1000 and $3000 a year had to assume the leadership in solving "America's problem for the twentieth century." Striking out against the attempt of the new middle class to imitate the wealthy, she emphasized the importance of reconciling "the uplifting tendency of the struggle to 'better one's condition' with the degrading result of striving to seem richer than one really is and to avoid the debilitating effect of luxuries." To Richards, adherence to moral values was critical in making sure the home would remain "the germ of Anglo-Saxon civilization." Income had to lead to "the fullest satisfaction of human wants" without unleashing "unreasoning impulse" that by "letting down . . . ethical barriers," brought "countless temptations to extravagance." Specifically, Richards suggested an "ideal division" of family expenditures: 25 percent for food, 20 percent for rent, 15 percent for operating expenses, 15 percent for clothing, and 25 percent for "Higher Life, Books, Travel, Church, Charity, Savings, Insurance."[43] These guidelines, in their crispness, their strict control of food costs, and their emphasis on elevating leisure, reflected her commitment to prudential values.

Richards imagined that most readers would believe that life under these circumstances would "not be worth living." Initially, she acknowledged, a family would struggle under such "bondage." However, "new habits . . . once fixed . . . maintain themselves." The "moral support" of keeping a household budget or having "some great ideal" such as the children's education would hold in check the "temptation to spend for things pleasant but not needful."[44] Indeed, adjusted for inflation, the lower end of her most modest estimate of the entry point into the middle class was remarkably close to Chapin's "normal" standard for the families of workers. This scale points toward the parsimoniousness she encouraged. Moreover, it reminds us that for Richards how one spent income, not simply the level itself, marked middle-class status.

For most categories of expenditures she combined an eye to practical detail with a sense of larger moral purpose. A house thus had to be not only well-planned and sanitary but also "an outer garment as it were, showing the taste and cultivation of its occupants." In seeing a house as "an expression of family ideals," she attempted to draw a clear line between the middle class and the wealthy. A family had to avoid trying to convey a higher social standing than it actually had, she reminded her readers, and emphasize instead moral and aesthetic elements. Operating expenses and food, the areas where "the tendency to extravagance" was most common, constantly threatened to become sieves because families did not carefully consider the long-term effects of their expenditures. The danger was that families with children, in order to control expenses, would choose to live in apartment houses, "a most extravagant luxury" that "causes deterioration in the race."[45]

Rather than incurring such risks, the housewife, like a scientific business manager, should seek the most comfort at the least cost. She could do this by taking care of the family's belongings, keeping in mind the costs of preserving purchased items, maintaining accounts in order to "check unrestricted expenditure on unessentials to the detriment of the fundamental needs," carefully balancing simplicity and convenience, and reducing the costs of household service by having children help or not hiring a "slow or slovenly maid." Food was a vitally important item because of both the potential waste involved and its "profound effect upon the welfare of the household." Again, practical and ideal considerations obtained. Economy and nutrition were important enough in themselves. With greater income, middle-class families thus had to remain frugal. With the father away at work and an emerging youth culture threatening to lure children from the home, Richards warned against the tendency to have family members eat their meals separately or outside the house. Though not justifiable on economic grounds, the family table was important because it "inculcated the virtues of self-control, self-denial, regard for others, good temper, good manners, pleasant speech."[46]

As with home and food, so with clothing: it was urgent to heed the call of prudence and refinement. It was important to pay attention to the practical, keeping the body comfortable, and the ideal, "self-respect and moral equilibrium," without giving up "one's own ideals" and relying instead "on the fashion-plates." Lacking the "absorbing occupations" that domestic industry once provided, modern women were constantly tempted "to allow free play to an untrained fancy in the clothing of themselves and their families." Richards remained confident that her readers were women from "the educated, cultivated families to whom the things of the intellect and of the soul are more than mere material show, to whom a decent exterior life which does not exhaust the energies nor debase the higher aspirations is sufficient."[47] Faced with more choice, income, and the example of people who spent with abandon, it was important for middle-class women to emphasize self-control and respectability, the path of the old middle class.

Expenditures for things other than food, clothing, and shelter comprised the principal battleground on which Richards hoped middle-class families would fight for the preservation of civilization through the strengthening of the self-contained and moral household. Poor families might survive on $500 to $800 a year because they obtained their pleasure through "communistic amusement and recreation" such as parks and vaudeville. Should the educated middle class go down the same road, the home, no longer where people experienced "the delight of living," would become "only a place of shelter and storage, to be left behind when real enjoyment is desired."[48] In her discussion of expenditures for "advancement," there was no careful balance between practical and ideal: the consequences seemed too important to bother with detail.

To preserve its values and sustain its place in American society, the middle class had to sacrifice luxury. Self-control and pursuit of higher things ensured that the home produced virtuous children. By spending on art, books, religion, and charity, rather than "frail articles, flimsy imitations," a middle-class family deliberately chose Culture over commerce and materialism. What demarcated civilized life was not simply income and possessions themselves but style, "the attitude of mind toward the objects with which we surround ourselves." Investment in a house, furniture, and art simultaneously accomplished several vital goals. It reinforced self-control and provided savings that would guarantee freedom from charity that "is essential to true manliness of character." It made it possible to surround children "at the impressionable age with those forms and colors and objects which shall lead them to choose the best things life has to offer."[49]

Above all, the bourgeois ideals of independence and individual ownership strengthened the home and inculcated middle-class values. Richards attacked people like Charlotte Perkins Gilman who were trying to break down the barriers between the individual home and the world around it. "The question confronting us," Richards asked "is, shall the same conditions of receiving the pleasures of life from the hands of the state be carried on into the more prosperous families, or is there a good and sufficient reason why each family should retain in its own control the needs of the intellectual life as well as of the animal?" What individual ownership of a home and its adornments promised was thus very considerable. It involved nothing short of the salvation of the family and civilization. Once the household income reached $800 a year, "the principle of paying for pleasure and education and comforts should be made a rule if for no other reason than because of the value of necessary cultivation of choice, of self-denial in one direction, of gratification in another." Again and again, Richards emphasized the role of women in preserving the sanctity of the nuclear family. She cautioned readers to distinguish themselves from "the mass of people" who

"take both their ordinary life and their pleasure in large groups, after the
fashion of the primitive communities." Although she recommended some
kinds of community activity, Richards made clear the importance of living
in individual homes, eating together as a family, and seeking pleasures that
involved ownership and strengthened the household.[50] Only these values
would help the nonimmigrant middle class, the family, and society to avoid
the dangers of socialism, the communal pleasures of immigrants and workers, and the debilitating luxuries of new-found wealth.

In her attempt to sustain an old-fashioned middle-class life, Richards thus
emphasized the centrality of the moral and independent home. The stric-
tures against participation in communal activities are familiar to anyone
who has read tracts railing against immigrant visits to saloons, nickelodeons, parks, and festivals. Richards broadened such concerns in several
ways. She warned civilized people to stay clear of places where the mass of
people swarmed. She cautioned against visits to libraries, museums, and
concert halls, places moralists had seen as the haven of the middle class and
the salvation of the unwashed. Even more surprising are her warnings
about the threat of the urban institutions that the middle class and wealthy
were beginning to utilize—clubs, apartments, and hotels. The concentration of population, she wrote in reference to the full range of urban institutions, had led to "provision for communistic amusement and recreation to
an extent somewhat startling to the moralist."[51]

What caused her to worry about the impact of communal pleasures was a
variant of the view of the middle class being pressed by the poor from one
side and the rich from the other. As Richards perceived it, the actual or
potential use by immigrants of museums and parks, along with the proliferation of restaurants, apartments, and hotels as urban institutions for the
wealthy, threatened to draw people from the home and thereby weaken the
nuclear family, the bulwark of Western civilization. In an effort to preserve
the family, Richards elevated woman's position. The housewife should
manage the house on an economical and business basis for spiritual ends. In
moderation middle-class consumers could enjoy some of the benefits of
affluence but had to do so not to impress others but to derive intrinsic
aesthetic and moral satisfaction. In these and other ways, Richards had
written a twentieth-century manual out of the mold of nineteenth-century
advice books. Household budgets were not to be described but to be pre-
scribed—and with an emphasis on constraints and higher values. Facing
changes in middle-class patterns of work and leisure that threatened to
erode traditional values, she insisted that the educated middle class remain
steadfast in its pursuit of a restrained style of living.

6   Inflation and the Middle Class: Comfort and Refinement, 1900–1916

In clear contrast to the party of prudence were those who struggled against inflation, recognized the importance of self-control, tried their best to economize, yet welcomed a new and rising standard of living. In comparison with traditionalists, these less severe moralists were more likely to be women than men and anonymous letter-writers rather than judgmental advice-givers.[1] The advocates of comfort were not primarily apostles of therapeutic self-fulfillment and mass culture. Rather, for them, refinement, benevolence, and commodities defined a middle-class way of life that would help American-born citizens achieve class and ethnic identity.

In the ten years beginning in 1906, Americans came to terms with the impact of inflation on middle-class household budgets. Reflecting the perspective of the older middle class, people like Ellen H. Richards counseled a continued exercise of prudence and restraint. Those people who adopted values of comfort and refinement responded differently. They wished to hold on to the new standard of living they had attained, something especially difficult for those whose incomes did not keep pace with rising prices. They recommended economizing without the sharp ethical imperatives of the conservative moralists. In justification of their own cost of high living in years with an increasingly high cost of living, they questioned the values of thrift and abstemiousness. Inflation and the new affluence thus helped undermine the dominant nineteenth-century outlook and foster the emergence of an ethic of comfort and refinement. These writers accepted new levels of consumption and yet continued to view negatively some of the moral effects of materialism.

Rising prices helped some middle-class people acknowledge the extent to which they had turned their backs on self-denial, rejected simplicity, and accepted a more comfortable way of life. "It seems rather absurd to complain of the alleged increased cost of living, does it not," commented William F. Dix, "when there isn't one of us who would go back to other times, other manners, even if it were possible to do so."[2] Rising prices and standards of living prompted a reexamination of the shibboleths of the nineteenth-century moralists. Inflation, in making some middle-class people worry less about savings, sacrifice, and self-control, helped them more readily accept new levels of comfort. This understanding of their own situation prompted some observers to think twice about questioning the supposedly extrava-gant and spendthrift habits of those below them on the social scale. Rising prices raised the question of whether middle-class observers could continue to castigate working-class families for pleasures they themselves struggled hard to attain. Thus more than the realism and sympathies of Progressives was responsible for weakening the old moralist tradition. Also at work were changes in the lives of members of the American middle class, specifically the challenges many of them faced in the early twentieth century as infla-tion wreaked havoc with expectations established by decades of declining or stable prices.

Again and again, writers denied the charge of middle-class extravagance. Even some of the those, like a New York doctor, who called for simplicity and greater economies admitted that it was "but natural that aspiration, imitation, and emulation should serve as incentives to raise the lower standards to higher levels" by stimulating the spending of money for a piano, phonograph, automobile, mortgage, telephone, or trolley ride. Often with some equivocation, observers writing for middle-class audiences argued that inflation must not prevent people from enjoying the standard of living they had attained. A writer in *Ladies' Home Journal* in 1916 acknowl-edged that "the pressure put upon both men and women by 'Keeping Up With Lizzie' is as disastrous as pathetic, but this habit has to be recognized as a definite factor in the adjustment of the budget." A "Housekeeper" from Ann Arbor whose large family had lived on $1705 in 1905 recognized that though "one must not sacrifice . . . future welfare to present convenience and pleasure, . . . a family must, above all things, be comfortable, healthy, and happy as they go along." To date, she observed, the family had "stemmed the tide . . . by still closer economy." However, she concluded, "something surely ought to be done in this wonderful country of ours to keep all the necessities and some of the pleasures and luxuries of life within reach of people with moderate incomes."[3]

For some who accepted the new standard of living, the problem was how to economize in a world where yesterday's luxuries seemed to become today's necessities. A school principal, his wife, and three children, who lived in a Chicago suburb on $2600 a year, recognized how much money was needed for proper living. They believed they were not extravagant, yet they had to cut back on rent, operating expenses, food, and clothes in order to have more to spend for aspects of "higher life" such as savings, charity, education, medical expenses, books, and "amusements." In short, many observers argued that though economizing was necessary to protect against inflation, the middle class had accepted an increasingly comfortable way of life. Helen Landon answered the question "Where Shall We Economize?" by suggesting that people do their own housework with the help of "modern conveniences," cut down on food costs ("probably the crucial point of the family extravagance"), use library books, and reduce expenditures for amusements. On some items, however, economizing was to be resisted. Life insurance, "gracious things of life, the friends at one's table sometimes, the occasional outing, the joy of giving to the needy"—these were "the real necessities."[4]

If Ellen Richards attempted to persuade the new middle class to adhere to the values associated with the old middle class, Martha B. Bruère (c. 1871–1953) came closer to describing and arguing for the acceptance of emerging patterns of consumption of the new middle class. Along with others who contributed to the women's magazines, Bruère spoke for those who welcomed the new standard of living. In effect, Richards and Bruère split the conservative moralist tradition. Both of them honored respectability, but Richards emphasized prudence and Bruère, comfort, refinement, and benevolence. Along with her husband Robert, Martha Bruère published letters in which middle-class people offered information on their household budgets. In the pages of the women's magazines, she went beyond description and offered her readers advice on how to consume. With her eyes on working-class and middle-class families, she criticized the overemphasis others had placed on savings and self-restraint. Instead, for the middle class especially, she advised spending for comforts and Culture. Unlike Richards, who hardened the dominant nineteenth-century ideology, the Bruères borrowed from it selectively. The Bruères rejected excessive parsimony and emphasized refinement and benevolence.

Martha Bruère took classes at Vassar and the University of Chicago, worked as a volunteer at Hull House and as an editor of *Good Housekeeping* and *Survey*. In 1907 she married Robert Bruère, an industrial counselor. Mrs. Bruère produced a series of articles for magazines like *Outlook*, *Woman's Home Companion*, and *Colliers*, that she and her husband brought together and analyzed in *Increasing Home Efficiency* (1912).[5] She provided detailed case studies that readers sent to the magazine, an approach that countered some of the limitations of working-class reports. Her evidence was impressionistic and her method raised all sorts of unaddressed questions, but she provided the first examination of middle-class household expenditures that presented a significant amount of material and analyzed it systematically. More than any other study of the early twentieth century, the Bruères' writing offers a window into the divergent styles of life of the old and new middle classes, as well as a criticism of the severity of the nineteenth-century moralist tradition. Though Bruère shared with Richards a sense of urgency about strengthening the middle-class home and producing respectable middle-class children, she advocated more spending and less saving. The Bruères' achievement paralleled the impetus behind the turn-of-the-century department store: the reconciliation of the opposites of refinement and pleasure in the midst of the transformation of bourgeois culture into consumer culture. In the process, the aspiration to consume rested in part on an appeal to ethnic and class pride.[6]

Previous studies had "discreetly passed by" the middle class, the Bruères argued, "because it is neither so rich as to dazzle the attention, nor so poor as to have to submit to investigation." "You can't investigate the middle-class, as you can the poor," they added, "without its free consent." The Bruères based their study primarily on letters people sent to them, letters in which families presented their budgets, explained their choices, and to which the Bruères responded with advice. Their sample was probably self-selected: magazine readers who kept records and were willing to reveal themselves, usually because success in making ends meet came with either ease or difficulty. Though the Bruères computed averages and developed guidelines for expenditures, the central focus of their study was a series of case histories. "Mythical average people," they wrote in an implicit criticism of the tradition of Ellen Richards, were "as detached from hampering peculiarities of temperament and locality as China dolls." Of the two hundred budgets they received from across the nation, they felt seventy-six bore "the stamp of truth." Mrs. Bruère acknowledged that such a small sample "of this character furnish[ed] slight basis for elaborate generalization." She insisted, however, that "the conclusions to which they lead are valuable as indicating the truth." In the final analysis the Bruères had to rely on the evidence they collected about "the real experiences of real middle-class people."[7]

Their definition of middle class rested on several criteria. In terms of income the range was from twelve hundred to five thousand dollars a year for a husband, wife, and children. The lower figure was "the line of decency which marks the entrance to the middle class." People with smaller incomes were outside "the realm of choice" and could do little more than sustain themselves physically. The list of occupations included "small landlords and better class mechanics and shop bosses, clerks and railroad conductors, accountants and secretaries, teachers and college professors, clergymen, journalists, physicians, horticulturalists and geologists, small capitalists and business men." Although they mixed skilled and white-collar workers, new and old middle classes, they directed much of their attention to the new salaried middle class of employees whose incomes, unlike those of entrepreneurs, were "about as elastic as New Bedford granite." Above all their definition centered not simply on income and occupation but on a style of life, a history of middle-class manners, and ethnic background. Households in their study with less than a thousand dollars in income, they reminded their readers, were not large immigrant families but those "that by tradition, feeling, association and intent belong to the middle class."[8] Like Richards, their principal audience was the urban, white, Protestant middle class of northern and western European background who were to be clearly distinguished from recent immigrants pouring into American cities.

Presentation of a few of their cases helps to convey a sense of the richness and diversity of their material. Mrs. Bruère considered the Wells family, living in "an almost fashionable suburb of Boston," an exceptionally good example of people who not only knew "what *they* want their home factory to turn out" but also succeeded in meeting their goals. This family's excessive emphasis on prudential virtues prevented it from producing cultured and aspiring children. Though the father was salaried, the family, in its background and style of life, typified the old middle class. Americans by birth and "by generations of tradition," Mr. and Mrs. Wells had inherited an "instinct of thrift that is the governing factor" in their lives.

Consisting of the parents and three grown children (two of whom still lived at home), the Wells family relied on the father's annual income of $2400 (expenditures shown in table 2). Years ago, when their children were younger and the husband's salary was much lower, the Wells family had lived by the rule of abstinence, "that you win by the things you go without." The father worked hard and the family economized, making it possible to save so that the children could get an education and move a "step above" the parents. The mother and father "believed that they had done this by pushing their sons into the clerical occupations." Now, with the children on their own, the parents continued to live frugally, saving 17.5 percent of their income and spending 1.6 percent of it on vacations, travel, books, and amusement.[9]

In contrast to the Wells family was another that the Bruères appreciated because it preferred comforts and enjoyment to prudence. The Parnells, a farm family of six with an annual income of $4000, had a style of living closer to the new middle-class suburbanite than to the old middle-class yeoman farmer. The mother and father had grown up in middle-class homes in Middle Western towns. Revolting "against the prospect of being clerks or struggling professional people," nineteen years previously they had moved to Kansas and "gradually changed their open prairie into field and farms."

Table 2 Budget of the Wells Family, 1911

Item	Amount in Dollars	Percentage of Budget
Food	504.00	21.00
Shelter (mortgage, repairs, taxes)	396.00	16.50
Clothes	192.00	8.00
Operating costs		
Help	120.00	
Heat and light	96.00	
Carfare	72.00	
Refurnishing	54.00	
Subtotal	342.00	14.25
Advancement		
Doctor, dentist, medicine	132.00	
Church, charity	168.00	
Vacations, travel, books, amusement	39.00	
Incidentals	89.40	
Insurance (fire and life)	117.60	
Savings	420.00	
Subtotal	966.00	40.25

Source: Martha B. Bruère, "What Is The Home For?" *Outlook* 99 (16 December 1911): 911.

Note: For the sake of clarity, the author has adapted the figures and modified the form for this table and subsequent tables.

Now living in a plain house which "four romping offspring" kept "dogeared at the corners," they worked hard and lived comfortably [10] (their budget is shown in table 3).

Consonant with a new middle-class pattern of life, the Parnells chose pleasures over parsimony. They economized by spending little on clothing and consuming some of their own poultry and dairy products. On most other items, however, they chose convenience and ease over frugality. To save the mother's time and energy so she could attend club meetings in town, the family had only a very small garden and used labor-saving devices in the home. That, Bruère reported, not only preserved the mother's "strength, but the mental wear and tear of getting servants; . . . she doesn't have to ask a vacuum cleaner if it wants to live in Kansas, or if it likes being a hired hand on the farm." Mrs. Parnell's mother, a doctor's wife from Evanston, Illinois, had commented that they "were as much suburbanites as she is." Mrs. Parnell bragged about her cosmopolitan orientation. The nearby city, she wrote, "has grown out toward us, and the trolley lines and good automobile roads have done the rest. I do not feel," she told Mrs. Bruère, "that I live in the country much more than you do. Why, I even belong to a club that is affiliated with yours in New York."[11]

Table 3 Budget of the Parnell Family, 1911

Item	Amount in Dollars	Percentage of Budget
Food	600	15.000
Shelter (taxes, repairs, improvements, etc.)	475	11.875
Clothes	450	11.250
Operating	625	15.625
Advancement		
College (son and daughter)	1000	
Insurance (fire and life)	148	
Vacation trips	200	
Gifts, charity, church	60	
Books, etc.	50	
Miscellaneous	182	
Savings	200	
Subtotal	1850	46.250

Source: Martha B. Bruère, "What Is The Home For?" *Outlook* 99 (16 December 1911): 913.

Note: Advancement expenditures do not add to $1850.

In the end, Mrs. Parnell considered herself "a Middle West country-woman." " 'Just think,' said an Eastern woman who was a school friend of Mrs. Parnell's, 'Clara is sending her children to a *Western* college! . . . Just think what they're missing—they'll never have the chance to be anything but farmers now! And Clara used to be *so* progressive!' " The Parnells were pleased with their children's prospects and their own lives. The agricultural college offered "a good practical working education," leading to "openings as farmers or foresters or agricultural experts of some sort." They themselves worked hard but had not "sacrificed themselves greatly." Their work "has consisted in living happily and fitting their children for the same sort of easygoing happy lives after them."[12]

A third family were Californians of the new middle class whose persistent work and careful spending Mrs. Bruère applauded because the goals were admirable—Culture and the raising of children who would enhance the Anglo-Saxon community. Mr. Allison earned $1800 as a schoolteacher and his wife ran "the whirligig of her little household in accord with the dancing of the happy world about the sun." Mrs. Allison, with what Mrs. Bruère thought was good business sense, placed "expenses almost at the level of subsistence, as you may say, and then made every expense beyond that tell for their business advantage" (table 4). The two largest items in the budget—the mortgage and savings totaled almost half of the expenditures—went toward ownership of a home, an investment on which they expected "to make about fifty per cent" when they sold. A couple without children, they

The Morality of Spending

Table 4 Budget of the Allison Family, 1911

Item	Amount in Dollars	Percentage of Budget
Food	216.00	12.0
Mortgage on home	360.00	20.0
Clothes	225.00	12.5
Operating costs		
Help	59.40	
Gas and electricity	41.40	
Telephone	23.40	
Carfare	70.20	
Laundry	14.40	
Subtotal	208.80	11.6
Advancement		
Insurance	91.80	
Church	10.80	
Books, etc.	64.80	
Amusements	50.40	
Incidentals	50.40	
Savings	522.00	
Subtotal	790.20	43.9

Source: Martha B. Bruère, "Experiments in Spending: The Budgets of a California School-Teacher and a Massachusetts Clergyman," *Woman's Home Companion* 38 (November 1911): 14.

were able to save for a time when their expenses would be higher. In addition, they tried their best to keep their food costs down. Mrs. Allison worked hard in the kitchen and in a garden that provided almost all of the fruits and vegetables they needed.[13]

Aside from "peaches, plums, apricots, oranges and pears in abundance," they ate plainly. Indeed on most nonfood items the family was parsimonious. Because "servants are hard to get here, and they are mostly Chinese when you do get them," the Allisons had little household help—a woman who came to wash and clean a half day a week and some laundry done commercially. The family kept its clothing budget (two-thirds of which was for the wife) to 12.5 percent annually by waiting for sales, taking care of what they had, and having "a few *good* things rather than a lot of cheaper ones." The $64.80 for books and periodicals was part of the husband's "equipment for his work." They were "sort of educational whetstones for his brains." The mortgage and saving aside, the Allisons lived on a modest $918.00 a year. To Mrs. Allison there was only one indulgence, tucked in under Incidentals. "I wasn't going to tell you about them," she wrote Mrs. Bruère, perhaps unsure whether such pleasures were acceptable to herself or to her audience, "but I will. They are mostly violets, lilies of the valley, and candy which my husband gets for me. I can't seem to break him of the habit, but, really, I don't object very much."[14]

Mrs. Bruère admired the choices the Allisons had made. She saw them as "a young couple trying to keep safely between the hedges which shut out the sea of debt . . . and the crags of killing hard work." However, she added, their "real life" was in the future: "intellectual achievement, children, and the chance to push the race ahead." They seemed realistic about their prospects, without "any illusions about fortunate speculations" or about increased income should Mr. Allison move up to college teaching. They saved for a future that combined admirable personal and social goals. Putting away money before they had children was the key to their future, for they fully realized "that their prosperity depends on what they can save out of their small but reasonably certain income."[15]

Though case histories were the basic building blocks of their studies, in *Increasing Home Efficiency* the Bruères gathered and analyzed all the statistics they had collected. Expenditures for food, they observed, ranged from $265.40 a year for families with less than $1000 in income to $572.57 for those in the $4000 to $5000 range. They noted "that the *proportion* of the income spent on food drops 4 1/2 per cent for every $1000 increase in income." Families of clergymen and mechanics spent more on food, the one because they entertained and the other because the father had to "replace [his] . . . physical wear." Due to transportation and marketing costs, food expenditures were lowest in small cities and highest in metropolitan suburbs and isolated towns. Families with incomes below the middle-class level of $1000 spent an average of $91.33 on shelter and obtained "inadequate housing." At the $1000 to $1200 level there was a "sudden jump" to 20 percent for shelter that demonstrated to the Bruères "how much the middle class value a decent place to live in." An increase above that level meant spending a decreasing proportion for shelter, dropping by 3 percent with every $1000 rise in income. The pursuit of "respectable shelter" was a mark of "place" in the middle class, leading "the salaried employee and the struggling professional man" to spend above an average amount. As with food, locale was important: high taxes and crowding caused the percentage spent on shelter to be highest in cities with a population of more than one hundred thousand.[16]

Unlike the costs of food and shelter, expenditures for clothing were stable, ranging from 9 percent to 12 percent and moving somewhat irregularly with changes in locale, income, and occupation. Only clergymen and physicians spent a "disproportionate" amount on clothes, something their professions "require[d]." For household operating expenses the situation was more complicated. On the one hand, though $200 to $400 appeared to mark a middle-class standard regardless of place, occupation, and income, the Bruères felt that in contrast with the expenses for shelter and clothing, "operating costs can go down indefinitely." On the other hand, when income increased, people appeared "to substitute the work of the laundry and the bakeshop and the clothing factory for the work of their hands." Even more clearly, the expenditures on household service varied with income: from $22.56 (slightly over 2 percent of income) in the lower range to $259.09 (5.2 percent to 6.5 percent) at the upper level, with $4000 the point at which employment of a full-time servant became possible and likely.[17]

Money spent for items other than food, clothing, and shelter enabled families to define their styles of living as different from those below them. The labor aristocracy may have wanted to separate itself from unskilled, immigrant workers and associate itself with the middle class. Yet many in the middle class wanted to sharpen the line between themselves and the working class. For the Bruères, discretionary income was critical in this respect. "It is under *Advancement*, however," the Bruères commented, "that we get the real significance of an increased income." They used a figure of $1000 to $1200 a year for a family of five to mark the lower edge of middle-class life, a calculation for which they relied on Chapin's 1909 study. At that level, they believed, a middle-class family was "capable of providing itself with the ordinary necessities of life." With that income, however, it would not be clear that a family could distinguish itself from the more comfortable members of the working class. With $1200 in income, "the pinch and the uncertainty" came in making provision for "those less material needs under advancement."[18]

How then did their respondents spend their funds on advancement and differentiate themselves from others? The upward curve, the Bruères wrote, rose in an unbroken line from $286.06 at the $1000 level to $2683.15 at the $4000 to $5000 level. To begin with, higher income meant the ability to make ends meet. The average deficit of $72.97 at the $1000 level turned into a break-even point above $3000. Above all it was "the margin above the decency line," the way the family spent its "surplus," that was important for middle-class families. Though they did not so label it, here the Bruères uncovered a difference between blue- and white-collar workers. Mechanics spent their average $503.97 surplus from a $1703.67 income on two and one-half children, better housing, savings, charity, and religion. In contrast, white-collar families of roughly similar income had fewer children and larger expenses for comfort and fashion. From an income of $1981.00, families headed by salaried employees spent their $747.63 surplus quite differently: $70.00 for better food; $100.00 more on housing; and double the mechanics' amount on clothing. Like the mechanics, these households put most of what they earned above a minimum into savings and insurance; unlike them, with one and one-half children, they spent none of their surplus on a larger family.[19]

Professionals, who averaged two children and whose incomes ranged from $1983.62 for educators to $2603.07 for clergymen, spent the "bulk" of their mean $1178.98 surplus on better clothes ("which might be called a professional requisite"), savings, and charity, while holding down expenses for vacations, travel, education, books, and professional improvement to $243.98. Here the Bruères pointed toward the difference between the new middle-class style of professionals and the old middle-class way of life of farmers. In contrast with this "generosity" of professionals, the Bruères noted the "niggardliness" of farmers who, with an average of 2.75 children, $2190.06 income, and $1012.34 surplus, made contributions equal to less than 3 percent of their income, put $267.38 into savings, and $156.88 into books, recreation, and travel. The Bruères believed this pattern meant that they chose "money in the bank," not "improvement or pleasure for themselves" and savings or education for their children.[20]

To the Bruères, small capitalists, representatives of the old middle class, presented the most dissatisfying pattern of expenditure, demonstrating as they did excessive self-control and insufficient pursuit of comforts. They preferred to live on their average income of $2666.66 "without exertion rather than enter any gainful occupation." "To follow their fancies," these families made a number of sacrifices. They had the fewest children, spent only $102.66 on service, and allocated an even smaller percentage than mechanics did to advancement. Compared with others with the same income but different occupations, they spent more on food and shelter. "They travel little," the Bruères noted in disappointment, "entertain little, give little; they simply continue to exist." The disdain the Bruères showed toward the group of small capitalists derived from how little they felt the group gave back to society in the form of offspring, charitable contributions, and the cultivation of the mind and spirit.[21]

Among middle-class families, those of businessmen had the largest margin "above the demands of decency" ($2251.20) and the largest incomes ($3343.81). They distributed some of their surplus "fairly evenly over the general cost of living." Most of their surplus of $1358.12 went for advancement, with 38 percent of that for savings and insurance, 16 percent for religion and charity, and 34 percent for education, books, and recreation. With an average of 1.7 children, businessmen had to choose between "running an automobile and sending a child to college. . . . Altogether," the Bruères concluded, "they have sufficient leeway, so that neither illness nor another mouth to feed need strike them with panic."[22]

To the Bruères, the best way to solve the problems facing the nuclear family was by ensuring that it broke out of its self-contained confines and entered the public world more fully than Richards recommended. Families should spend more expansively on material goods and on refinement; exhibit a spirit of generosity, especially through charitable contributions; and bring into the world children who were refined and ambitious. Against the yardstick of a family's contribution to society, the Bruères found many in their sample of seventy-six lacking. Three-quarters of the households put church and charity in one category "as though they did not give to religion for value received, but as a gratuity to a mendicant." Only six of those who listed it separately gave to religion as much as they did to charity—and half of these were clergymen's families. Equally disturbing to the Bruères was the average, for all in the sample, of slightly more than three hundred dollars for savings and insurance. Perhaps, they thought, people would have more children if they did not have to put aside so much money for their old age. Society and individuals need to plan, they concluded, "and perhaps the most important result of all budget-making will prove to be the harmonizing of our individual plans with a program of social welfare."[23] Like Ellen Richards, the Bruères wished to have the family serve larger social ends. Yet their notion of public service was more expansive, involving as it did a number of strategies for breaking down the barrier between the nuclear family and the larger society.

The Bruères were attempting to do much more than simply describe the lives of their middle-class respondents. Central to their definition of virtue was their use of the term *Advancement*. Though they never explained the phrase, it is likely that it had two meanings that united individual and national goals: social mobility and Culture, with the pursuit of both promoting the Anglo-Saxon race. Indeed, like the working-class studies, it may well be that the Bruères structured the answers to make a point: families that spent freely on advancement would move the society and themselves toward civilization. Quite obviously the Bruères evaluated what they reported. If the tone of the working-class budget studies carried out by middle-class reformers was often severe and judgmental, the Bruères' approach was chatty, personal, familiar, and, on a good number of occasions, chastising. However, what came in for the most consistent criticism was saving too much and giving too little to society. In reviewing how the Wells family spent its money, they cautioned the wife against making all her clothes at home and considering her savings "too carefully" when purchasing a hat. In being so thrifty, Mrs. Bruère remarked, the family had done little more than turn "loose an ugly home and ugly clothes on an unprotected community."[24]

The Bruères opposed excessive thrift, not thrift itself. "Now saving for its own sake isn't an inherent trait in any normal being—praise be!" Mrs. Bruère wrote in reference to a Massachusetts minister and his wife who were "reaping the harvest of comfort and content" of a quarter-century of putting money aside for late in their life. "Nobody ought to enjoy doing without things, else we should become a race of misers, each sitting on his little separate store of gold." Because economy was "not how *much* you can get out of a dollar, but getting what you *want* out of it," it was admirable to save "to enjoy a thing in the future which is more precious than any present indulgence."[25]

For the Bruères the most problematic kind of excessive saving occurred when middle-class people limited present pleasures in order to provide for retirement. The fear of poverty in old age, they believed, was "paralyzing" the middle-class home. "Is all one's life," they asked rhetorically, "to be a preparation for possible misfortunes?" "Wouldn't a man run better in the joyous hope of taking an Olympic prize," they answered with another question, "than in the deadly fear of pursuing growls in the forest?" The $300 (12 percent of income) that the average middle-class family put aside for savings and insurance, their "most serious financial mistake," forced them to "cut off $300 a year from their pleasure and usefulness."[26]

One consequence of the Bruères' opposition to too great a pursuit of individual virtue was a recognition of the pitfall of private solutions to all the problems a household faced. Studies of working-class expenditures written at the same time had treated the family as an isolated unit, as if the decisions it made privately would resolve some of the difficulties it encountered. The Bruères treated the middle-class family quite differently. When one woman wrote to complain that she had no control over her family's destiny, the Bruères responded that she was wrong in assuming that "any individual industry, intelligence or thrift" would allow her to meet the forces of corporations and public school systems "single handed when they meet her in combination."[27]

In becoming citizens, women would realize the limitations of private solutions. Through pure food laws, garbage collection, milk inspection, they would help contribute to "the domestication of business and the socialization of the home." Above all, families, which had already begun to work "collectively through the state" for some kinds of social insurance, should cooperate in providing for old age. "We still labor under the delusion that we can provide" individually for retirement, Mrs. Bruère cautioned.

"These old people," she remarked, "are pensioned without honor, and yet every one of them who has lived in this country, who has paid for the products of industry, who has ridden on the railroads, has contributed to the government. Suppose they had contributed directly their $300 a year savings, would they not then be sure of incomes in their old age, whether their individual judgment on investments was good or bad?"[28]

The Bruères recognized the limitations of private prudence but they hardly approved of cooperative living. The budget, "to the housekeeper what a set of blue prints is to the builder," was essential to the efficient running of a household, which could no longer be "left to instinct, moral sentiment, and romantic inspiration." Because society gave middle-class homes a "financial surplus," these families in turn owed the community an "adequate social return," something achieved through children. The Wells family had failed in this regard, for its excessive parsimony had meant that "the output of their domestic factory so far is two sons able to earn living salaries, who are useful to the community undoubtedly, but as easy to replace, if damaged, as any other standard products that come a dozen to the box." "The products of the home are of three kinds," the Bruères argued, using the analogy of an efficient industry: "happiness; service to the community, usually through the occupation by which we get our living; and children of the right sort."[29]

For the Bruères, the crux of the problem of the American home was that a rising standard of living and the necessity to provide for retirement had "compelled" middle-class families "to limit their output." With a household run efficiently and a pension assured, a family would be free to spend its income on making the home efficient "as a factory for the production of citizens." These concerns reflected changes in the American family, especially the declining birth rate of nonimmigrant families and shifting expectations about who would care for the elderly. In the final analysis, the question for the Bruères was whether society, by not making provisions for old age, was preventing respectable couples from having large families.[30]

Even though there was an anxious dimension to their response to the problem of the high cost of living and the cost of high living, these very forces made the Bruères more understanding of the plight of the working class. Ellen Richards, with her strict moralism and her exaggerated sense of the possibilities of curbing waste and increasing efficiency, assumed that a middle-class family could live decently on less than what many workers earned. The Bruères, in contrast, recognized that if a minister or teacher could have few comforts and hardly make ends meet on twelve hundred dollars a year, then it was unreasonable to expect a laborer to do better on less. If recreation, vacations, and the prevention of children working at too early an age were "good for some of us, why are they not good for the rest?" Attacking those who criticized the poor for mismanaging themselves into debt, the Bruères argued that the evidence proved higher incomes, not better character, enabled the more prosperous to balance their budgets. Why, they asked pointedly of ministers who preached that the meek shall inherit the earth, "should these advocates of the Spirit of Brotherhood take it for granted that the things necessary to the efficiency of their own households [with an average income of $2603.07] are not necessary for the rest of the race?"[31]

The experience of inflation and the acceptance of new comforts were among the factors that prompted contemporaries of the Bruères to reexamine the notion of what standards of economic morality would be applied to workers and immigrants. If observers of the middle class looked upward with a mixture of blame, envy, and admiration, like the Bruères some of them looked below to workers and immigrants with a new degree of sympathy. The situation in which the middle class found itself—budgets frequently pinched by inflation, struggles to maintain a comfortable standard of living, and confrontation with an array of new consumer goods and experiences—encouraged a fuller appreciation of how those with lower incomes struggled to make ends meet. Defending themselves against the charge of extravagance and rethinking the wisdom of thrift, some middle-class observers now approached the question of working-class prodigality with greater sensitivity and lessened censoriousness. Inflation, rather than making them turn to those below as scapegoats, encouraged in some middle-class observers a greater understanding of those whose economic situation was even more strained than their own.

On a number of critical issues, observers paralleled the Bruères in rethinking the familiar castigation of the working class for its prodigality. Around 1912, scientific studies of nutrition began to contribute to the shift from a class-stratified notion of food needs to a standardized one. Moreover, perhaps independent of the impact of inflation, some surveys had pointed out how little room was left for extravagance in working-class budgets. Consequenty, the "plea for economy" was for some "a plea for a lower standard."[32] In 1913, Margaret F. Byington raised doubts about the effort to use surveys of household expenditures of the families of workers to devise a scientific minimum standard of living. "Has anyone the faintest idea," she asked, "what a minimum sane expenditure for sundries would be? Yet in this item we include all the subtle expenditures that go so far toward making life wholesome; . . . [those] for schools and newspapers, for church, for amusements." Noting that in the families she studied an 80 percent rise in expenses for sundries accompanied an increase in income from under $625 to over $1040, Byington sensed that the added expenses were "wholesome and in the long run tended to create physical well being and more intelligent citizenship."[33]

Inflation played a critical role in the realization of the similar situations of divergent social groups. Two writers who believed that the increase in the cost of living had begun before 1906 saw inflation as something that gave the working class and the middle class a common experience. "Steel workers," wrote John A. Fitch in one of the volumes of the Pittsburgh Survey, "in common with all consumers in America, experienced" beginning in the 1890s "an unprecedented rise in the cost of the necessaries of life." Arthur B. Reeve, an editor of *Charities*, in 1907 remarked that the smallest wage increases had gone to "the workers of the middle class, unorganized, whose affiliations and tastes" were with capitalists but whose "interests" were with organized labor. "What must be the condition of the Under Half," Joseph Jacobs asked in the same year, if "the Middle American, the mid-most man in the nation's ranks" could not afford to travel, buy books, or attend theaters. For all those, such as urban laborers, salaried employees, and professionals, who earned a living by their labor and not by ownership of capital, wrote the radical economist Alvin S. Johnson, the "objective conditions of thrift" were becoming increasingly less favorable. Consequently it was necessary to challenge the view "that one of the best tests of the worth of a man is his power to sacrifice present enjoyment for the sake" of his family's future.[34]

In the early twentieth century, the advocates of prudence, best represented by Ellen Richards, and those who spoke for comfort, best represented by Martha Bruère, offered two different ways of studying the changes in middle-class patterns of consumption: the one mostly prescriptive; the other, mixing reportage and advice. Richards and Bruère defined class as much by ethnicity and "respectability" as they did in terms of occupation and income. To them social position was inextricably linked with styles of living based on ethnic origins. Yet though they pointed down different paths, both Richards and Bruère conveyed a sense of the crisis confronting American society. For both of them, economic and social changes threatened the home as the center of civilization and the producer of children. Facing declining birth rates for "respectable" families, they worried about the conditions for raising children who would be a credit to what they perceived as middle-class values. They both viewed the household budget as an instrument in the battle for self-preservation that "good families" had to wage.

Richards and Bruère saw the middle-class family threatened, with their worries focusing largely on the effects on society of a declining birthrate among respectable people. However, they offered different survival strategies. Richards believed that adherence to the values of the old middle class would strengthen urban, white-collar families in their effort to remain differentiated from what she saw as the profligate behavior of immigrants and the wealthy. Generally less fearful, the Bruères saw prudential values as the problem, not the solution. The sharp contrast between Richards' suggested budgets and the ones the Bruères actually collected underline the divergence in expectations (see table 5). The Bruères' respondents spent less than Richards suggested on food, clothing, shelter, and operation and much more than recommended on higher life or advancement. In other words, to the extent that the Bruères' data are reliable, Richards' guidelines were at odds with what middle-class American families spent on savings, amusements, vacations, medical care, reading material, church, and charity.

Behind the differences in the budgets of Richards and the Bruères lay fundamentally divergent views of middle-class life in America. They all defined their most important audience as the new urban middle class and a middle-class style of life as one that proper native-born people would pursue. Richards attempted to encourage the new middle class to accept the virtues of self-control in consumption long associated with the way of life characteristic of people who lived on farms and in small towns, for whom work and property ownership went hand in hand. Fearful of the masses, Richards worked to cut respectable people off from any association with the institutions that the families of workers and immigrants frequented. The Bruères felt that all Americans deserved the margin of comfort available to middle-class families. To some extent the Bruères' evidence pointed to an emergent new middle class, small urban families who valued spending, comforts, and display. Yet neither what they advocated nor what their case studies revealed was a consumer culture in full bloom.

Where Richards spoke for traditional and parsimonious values, the Bruères represented a new middle class, one that was in many ways optimistic about its position and expansive in its consumption patterns. If the one emphasized the importance of individual thrift and the danger of excessive extravagance, the other hardly ever mentioned waste or worried about expenditures. Where Richards preferred a retreat from "socialized" recreations, the Bruères accepted public amusements and advocated a community solution to the problem of retirement. To the Bruères, comfort, respectability, and Culture marked the new middle class. Self-control still balanced self-expression. In the world they preferred and described, social class was becoming a matter of respectability based on new patterns of consumption that in turn relied on a sense of propriety. Social background heavily influenced their sense of proper modes of consumption. Perhaps more to the

Table 5 Comparison of Budgets Presented by Richards and the Bruères

	Richards		Bruères	
Category	"Ideal Division"	$2000–4000	Average of $2552.62	Average of $3623.83
Food	25%	25%	20%	14.84%
Rent or shelter	20	20	16	12.16
Operation	15	15	14	9.12
Clothing	15	20	10	14.19
Higher life or advancement	25	20	35	45.62
Incidental			5	4.05

Source: Ellen H. Richards, *The Cost of Living as Modified by Sanitary Science*, 3rd ed. enlarged (New York: John Wiley and Sons, 1910), p. 39; Martha B. Bruère and Robert W. Bruère, *Increasing Home Efficiency* (New York: Macmillan, 1912), p. 315.

Bruères than to their respondents, refinement was of greater importance than mass culture. In their preferences and in what they uncovered, the Bruères to a considerable extent envisioned a new middle class that was less parsimonious than the old middle class but more cultivated than a standardless one dominated by mass culture. Richards represents one of the last gasps of the conservative moralist tradition. The Bruères stood for a group that had abandoned some but not all of that tradition. They did not envision a mass, middle-class America. In their attack on parsimony and their embrace of comfort, they departed from the strict moral tradition. In their preference for refinement and benevolence, the Bruères stuck to a moralist position.

If the studies the Bruères produced were different from those of Richards, they also differed from the Progressive investigations of working-class consumption. The richness and the uniqueness of Bruères' effort lay in the case studies they presented. The diversity of family histories and expenditures is immediately striking. To some extent this was inherent in their method of collecting information. Unlike those who caried out virtually all working-class studies, the Bruères did not confine themselves to either one locale or to strict income, family, and occupational requirements. Thus, their articles juxtaposed families from farm and city, those with and without children, and households that earned slightly more than six hundred dollars with those having incomes in excess of fourteen thousand dollars. Moreover, the case history, based on long and discursive letters, enabled subjects to convey their perception of the texture of their lives, where they had been, and where they hoped to go. Though the Bruères offered a statistical summary that demarcated patterns and even on occasion discussed the standardization of middle-class expenditures, their implicit message was quite different.[35] The case histories, with their pictures of how individual families saw themselves, conveyed a sense of the uniqueness, choice, and color of the lives they described. Their subjects were distinctive individuals, in sharp contrast to the more anonymous members of the working class who only occasionally peeked out from behind the surveys of Progressive social reformers.

The distinctiveness of the individual portraits, however, did not emerge only from the method of collecting data. For the higher incomes of middle-class families also allowed more diverse ways of spending money. As incomes rose, a number of choices became possible. Families could purchase fresh fruits and vegetables (even when out of season), dairy products, meats, and confections. Larger and more varied wardrobes also became possible. Families living well above the minimum comfort level could afford larger residences, located in better neighborhoods, and equipped with indoor plumbing, electricity, and central heating. Above all, the Bruères' respondents made their mark with expenditures for things other than food, clothing, and shelter. The scant 14 percent and $113.89 that the average $800 to $900 family spent on insurance, health care, and sundries in the Chapin study of New York City workingmen's families stood in clear contrast to the nearly 50 percent and $1670.12 that the average businessman's family in the Bruères' sample spent for advancement.[36] The change in terminology was obviously important, from Sundries, suggesting something scattered and directionless, to Advancement, giving a sense of concerted self-improvement and refinement. Marks of affluence included servants, insurance, home ownership, vacations, excursions, entertaining, movies, education, and automobiles. If the confessions in the women's magazines are at all accurate, then with extra income middle-class people strove to save for defensive purposes and to spend on comforts. They reported they were actually able to allocate a major portion of their additional income for what workers and their families only hoped to do: put money into savings, insurance, organizational life, and benevolence.

Nonetheless, even more so than for the working class, with the middle class it is difficult to separate the truth from perceptions that lay behind the gathering and presentation of information. Nowhere is this clearer than in the fact that in the same period working-class and middle-class families of roughly comparable incomes reported spending widely divergent percentages of their incomes for food and miscellaneous. Juxtaposition of Chapin's budgets for working-class families with the Bruères' for the middle class at two different levels, in two years between which prices changed little, demonstrates the differences (see table 6). Even with similar incomes, people reported quite different expenditure patterns. Compared with workers and

Table 6   Comparison of Budgets Presented by Chapin and the Bruères

Survey	Income Level	Percentage for Food	Percentage for Shelter	Percentage for Clothing	Percentage for Miscellaneous
Chapin	$900–999 (ave., $942)	44.70	24.10	14.60	16.60
Bruères	Under $1000 (ave., $960)	27.65	9.51	9.05	46.19
Chapin	$1500–1599 (ave., $1518)	36.80	20.40	16.80	26.00
Bruères	$1000–2000 (ave., $1510)	24.99	18.99	10.99	44.97

Source: Robert C. Chapin, The Standard of Living among Workingmen's Families in New York City (New York: Charities Publication Committee, 1909), p. 70; Martha B. Bruère and Robert W. Bruère, Increasing Home Efficiency (New York: Macmillan Co., 1912), p. 315.

Note: At the Bruères' level under $1000, there was a deficit of 7.6 percent.

their families, middle-class people reported using greatly lower percentages for food and greatly higher proportions for miscellaneous items.

What accounts for these differences? Because at both levels Bruères' families were smaller than Chapin's, some of divergence stemmed from variation in family size. Doubtlessly fewer offspring put less claim on expenditures for food, shelter, and clothing and therefore allowed for greater miscellaneous spending. However, extra children were unlikely to account for all the differences, although it is possible that place in the life cycle was a factor. Any explanation of the difference would have to include the likelihood that the middle class overemphasized economizing and aspirations for Culture.

An examination of budgets from middle-class families with incomes below $1500 gives some clues as to how middle-class families claimed they made ends meet. In 1913, Ladies' Home Journal presented the story, of one family of four living on $800 a year, that stands in clear contrast to the families in Chapin's sample at the same level, a level that he had defined as below "a normal standard, at least as far as the physical man is concerned" [37] (see table 7).

How did the Journal's household accomplish what it reported, enabling it to "entertain considerably, have all the necessities and some of the luxuries," even though its income was quite low? Mostly, the family said, by being very economical. It had purchased a home and paid off much of the mortgage, shopped with great diligence, produced some of its own food, used public facilities to provide "opportunity for intellectual advance-

Table 7 Comparison of Budgets Presented by *Ladies' Home Journal* and Chapin

Survey	Income Level	Year	Percentage for Food	Percentage for Shelter	Percentage for Clothing	Percentage for Miscellaneous
Ladies' Home Journal	$800	1913	32.5	14.5	12.5	40.5
Chapin	$700–799	1907	45.6	26.9	13.4	14.1

Source: Robert C. Chapin, *The Standard of Living among Workingmen's Families in New York City* (New York: Charities Publication Committee, 1909), p. 70; "How Other Folks Live," *Ladies' Home Journal* 30 (February 1913): 74.

ment," and spent only $124 on items other than food, clothing, shelter, insurance, and saving, and all but $14 of that on carfare, church, and medical care. Others wrote to the magazine with similar stories in which gentility, systematic bookkeeping, financial planning, and strenuous economies were the keys. "Our simple manner of living satisfies and has become a habit and a pleasure to us," wrote a Massachusetts housewife who shared an income of $780 a year with her husband, "and we have learned . . . that 'it is better to desire the things we have than to have the things that we desire.' "[38]

Even if households such as these were atypical, it is unlikely that, except in unusual circumstances, working-class and middle-class families of roughly comparable incomes spent such divergent percentages of their income on food and miscellaneous. At issue here is the context in which households offered their budgets to an audience. Working-class families, faced in the same years with social workers who asked about their way of life, probably minimized the expenditures they reported for miscellaneous items, especially liquor, tobacco, church, unions, and social clubs. Conversely, the middle-class women's magazines elicited exceptional stories of the heroics of genteel poverty or genteel comfort, of individuals who were proud of how they economized and yet managed to live respectable lives. The women's magazines may well have attracted respondents who emphasized self-restraint and refinement, not self-indulgence. The magazines may well have wished to romanticize the economical life in order to provide an example to readers. Still influenced by aspects of moralism, writers and editors promoted prudence and Culture as choices that made the middle class different from (and reputedly better than) those below.

In level and content of expenses, the bottom of the middle class and the top of the working class touched and often overlapped. However, reading the social workers' surveys of the one group and presentations in the women's magazines of the other brings the reader into distinctive worlds. In one, choice was limited and anything beyond a minimal level of comfort relatively rare. Farther up the social scale was a world not without considerable uncertainties but filled with a more expansive sense of choice and greater comfort. Even if the real differences were small, their symbolic meaning was considerable. Having experienced a sudden drop in income to fifteen hundred dollars a year, a Brooklyn family gave up a commodious house and a maid but still managed to live "if not in luxury, yet with reasonable comfort," though "not in a tenement neighborhood." As in the choice of locale, status was important in defining a middle-class style of living. A number of budget items made "just the difference to us between poverty and comfort": the husband's lunches out, life insurance, and a church pew, which "makes us feel a certain self-respect," fulfilled a "duty towards our children," and brought "delightful friendships we could not spare." Finally, the "incidentals" on which they spent one hundred dollars meant "a little vacation in summer, many a picnic, a new book now and then, and a little recreation of one sort or another," all of which were "as needful to real life" as food and shelter.[39]

During the late nineteenth and early twentieth centuries, middle-class styles of life did change, often in ways that made them distinctive. Although new items did come to signify a middle-class life, many observers continued to envision a world shaped less by modern commodity consumption than by the emphasis on refinement. Yet if the commentary in the women's magazines is at all representative, middle-class self-perception may have changed less than reality. Old notions provided the way of interpreting new possessions and experiences. To a significant degree, the moralist tradition still shaped the ways that observers comprehended new patterns. The preference for prudence and Culture influenced the advice given and the budgets collected. "Advancement" to a considerable extent remained something these observers held out as a goal principally for their own middle-class peers. Moreover, though they had some recognition of the arrival of important elements of mass consumption, they assumed that the middle class still sought the "higher life" of education, medical care, Culture, and charity. The middle class was going to movies, taking vacations, employing servants, and purchasing automobiles, something the stories in the women's magazines did not fully reflect. Although status was coming to be connected with a package of consumer goods, the belief in refinement and respectability shaped the meaning of such new consumer goods and experiences as commercial leisure and mass culture.

Despite whatever place it had in people's lives, mass commercial culture entered discussions of middle-class household budgets to a surprisingly small degree. Movies, amusement parks, cameras, phonographs, automobiles, and popular books and magazines played virtually no role in the

Bruères' definition of a respectable standard of living.[40] Mass culture rarely emerged as a separate category in budget discussions. Even those respondents who recognized specific items tended to see them within a framework that traditional language shaped. One observer talked of phonographs as an example of the shift from work to pleasure as the principal object of life but placed his discussion within the context of the rise of extravagance and the demise of frugality. Another observer spoke of increased spending on automobiles and movies as "unproductive consumption." On the relatively rare occasions that budget professionals mentioned the impact of mass culture on middle-class life, they expressed concern with how new forms of commercial entertainment—movies, nickelodeons, amusement parks—threatened to undermine traditional institutions.[41]

A number of factors shaped the perceptions of observers, but especially influential were concerns about race suicide, social mobility, and respectability.[42] Even those who welcomed a rising standard of living did so not primarily because they embraced narcissistic self-realization or mass culture but because they thought of themselves and their peers as people who lived refined and comfortable lives. Budget studies served to remind people who thought of themselves as members of the middle class that their lives were different from workers and immigrants. The divergence in the methods of the two kinds of studies underlined the importance of a search for distinctiveness. As skilled workers and some immigrants earned larger incomes, it was all the more important to locate the boundaries between people with roughly similar household budgets and to encourage the middle class to seek respectability. The search for distinctive styles of life thus became more crucial. The values of the American-born middle class—refinement, taste, comfort, and Culture—became the markings of a respectable and virtuous life.

Interest in the standard of living and household budgets was in itself part of an effort to define middle-class styles of living in new situations. A rising standard of living, the emergence of the new middle class, and the proliferation of consumer goods and experiences made it imperative to understand distinctive styles. Household budget studies, of whatever class, were morality plays, reminders of the dangers of behavior that was imprudent and improper for aspiring and respectable people. As work became more problematic as a source of meaning, middle-class observers wondered how consumption might make lives worth living. Even in studies of workers and immigrants, a tradition that originated in a desire to discover how the poor got by, the subtext may have been the survival of the middle class.

Affluence strained the connection that nineteenth-century moralists had established between prudential values and the social order. Over time the conflict intensified between hard work and the excessive enjoyment of its results. Rarer and rarer became the claim that wealth would bring about the demise of civilization. A clear alternative, however, had not emerged. With mass consumption hidden under "higher life," the categories were breaking down and the distinctions were harder to maintain. The new formula uneasily contained comfort, materialism, and mass culture, along with an expectation of cultivation and refinement. What emerged was a redefinition of a higher standard of living that located the source of anxiety not in weak character or mass culture but in the chase after a continual escalation of desires. What persisted was a dream of rejecting the new material comforts not for the sake of the Protestant ethic's self-denial but for the restraint that simplicity brought. The pre–World War I middle class may have behaved like dedicated consumers but tended to see itself not as incipient Babbitts but as potential Thoreaus or cultivated citizens.

7   Double Digits: World War I, the Red Scare, and Attitudes to Consumption

From the perspective of 1918 or 1920, the inflation of 1906–16 would seem mild. Between 1914 and 1921, the cost of consumer goods doubled. When the war began in Europe, prices, according to one index, stood at 120. Two years later they began to register five years of hefty increases: to 130 in 1916, 153 in 1917, 180 in 1918, 207 in 1919, and 240 in 1920. Then prices broke and fell—to 214 in 1921, and 200 the next year—and remained in the low 200s throughout the 1920s.[1] Wartime increases reopened old questions and brought new realizations. Until World War I, reconsideration of the conservative moralist tradition proceeded slowly. In the cauldron of wartime and immediate postwar events, discussion intensified but produced no clear resolution. Public debate over wartime priorities, budget-planning advice, and studies of household expenditures reveal the ways that observers viewed changing patterns of consumption. The claims of patriotism, the strains of class relationships, the impact of double-digit inflation, and complex developments in American capitalism fostered a simultaneous reassertion of the need for prudential virtues and acceptance of new patterns of spending. In discussions of middle-class standards of living, traditional rhetoric did not succeed in covering up new ways of consuming.

The treatment of working-class spending was more complicated: wartime sympathy for a more generous standard quickly turned into postwar antagonism. Observers differentiated among styles of living and defined social position in terms of ethnicity and divergent kinds of consumption. However, what at the time looked like a resurgence of nineteenth-century moralism, in retrospect was more one of its last gasps. The swift and contradictory changes of the years around World War I undermined the old tradition and prepared the ground for a new vision of a consumer society that emerged in the 1920s. At the point of transition to a new outlook, the strain was greatest in the old.

For households, the meaning of rising prices depended on a number of things, including what happened to income in the same period. One astute contemporary noted that the air was "filled with lamentations, while of rejoicing over good fortune little is heard."[2] The effect of inflation varied in another way: prices for categories of expenditures rose at different rates. In the five years beginning in December 1914, the cost of living in large cities increased 91 percent for food, 198 percent for clothing, 25 percent for rent, 52 percent for fuel and lighting, 175 percent for furniture and furnishings, and 92 percent for miscellaneous.[3] In response to such wildly divergent rates of change, people adjusted their expenditures. Those whose incomes rose proportionately faced little real sacrifice in their standard of living. Others whose incomes remained relatively stable had difficult decisions to make. What actually happened to real earnings in the period is complicated. The real incomes of unskilled workers rose sharply and those of skilled workers and the middle class tended to rise more modestly and in some cases actually declined. The most significant change is that the income differential between unskilled laborers and those above, which had been widening for almost two decades before World War I, now reversed itself. This unprecedented and sharp change in the nature of income relationships made the middle class feel it had some reason for complaint. In addition, except for the most fortunate, such rapidly spiraling prices were doubtlessly disorienting. One commentator in 1920 argued that the recent inflation had caused "disturbances, material and psychological, so grave as to be comparable with those directly caused by the waste and destruction of the war itself. The unsettled condition of people's minds in relation to the familiar concerns of daily life, which has attended the disarrangement of price relations," he remarked at a time when newspapers were reporting revolutions, strikes, and repression, "has contributed no inconsiderable share to the social unrest with which the world is beset."[4]

The 1915–17 household expenditures of the family of Stuart Chase convey the impact of inflation on the life of one unusual upper-middle-class household. For Chase, twenty-seven years old in 1915, wartime inflation was the catalyst that prompted him to change from a prewar Progressive concerned with the lives of the workers (he and his wife spent their honeymoon pretending they were unemployed and looking for work) to a postwar consumer advocate interested in the impact of a rising standard of living on middle-class Americans. In *Good Housekeeping*, Chase presented the budget he and his wife had prepared (see table 8).

Both from well-to-do families, in 1915 the Chases established their first household in a three-room Boston apartment and lived on his earnings as an accountant and income from other sources. At the end of the year, Stuart Chase looked back on the experiment with some satisfaction. He and his wife had adopted a plan and kept to it reasonably well. They had

Table 8 Budget of the Chase Family, 1915

Item	Amount in Dollars	Percentage of Budget
Rent, light, gas, janitor	500	24.0
Food	350	16.8
Clothing		
M.H.C.	100	
S.C.	100	
Subtotal	200	9.6
Operating expenses		
Household, general	100	
Laundry	75	
Health	75	
Telephone	40	
Sundries and lunches—S.C.	125	
Sundries—M.H.C.	75	
Subtotal	490	23.5
Advancement expenses		
Insurance	100	
Recreation	37	
Education	38	
Books and periodicals	25	
Gifts and contributions	50	
Vacations and trips	100	
Subtotal	350	16.8
Total estimated expenses	1890	
Furnishings and savings	195	9.4
Total estimated income	2085	

Source: Stuart Chase, "Budget Building," *Good Housekeeping* 62 (April 1916): 511.

managed to put aside $146.47, over half of which they spent on furniture. Their "domestic partnership" was a success: they worked "equally hard," he at the office and she at home. Each had the same power to decide how to spend common funds because the notion that the husband as prime income earner should control allocation of all expenditures was "a quaint barbaric survival that we must outgrow as we have outgrown chattel slavery." They kept their costs down by not having a full-time maid; by not entertaining very much; by seldom going "to the theater or to other purely social functions"; and by having "despoiled" their families for a large number of Sunday dinners. At the end of the year, it was clear to them that a childless couple from their backgrounds needed at least $1800 a year to live in a city and "keep up a semblance of their former social standard." As 1916 began, they were confident that the past year's experiences enabled them more accurately to plan for the future.[5]

Two events—the birth of a child in 1916 and the acccelerated rate of inflation—undermined their predictions. Careful economizing and an installment loan enabled them to move to a six-room apartment farther from the city center and finance the addition to their family while maintaining "*our middle class standard of living.*" When they came to plan for 1917, they hoped that a significant rise in salary would enable them to afford greatly increased food expenses and "to cover the maid and that even greater tyrant—the High Cost of Living." Cautioning against making it appear that he and his wife were doing more than keep up "some semblance of appearance," Chase asked his readers to look at "the 'Recreation' item and figure silently how many theater tickets, concert tickets, taxicabs, fresh flowers, country-club dues, and quiet little dinners in town you can get for $25 a year."[6]

Less than four months later, Chase announced that the war had raised "havoc" with his budget (see table 9). Chase noted that the increase in expenses was not as great as that reported in national indexes, because the rent had remained stable and the family had eliminated meat from its diet.[7] Escalating prices had done their greatest damage to plans for Advancement expenses, with $150 budgeted and $243 actually spent. "We did not have the grit," Stuart Chase confessed, "to sacrifice the moderate extras that our middle-class standard of living has accustomed us to." Books, magazines, a winter vacation in the mountains, an occasional play or concert, and "recklessly small checks for unpopular causes"—these were the items that Chase with tongue in cheek said represented "wanton extravagance."[8]

America's entry into World War I in April 1917 convinced Chase that it was "not only a personal necessity but a patriotic duty to eliminate waste and extravagance" by cutting back on luxuries. The war thus prompted him to consider personal and political responses to escalating prices and more fully embrace self-discipline. Chase explored ways that families could solve their budgetary problems. They could grow more food in home gardens; try to reduce waste, especially in the preparation and serving of food; and decrease the consumption of luxuries. He also went beyond the emphasis on an individual solution and suggested how society might enforce virtue. In one of the first references to taxes in the period's household budget discussions, he considered new levies on luxuries and excess profits. Moreover, Chase, like others who had anticipated the beneficial side effects of earlier wars, felt that this one provided a chance "to revolutionize the whole economy of luxuries." He believed that the nation could cut back on "baubles, surfeits, and poisons that serve no rational human need, and only succeed in polluting and perverting our national life and character." The elimination of such expenditures, "the product of grave injustices in the distribution of wealth," would end "progressively the more bizarre and the more vicious elements of luxury." Radically changing the way Americans

Table 9 Budgets of the Chase Family, 1916–1917

	Six months ended May 1, 1916 Actual Expenses	Six months ended May 1, 1917		Percent Increase 1916 Actual To 1917 Actual
		Budget	Actual	
Food	$ 168	$ 185	$ 266	58
Shelter	297	300	313	5
Clothing	164	200	224	36
Operating	246	250	334	35
Advancement	211	150	243	15
Total	$1086	$1085	$1380	27
Income	1150	1250	1305	13
Surplus	$ 64	$ 165		
Deficit			$ 75	

Source: Stuart Chase, "A War Budget for the Household," *Independent* 91 (4 August 1917): 169.

produced and consumed, with a new stress on the necessary and "whole-some," would signal "the beginning and the end of all sane spending, in peace no less than in war."[9]

Nothing so well illustrates the contradictory nature of his (and his con-temporaries') reaction as Chase's simultaneous call for purification and consumer comfort. He was unwilling to consider tax policies that might have significantly redistributed wealth or limited consumption. In his hypo-thetical analysis of a budget, he mentioned only one specific item he was willing to eliminate, two dollars spent at an after-theater cabaret. He drew back from a full attack on materialism. A moderate amount of luxury, Chase felt, was "necessary to any sort of civilized life." Moreover, he argued, a sudden decrease in the use of luxuries such as jewelry, costly millinery, limousines, opera boxes, and movies would be "disastrous to the general business of the country, however excellent its effect on the character of the individual."[10]

As the United States entered World War I, Stuart Chase voiced most of the major American preoccupations with the relation between the war, heightened inflation, and the standard of living. Like many families that lived well above subsistence, the Chases experienced a renewed interest in curbing waste and in becoming more self-reliant. Along with many of his contemporaries, he approached these tasks as economic and patriotic necessities, not individualistic moral imperatives. Similarly, almost in the same breath Chase attacked and accepted luxuries, embraced moralistic values and welcomed a new level of material comforts. In all these ways, Chase was participating in a national debate that linked private concerns about the household budget to public policy questions concerning national priorities and how to achieve them. The war was one of those moments when traditions and new possibilities stood uneasily side by side and thus produced an especially intense and often contradictory examination of the meaning of a higher standard of living.

World War I provided a backdrop for statements by the parties of prudence and comfort. To a considerable extent the war offered moralists an opportunity to revive commitments to thrift and simplicity among comfortable and affluent Americans.[11] However, closer examination of rhetoric shows important modifications of the inherited ideology. If the moderate inflation of the dozen years before the war caused many middle-class families to feel pinched, the much more severe wartime rise in prices provoked some members of the "unprotected 'middle class' " to feel "constantly being ground to the point of desperation." Some responded by linking profligacy to impending disaster, from which the nation could be saved only by renewed emphasis on industriousness, frugality, self-sacrifice, and self-improvement. The embrace of false standards, commented one U.S. senator, and "this revelry in extravagant habits, this unquenchable demand for amusements, for continuous mental intoxicants" threatened to bring the nation to its knees.[12]

Many writers emphasized the connection between thrift, simple living, and the war effort. As early as 1915, one observer hailed the war as a blessing in disguise that would bring a revival of "the frugality and self-restraint that makes for character." As American participation in the war increased, others celebrated the thrifty—women especially—as national heroines who would redeem themselves by renouncing their extravagance. Struck by wartime economies and the specter of Bolshevism, in late 1918 Katharine F. Gerould argued that the salvation of the middle class depended on the rejection of materialism. "We shall learn to take pleasure in beautiful things that do not and never can belong to us," she wrote, "and we shall purge ourselves of the ignoble passion of envy." Especially when the war's end unleashed pent-up demand for consumer goods and intensified social unrest, observers called for the renunciation of excess. "We have all been participants," Christine Frederick wrote in 1921 in reference to the war's immediate aftermath, "in a wild, bacchanalian orgy wherein we cast aside our usual sense and caution and flung our money insanely to the winds, gorging ourselves on every delicacy and indulging our desire of licentious spending until we finally achieved an economic debauch."[13]

The proponents of thrift rested their case on a combination of patriotism and prudence. Representatives of the industrial, banking, and investment communities saw more careful expenditures and greater thrift as critical to the war effort. Bankers especially took the lead in organizing nationwide thrift campaigns. Those who called for savings appealed especially to house-wives, arguing that "the most patriotic woman will be the one that finds happiness in what she does without rather than in what she consumes." Economy became the moral equivalent of fighting. "The woman who is handling the food supply in the home," wrote the meat-packing industrial-ist J. Ogden Armour in 1917, "is equal in importance to the man who handles the gun on the battlefield." At times, however, the rhetoric sug-gested that abstemious behavior involved more than necessity and patriot-ism. Some observers linked thrift with personal success. Others argued that thrift will "permanently elevate and strengthen" character. Individual responsibilty, self-control, stability, character, and sacrifice—these became the touchstones of thrift campaigns.[14]

Embedded in the thrift discussion were important changes in attitudes. Some contemporaries went so far as to turn their backs on self-sacrificing, individualized thrift and embraced increasing wants as the engines of pro-gress. The young economist Alvin Hansen, who mentioned the writings of George Gunton and Ira Steward, asserted that free spending on items such as housing would increase a family's standard of living. Even advocacy of savings rested on a distinction between constructive and destructive spend-ing. In *Investment Weekly*, for example, one writer used self-serving logic to attack consumption of luxuries such as "cigars, cocktails, theater tickets beyond reasonable requirements of relaxation, [and] a motor car to be used for pleasure only" as kinds of transient gains of "no permanent value." He contrasted this with cutting down on spending in order to save, something that would enable banks to encourage the production of things of lasting quality and thus help "contribute to an increase in the country's business." Thus, often side by side with the appeals to the familiar and individual values of conservative moralists, promoters of thrift acknowledged that savings supported national goals of investment and productivity. More-over, contemporaries saw more widespread stock and bond ownership as a factor that would help lessen strife between labor and capital.[15]

The criticism of thrift campaigns illustrates the contradictory impulses within the business community. The rhetoric used to oppose savings often reflected the change in the view of the worker from someone who labored hard and who saved to a purchaser who used the installment plan to consume. Some, often representatives of savings and investments interests, reiterated traditional arguments for self-control. Others, frequently speak-ing for industries that would suffer from cuts in spending, attacked excessive thrift. During the war, department stores and clothing manufacturers were among the special interests that feared excessive savings would hurt them. Executives in the automobile industry were particularly nervous about decreased consumption. One company took out advertisements encouraging people to spend freely, especially on its products.[16]

Once the war's end severed the close connection between loyalty and savings, some businessmen organized the National Prosperity Bureau and used xenophobia in an attack on thrift "which inevitably reduced the living standard of American workingmen to the niggardly requisites of certain immigrants." Opposition to the thrift campaign was more profound and widespread than such expressions of specific self-interest indicated. The discovery of malnutrition among military recruits was among the factors that prompted one nutrition expert to attack savings that sacrificed the standard of living. Recognizing that the thrift campaigns benefited bankers, he cautioned people to avoid "sordid economizing" that could "result in the wilting of worthy ambition, the dwarfing of soul and the stunting of the mind and body."[17]

An examination of wartime and postwar federal policies provides an additional way of understanding the conflicting pulls of self-restraint and pleasure. Policy debates reveal the difficulty of drawing an exact line between a high standard of living and extravagance. In levying excise taxes, Congress showed what it thought were nonnecessities or luxuries. As American involvement in the war intensified, levies on liquor and tobacco increased and the government imposed or dramatically raised taxes on a number of items, especially those associated with amusement, recreation, and personal adornment. Interest groups and national security considerations obviously influenced some of these choices. By placing an especially heavy tax on liquor, tobacco, theaters, museums, music halls, circuses, street fairs, club dues, cameras, sports equipment, pleasure boats, art works, and expensive clothing, the immediate postwar legislation made it clear that military priorities were not the only issue.[18] Legislators had lumped together a curious melange of what they considered superfluous luxuries: things like liquor and events like street fairs, both long identified with pleasure-seeking immigrants and workers; museums and art, associated with the pursuit of Culture; yachts, the playthings of the rich; and cameras and sporting goods, new items of mass, commercialized recreation.

Other policy considerations revealed an equally confused understanding of how to distinguish between luxuries and necessities. Under the direction of Bernard Baruch and the War Industries Board (WIB), the government tried to decide upon wartime production priorities. The WIB failed in its effort to define "less essential" or "nonessential" industries in order to curtail them. Public debate usually reflected similar uncertainties.[19] In most cases those who advocated the use of public policy to curb expenditures on luxuries came up against a reluctance to injure specific industries, to challenge the economic system, or to call on Americans to endure more than a modicum of sacrifices.

Amid the confusion, Thorstein Veblen was unusual in his ability to spell out an unequivocal position on extravagance and explore the radical potential of puritanism. The "edifying talk" about the priority of war demands, he noted in 1918, had resulted in "surprisingly little" action. "Popular interest and administrative policy," he had to conclude, "are still bent on the maintenance of the domestic status quo,—the status of competitive gain and competitive spending." To democratize sacrifice, Veblen proposed a sharply progressive tax on "menial" servants whose principal function was to provide their masters with a "sense of self-complacency and invidious distinction." Anticipating the objection that such a policy might make it difficult for the rich "advantageously" to inhabit "superfluously large houses," with his typical ironic touch Veblen suggested that mansions could be used as homes or places of recreation for workers and their families.[20]

Like the issue of national priorities, contemporary discussion of budget planning for middle-class households illustrates the complex pulls engendered by the 1916–21 experience with war, inflation, and social unrest. Budget experts questioned the wisdom of extravagance and pretense while often acknowledging their existence in a matter-of-fact manner. C. W. Taber offered the most revealing approach to the question of the balance between self-discipline and excess. On the one hand, he argued that with the high cost of living destroying the middle class, it was advisable to turn to the pursuit of higher things because there was nothing "in any material thing that can or will bring us lasting happiness." On the other hand, he attacked excessive thrift. If too much savings meant "enforced self-denial and the absence of bodily comforts or the starving of mental cravings and the sacrifice of spiritual developments," he argued in 1918, "then the price of increased bank deposits is too high."[21]

Implicitly, Taber found the path to a nonluxurious "abundant living" by subsuming participation in mass commercial and materialistic culture under experiences that led to "development of the mind and the growth of the soul." He insisted that vacations should involve the pursuit of Culture and not be "merely an excuse for letting down the bars of self-control." Similarly, though he was among the first to mention movies as a regular budget item for middle-class families, specifically as a way of celebrating holidays and special family occasions, he cautioned readers to see only films "of unusual worth." He likewise included movies, along with theater, parties, and socials, under "mental activities," automobiles under travel, and resorts under "out-door activities."[22] Indeed an examination of Taber's budget guidelines indicates that, though his language suggested pursuing a "higher life," compared with those who gave advice to the middle class early in the twentieth century, he actually embraced a more materialistic standard of living. One of his model budgets included 4 percent of total expenditures for "luxuries." Moreover, under the umbrella of "higher life," he included phonographs, player pianos, "amusement," "personal indulgences," automobiles, and motor boats.[23]

The wartime and postwar studies expanded the categories of spending in other ways. One person advised three levels of expenses (see table 10). The addition of new categories undermined the old ones. The traditional division, wrote Isabel E. Lord, meant that "by a grim jest that few appreciate, the doctor and the dentist get charged to Higher Life." The proliferation of new headings also highlighted a host of additional items, such as children's allowances, flowers, parcel post, meals outside the home, postage, interest on debt, stationery, taxes, telegrams, and lawn care. A greater sense of relativity and choice accompanied this expansion of the notion of what a budget might contain. Again and again observers struggled to define extravagance and usually concluded that there were "no-hard-and-fast rules governing the spending of an income." By making the distinction between luxury and "abundant living," budget planners suggested that people could make choices without overstepping the boundaries of a moral life.[24]

Thus by 1918, "higher life"—which to traditionalists had meant benevolence and Culture—included items such as automobiles, amusements, phonographs, and "personal indulgences." For the middle class, more expensive, "elevating" consumer goods and experiences were coming to define their way of life. Rapid inflation and the income gains of labor made members of the middle class run to stay even in the race for greater material and commercial pleasures. As the connection between social background and income became more blurred, the American-born middle class still thought of itself as seeking an ennobling way of life that had more than a hint of ethnic superiority. The middle class was moving away from viewing itself as pursuing self-restraint to a more complex view that acknowledged a higher standard of living but continued to insist that more consumption involved the pursuit of "higher" goals. The persistence of notions of a more refined life allowed ethnic identification to cover up the coincidence of income, consumption packages, and social position. Morever, the transition to a new sensibility was still incomplete, as evidenced by the advertising executive Bruce Barton's simultaneous embrace of luxuries as a spur to ambition and the wisdom of Henry David Thoreau.[25]

Nonetheless, a number of changes reflect the increasing realization that the middle-class way of life had moved well beyond necessities and restraint:

Table 10 Three Suggested Levels of Expenses, 1921

	Food	Clothing	Shelter	Housekeeping Expenses	Development
Charges fixed			Rent Interest on mortgage	Water (if not metered) Service Telephone Chore man	Church dues Club dues Magazine subscription Newspaper subscription Tuition Personal allowances Automobile Garage License Registration
Charges possible to estimate	Groceries Ice Milk Meat Vegetables Fruits	New materials New clothing	Taxes Business carfare Insurance (fire)	Water (if metered) Coal Wood Gas Electricity Household supplies Laundry	Philanthropy Amusements Concerts Carfare (personal) Automobile Running expenses
Charges necessary to limit	Outside meals Out-of-season foods	Cleansing Repairs	Repairs	Extra service Long-distance telephone Repair and replacement of equipment Extra laundry Incidentals Express Postage House carfare, etc.	Doctor, dentist Travel Books Gifts Automobile Repair Equipment Entertaining New equipment

Source: S. Agnes Donham, "Your Income, and How to Spend It," *Ladies' Home Journal* 38 (March 1921): 107.

the wartime linking of thrift and productivity; the shift in emphasis from individual character to national investment; the increasing number of special interests with a stake in greater consumption; the explosion of categories and items in recommended budgets; and the difficulty of drawing a line between luxuries and necessities. Even with the general dislocation and the stringencies caused by inflation, middle-class Americans embraced a higher standard of living. Looking over their shoulders at workers and immigrants who were capable of purchasing elements of a higher standard of living, people who wrote for a middle-class audience embraced a more self-indulgent way of life at the same time that they stressed simplicity and refinement.

Indeed, inflation itself was in part responsible for the hectic chase after greater comforts and more luxuries. If in the 1970s inflation prompted millions of Americans to save less and spend more before rising prices eroded their savings and purchasing power, something similar may well have happened earlier, especially after the Armistice severed the connection between prudence and patriotism. "What has led to the 'orgy of extravagance' concerning which we hear so much?" Bruce Barton asked in 1920. Inflation had, he answered, noting that it was "inevitable that dollars that have little purchasing power should be lightly regarded." Much of what critics labeled extravagance, Albert W. Atwood noted in the same year, was the unleashing of spending held in check by World War I, when people craved "vanities and fripperies" only "with a feeling of guilt," while other excesses were actually "frenzied buying" in anticipation of still higher prices.[26] Feeling the pinch of inflation, recovering from the strain of forced savings, and envying workers whose rise in income outpaced prices, people who spoke for the middle class welcomed a greater degree of material pleasures, albeit often under the cloak of "higher" things or with a criticism of excess.

How did budget experts treat working-class spending habits in the years surrounding World War I? The importance of labor in the war effort, the Russian Revolution, activity of unions and radicals in the United States, and the actual results of increased purchasing power of many working-class families made these years critical in the development of middle-class attitudes toward the consumption of those below them on the social scale. This period produced several landmark studies of working-class budgets, many of them geared to the introduction in 1919 of the Bureau of Labor Statistics' Consumer Price Index. The federal government expanded its activity in the collection and analysis of data on how price changes affected the way people spent their money. In 1918, the federal government undertook a massive and elaborate survey of household budgets, one that documented new patterns of working-class consumption. To devise a consumer price index in a period of rapid inflation, the Bureau of Labor Statistics studies became more sophisticated methodologically.

Simultaneously, the government attempted to define a "minimum comfort" budget above the subsistence level. Pressure from organized labor, effective during a war when demands for workers and for industrial peace were high, prompted a reevaluation of notions of adequacy of existing standards of living and made some observers more appreciative of new patterns of working-class expenditures. The postwar reaction to labor's gains in turn led the government to reverse itself and establish a norm that reflected the hold of the conservative moralist tradition more than it did newly emergent patterns of consumption. Once again, middle-class writers used asceticism to accuse the working class of extravagance.

In 1918 and 1919, the Bureau of Labor Statistics, in cooperation with the

War Labor Board, carried out the most extensive and sophisticated survey of household budgets to date. To help resolve disputes over whether wages had kept pace with rising prices, the government investigated the expenditures of nearly thirteen thousand families in American cities and towns.[27] The study focused on wage earners of any income level and "low or medium salaried families." Even compared with the forms used in working-class studies ten years earlier, there were more entries for vacations, travel, excursions, movies, education, taxes, and vehicles. Yet the gap persisted between categories used in working-class and middle-class investigations. The term *miscellaneous*, instead of *development* or *higher life*, remained appropriate for those low on the social scale. Similarly, the sense of choice was still a middle-class prerogative; for them but not for workers, "personal indulgences," "extras and excess expenditures," and "personal allowances" appeared in lists of budget items.[28] For each household the investigation collected information on an eleven-page form (see Appendix C for the cover sheet and page on miscellaneous expenses for a Fall River, Massachusetts, family).

The data in the 1918–19 study described working-class families that spent a good share of their income on a wide variety of items other than food, clothing, and shelter. In Carroll D. Wright's 1875 report, most families allocated 3 percent to 10 percent of their expenditures to sundries. In 1918–19, families earning $1200 to $1499 spent an average of 25 percent or $324.35 for furniture, furnishings, and miscellaneous (see Appendix A). In 1875 most of these funds went for newspapers and organizational life. More than four decades later, the list of frequent expenses, those for which more than half of the families at the $1200 to $1499 level allocated any money was varied: life insurance, church, "patriotic purposes," gifts, streetcar fare, movies, newspapers, postage, physician, medicine, tobacco, "laundry sent out," cleaning supplies, "toilet articles and preparations," and barber (see Appendix B). Some of these families were coming to benefit from indoor plumbing, as well as gas heating and lighting. Moreover, making ends meet with less difficulty was one of the differences that marked an improved economic situation.[29]

Yet at the end of World War I, a very substantial percentage of Americans were hardly living a life of ease. Of the "wage-earners and the low or medium salaried families" that the BLS surveyed in 1918–19, approximately two of every five were below the "subsistence level" of $1386.00 and about three of four were under the level "above minimum subsistence" of $1760.50. The income of the head of household did not usually provide enough money for most families. At the end of the war, about 75 percent of the individuals who reported earnings took home less than $1575.00 a year.[30]

The families of most workers, though they spent a larger percentage of their income and more real dollars on household goods and miscellaneous items than their predecessors, had relatively small amounts of money for paid recreation, movies, excursions, vacations, household help, or vehicles. Most workers made most of their household and miscellaneous expenditures in ways that reflected old, defensive, and communal patterns more than they foretold new, accumulative, and artificial ones (see Appendix B). Not even at the range of $1500 to $1799 of household income did people experience considerable comforts and mass consumer culture. With that income, 80.7 percent of families spent an average of $10.73 a year on movies; 18.6 percent, an average of $7.36 for excursions; 27.6 percent, an average of $30.24 for vacations; 16.2 percent, an average of $108.75 for automobiles, motorcycles, and bicycles; and 18.1 percent, an average of $26.39 for household help. Even above $2500 only one of every four families reported spending any money for excursions, two of every five for vacations, one of every three for a vehicle, and one of every four for household help.[31]

In addition to collecting large amounts of data on how Americans spent their money, the federal government attempted to describe a budget level above subsistence, something that had begun to interest survey takers in the Progressive period. The most important efforts along these lines took place just before and during the war, when labor's political power was at its height. Many observers continued to charge the working class with profligacy. In the effort to legitimize a higher standard of living, Royal Meeker, the head of the Bureau of Labor Statistics, played a critical role. In 1916 and 1917 he supervised a study of the cost of living of slightly more than two thousand families in the District of Columbia. Discovering that almost 40 percent of the households had incomes of less than nine hundred dollars a year, he spoke of the "shocking state of economic indecency" and the "pinch of economic distress." Under such a "crushing load of poverty," he concluded, it was impossible for many working-class families to live decent lives. "To preach to such families the 'gospel of the clean plate,' or to offer them dietary advice," he remarked, "would be bitter irony."[32] Consequently, an upward revision in notions of what was acceptable was in order. Recognition of a new level for laborers involved denial of working-class extravagance, an attack on the view of the worker's wife as a heroic economizer, and a belief that it was more appropriate to adjust budget levels than to try to change consumers' habits.[33]

By the summer of 1919, the BLS studies had convinced Meeker that it was necessary to question not only the notion of worker profligacy but also the idea of a uniquely American standard of living. Although he expressed some unease when it came to the question of expenses for amusement,

Meeker argued that the data did not bear out the charge of worker extravagance in clothing. Indeed he accepted the idea that what workers and their families wore "should possess something of that subtle something called 'style.'" He found it "repugnant" to society's "sense of right" that "the working classes should dress in a way to set them apart from the more well-to-do." Since clothes were in fact for adornment and society accepted the "ridiculous and often health-impairing standards of dress" established by designers, the nation had to offer the worker wages high enough "to enable him to conform to the accepted fashion." Thus Meeker had come to doubt that there was any such thing as "the American standard of living in the sense of a very superior standard giving all the necessaries, many of the comforts, and a goodly supply of the luxuries of life." Do not be "fooled by the cry that the American standard of living is the highest in the world." The budget studies had revealed that a different goal lay ahead, making the "minimum standard in America one that will support life in decency and health."[34]

Though the definition of *decency* or *comfort* remained elusive, the development of a higher norm represented an important step toward the fuller acknowledgement of a new standard of living for workers and their families. On occasion, those who tried to describe *minimum comfort* admitted that it was not significantly higher than the subsistence plus level established in key studies carried out during the Progressive period. The new level nonetheless represented a clear gain over what Robert C. Chapin's authoritative work had established as a "normal standard."[35] Though contemporary studies were noticeably vague on differences in occupations, the distinction between subsistence and comfort to some extent paralleled the difference between unskilled and skilled laborers.[36] What people like Chapin had pegged as "subsistence plus" was now recategorized as a subsistence level. Below it was placed a poverty category; above, "health and decency" or "comfort." Thus instead of an earlier period's attempt to establish one budget level for workers, researchers suggested three: poverty, where the family received charity or incurred substantial debt; living or "minimum of subsistence" wage representing "mere animal existence" and allowing "little or nothing for the needs of men as social creatures"; and the "minimum of health and comfort" or "decency" level.[37]

In 1918, under the auspices of the National War Labor Board, William F. Ogburn directed an investigation that incorporated a relatively generous standard of living for workers. This study offered budgets for the two levels above poverty (see tables 11 and 12). Its "minimum budget" drew on the actual expenditures of several hundred shipyard workers in the New York City, while its "level above minimum subsistence" used the expenditures of

Table 11   Subsistence-Level Budget, NWLB, 1918

Item	Amount in Dollars	Percentage of Budget
Food	615	44.4
Clothing	234	16.9
Rent	180	13.0
Fuel and light	62	4.5
Insurance	40	2.9
Organizations	12	0.9
Religion	7	0.5
Streetcar fare	40	2.9
Papers, books, etc.	9	0.6
Amusements, drinks, tobacco	50	3.6
Sickness	60	4.3
Dentist, oculist, glasses, etc.	3	0.2
Furnishings	35	2.5
Laundry	4	0.3
Cleaning supplies	15	1.1
Miscellaneous	20	1.4
Total	1386	

Source: U.S., National War Labor Board, *Memorandum on the Minimum Wage and Increased Cost of Living in the United States* (Washington, D.C.: GPO, 1918), p. 10.

New York shipyard workers who received higher incomes. There were important differences between the subsistence level and the one above. Though expenses for shelter, clothing, and utilities stayed roughly even, at the higher level those for food decreased from 44.4 percent to 35.5 percent and for Miscellaneous increased from 21.3 percent to 30 percent. Moreover, the subsistence level's allocation to Amusements, Drinks, and Tobacco nearly doubled. In addition, at the higher level this category split in two: Comforts and Recreation. Moreover, Education appears for the higher income level, perhaps including what was under paper, books, etc. for those at the lower level. These changes signified a more positive attitude toward such expenditures when made by people with higher incomes. Equally notable is the kind of spending that a higher income permitted: no significant difference on health care; somewhat more on organizational life, carfare, and furnishings; and much more on savings, insurance, recreation, education, and miscellaneous.

If wartime conditions had prompted the federal government and some middle-class writers to make a relatively generous estimate of labor's standard of living, the postwar situation pointed in the opposite direction. Even during the war, middle-class sympathy for workers was obviously far from complete and accusations of profligacy never totally disappeared. As the

Table 12 Level above Minimum Subsistence Budget, NWLB, 1918

Item	Amount in Dollars	Percentage of Budget
Food	625.00	35.5
Clothing	313.50	17.8
Rent	220.00	12.5
Fuel and light	75.00	4.3
Insurance and savings	150.00	8.5
Organizations (church, labor, others)	24.00	1.4
Carfare	55.00	3.1
Education	20.00	1.1
Comforts (tobacco, candy, gifts, etc.)	43.00	2.4
Health	60.00	3.4
Recreation	50.00	2.8
Furnishings	50.00	2.8
Miscellaneous (cleaning, stamps, barber, etc.)	75.00	4.3
Total	1760.50	

Source: U.S., National War Labor Board, *Memorandum on the Minimum Wage and Increased Cost of Living in the United States* (Washington, D.C.: GPO, 1918), p. 14.

war neared its end and especially after the Armistice, many observers revived the charge that workers spent carelessly. An important BLS report issued in late 1919 lowered the official estimate of a standard of living above the subsistence level. The renewed advocacy of self-control came in response to the perception that, in comparison with other groups, laborers were gaining power and social status.

With purchasable styles of consumption rather than inherited class and ethnic identity threatening to define social position and with some workers apparently overstepping critical boundaries, representatives of the middle class reacted strongly. Once again frugality became a familiar shibboleth. Also at work was the impact of the reactionary mood of the Red Scare years. Especially as organized labor pressed its demands in the fall of 1919, influential groups opposed the gains they thought workers had made. Events of 1919—the Seattle General Strike in February; bomb explosions in April, May, and June; the formation of radical parties in September; strikes by the Boston police and by steel workers in the same month, and by coal workers in November—proved to many that Bolshevism was coming to America. In short, with the definition of needs and adequacy reflecting shifting strengths of competing groups in the society, middle-class citizens and business interests seized the initiative and tried to reverse some of labor's wartime advantages.[38]

In 1919 and 1920, only rarely did writers with middle-class audiences sympathetically welcome working-class adoption of what were coming to be defined as middle-class styles of living. One such reaction came from a settlement house worker who noted that the rich who have several houses and automobiles would have to lessen their "extravagant standards" to meet the rising aspirations of workers as expressed in a quest for better food and clothing, greater privacy, bathing facilities, education, and recreation.[39] However, most middle-class observers chastised workers for their supposed extravagance. As wartime conditions began to ease, Katherine F. Gerould, who urged middle-class people to accept a nonmaterialistic "new simplicity," felt that never before had skilled labor been "so pampered, so flattered, so kow-towed to" as during the war, when its work was strategic. Consequently, workers were "demanding money, not for the necessities of life, but for the luxuries—just like the capitalists they have so inveighed against." As examples, Gerould listed such luxuries as "motor-cars and the delicacies of the table, the jewels and the joy rides." [40]

Albert W. Atwood's critique of working-class extravagance made apparent the ideological and cultural assumptions behind the postwar reaction. Across America, he announced in 1920, wage earners "are to-day gratifying wants long felt and never before possible of realization." Though he found it difficult to distinguish between necessities and extravagance, in the end Atwood criticized members of the working class who seemed to use consumption to mark their rise above their station. He told of a factory girl who bought a three-hundred-dollar cloak, another who sold her fifty-dollar war bond and picked out "a pair of fancy dancing pumps and a couple of waists," and workingmen who purchased twelve silk shirts at ten dollars each. "A colored woman in a cotton dress and shawl," he reported, went to a store and asked to see a pair of shoes. When the salesman asked if she knew they cost twenty-five dollars, she replied "I didn't ask you the price" and proceeded to purchase two pairs. For Atwood, the issue of extravagance was not one of price but style. Like others who were newly rich, he argued, workers were imitating those above them and spending without any sense of taste and restraint. Artists and scientists "advertised" their "importance" in appropriate ways, he wrote, while manual workers, with "no real personal distinction" coming from their work and not knowing how to show "social distinction" by joining clubs, going to concerts, or giving to charity, had no choice but to put their money "into mere show, into clothes, diamonds, and the like." There was an ideological dimension to Atwood's call for working-class frugality. He agreed with Attorney General A. Mitchell Palmer's argument that, by helping in the war against hunger, economizing would quell the social unrest that threatened to engulf America.[41]

Against the background of labor militancy, middle-class fear, and corporate power, the BLS prepared the *Tentative Quantity and Cost Budget Necessary to Maintain a Family of Five in Washington, D.C., at a Level of Health and Decency*, one of its most important reports on working-class standards of living. The months preceding its publication in December 1919 were critical in shaping its tone and conclusion. At its convention, the American Federation of Labor had hailed the BLS efforts to collect data and establish budget standards. However, with the war over and organized labor pressing its demands through strikes, key sectors of public opinion turned against the bureau's efforts to support the aspirations of workers for a higher standard of living. In late 1919 Congress authorized appropriations of only 1.5 percent of the special funds the BLS had requested.[42] Many representatives of the business community doubtlessly took the position the National Industrial Conference Board articulated in 1921, that the minimum comfort level was an ideal to be attained and not "a minimum of prevailing conditions which can be considered acceptable and by which all others are to be measured."[43]

In late October 1919 the *New York Times* typfied the attack on the direction in which the BLS had been moving. On a page with editorials that labeled the threat of a coal strike "unreasonable" and welcomed a "campaign against anarchistic propaganda," the newspaper chastised the BLS and Royal Meeker for the conclusions drawn from the 1918–19 study. The BLS, the editorial noted, was tending "to raise an ideal standard, a standard incapable of being realized in any nation, and especially in the present acute industrial crisis." Not only were workers spending "sums on amusements—including movies, theaters, and vacations," but in demanding more, the editors stated, well-paid laborers threatened to impose more of a burden on the other half, people who were "already suffering deprivation."[44]

Compared with wartime studies, the December 1919 *Tentative Quantity and Cost Budget* thus reflected a less generous and more censorious estimate of the aspirations of workers. In determining expenditures, the study called for "a sufficiency of nourishing food for the maintenance of health, particularly the children's health."[45] On clothing, the report was even more severe, acknowledging at one point that it recommended a level "cut down to what amounts to almost a subsistence budget." "While admitting the desirability" of a "more generous wardrobe" that made possible a regard for "style" and "mental satisfaction," the BLS in fact allowed "only those quantities of clothing consistent with the *minimum* requirement for health and decency, and, where a doubt had existed," preferred "to err on the side of conservatism rather than to present an opportunity for the criticism of extravagance." In the Miscellaneous category, BLS officials likewise chose the low side. There was no provision for savings, and the life insurance, which would have provided the surviving wife and children only three hundred dollars per year, would hardly permit replacment of lost earnings. The report emphasized "wholesome amusement" that "arises naturally within the circle of a family and its friends and costs nothing" and did not include money for a vacation even though the survey on which the recommendations were based revealed that twenty dollars a year was a normal expenditure. Similarly, the report made no allowance for magazines, books, education, or membership in organizations other than churches and unions.[46]

Overall, the report tended to value economizing more than comforts. It took swipes at the severity of moralists, pointing out that "no housewife can reasonably be expected to perform more than one miracle of domestic economy each day." It nonetheless presented almost $250 of expenditure cuts that would enable the family to maintain a "minimum of health and comfort level" on less income. Reliance on the wife's skills and "extraordinary ingenuity . . . in economizing" would make possible the reduction in spending on food, clothing, and shelter. In dollar and percentage terms, the report's authors saw the largest potential for savings in the Miscellaneous category, which they envisioned reducing almost 20 percent. By living within walking distance of the husband's job and by being "exceptionally fortunate," the family could lower its expenditures for things other than food, clothing, and shelter. Through the exercise of "extreme thrift, of high intelligence, great industry in shopping, good fortune in purchasing at lowest prices," and by having the wife "do a maximum amount of home work," the family could cut its total expenditures almost 11 percent.[47]

The report's relative lack of generosity was not only rhetorical, as a comparison with other major budgets above subsistence demonstrates (see table 13). Though these studies relied on records of what people actually spent, they also represent their authors' sense of what workers deserved. The percentage allocated to miscellaneous is an especially sensitive barometer. The two 1917 studies, completed on the eve of American entry into the war, allotted 24 percent and 24.3 percent to this category. In the 1918 War Labor Board memorandum, coming at the apogee of labor's wartime power, that figure rose to almost 30 percent. In the postwar reaction, however, the miscellaneous figure fell to 24 percent and even lower, to 21.8 percent, for the economizing budget. Once again, household budget experts used their craft to sharpen social hierarchies rather than to soften them.

The expenses listed in the minimum comfort budgets provide evidence of the nature of the recommendations of experts and the expenditures of workers and their families. For the War Labor Board's 1918 study, at the level above minimum subsistence 63.6 percent of the miscellaneous funds

Table 13   Expenditures in Selected Budgets, 1907–1919

Survey	Percentage for Food	Percentage for Clothing	Percentage for Shelter	Percentage for Miscellaneous
Chapin, 1907 ($811.88)	44.3	14.0	25.7	16.0
Ogburn, 1917	35.4	19.3	20.9	24.3
Peixotto, 1917	36.6	19.5	19.9	24.0
WLB, 1918	35.5	17.8	16.8	29.9
BLS, 1919	34.2	22.7	18.9	24.2
BLS, 1919 (economizing)	35.5	22.9	19.7	21.8

Sources: Robert C. Chapin, *The Standard of Living among Workingmen's Families in New York City* (New York: Charities Publication Committee, 1909), p. 70; U.S., National War Labor Board, *Memorandum on the Minimum Wage and Increased Cost of Living in the United States* (Washington, D.C.: GPO, 1918), pp. 14, 17–18, and 48; U.S., Department of Labor, Bureau of Labor Statistics, *Tentative Quantity and Cost Budget Necessary to Maintain a Family of Five in Washington, D.C., at a Level of Health and Decency* (Washington, D.C.: GPO, 1919), pp. 10 and 39–44.

were for savings or insurance, health care, carfare, education, and furnishings. With another 8.2 percent for "comforts" (tobacco, candy, gifts) and 14.2 percent for such things as cleaning, stamps, and barber, only 9.5 percent of miscellaneous (or 2.8 percent of all expenditures) went for recreation. Even though it was less generous, the 1918–19 Bureau of Labor Statistics study, with its greater detail, makes even clearer the smallness of expenses for commercial recreation. In that case, 81 percent of the miscellaneous expenses paid for defensive purposes, maintenance, or work-related things: upkeep, insurance, laundry, cleaning, health, and carfare. An additional 5.6 percent went for newspapers, labor dues, and church contributions. Another 9.5 percent went for Incidentals, a category that included moving, burial, stationary, telephone, telegraph, gifts, charity, and tobacco. That left 3.7 percent of miscellaneous (and 0.88 percent of all) expenditures for "amusement and recreation."[48]

The aggregate and individual budget statistics and the wartime minimum comfort budgets point to the extent of the transformation of America into a modern consumer economy before the 1920s. To begin with, it took time for people to accustom themselves to new earnings, especially since they usually were still familiar with the problems of subsistence and survival. Some workers did come to see life in terms largely apart from work, but for many families traditional patterns of consumption persisted.[49] At least for the families of workers, the evidence does not point to a new world of ease and mass consumption. Shifting our perspective from elites who promoted or attacked new patterns of consumption to workers and their household budgets, a more traditional and constricted pattern of consumption emerges.

Clearly, however, for many if not most American workers and their families, the world of 1919 was different from that of 1875. Well before the last quarter of the nineteenth century, most Americans to a very considerable extent entered the marketplace for goods and lived in a world where experience with commodity consumption was a daily occurrence. Between 1875 and the end of World War I, a number of things changed (see Appendix A). With the arrival of indoor plumbing and new kinds of heat and light, the residences of working-class families became more comfortable, though not necessarily more commodious. Diet improved as an agricultural revolution brought food prices down and scientific nutrition gained in impact and sophistication. Well-situated families could decrease their consumption of grain products and eat more meat, vegetables, fruits, and dairy products. With a smaller percentage of income going to food, clothing, and shelter, people had more money to spend on other items and, in many cases, more time to spend it. Newspapers, telephones, movies, excursions, and vacations, as well as more traditional pursuits such as labor union activity and church attendance, introduced millions of people to a world outside the household and, less often, outside the community. The family remained central to most of these new patterns of consumption, yet people were spending less time and money on home-centered activities.

Though the investigations of household budgets of workers and their families for the period between 1875 and 1919 reveal major changes in patterns of consumption, they do not show a clear shift from defensive to accumulative patterns, from a producer to a modern consumer economy. The most fortunate of working-class families, often those where the employment of the father, mother, and several children brought in considerable total income, spent their marginal money in a number of ways. With savings, insurance, and health care, they sought to combat present and future adversity. The purchase of furniture and appliances may have represented their entry into a world of modern consumption, but it just as likely that these items also involved a desire to put savings into goods in relatively good times.

Nor do the data clearly point to a world in which mass culture and commercialized leisure dominated the lives and budgets of most families with low to moderate incomes. Movies were the most important item that indicate an involvement with mass culture. Given the patterns of movie attendance—its close relationship with other kinds of out-of-the-house pursuits, as well as the relatively small amount of time and money involved—its importance must hinge on its magical power or its meaning as a harbinger of commercialized mass culture (see Appendix B). Its significance as a leading edge of change is probably greater to historians than it was to most people who experienced it before 1920. We have usually understood the meanings that commercial recreation and leisure had for workers and their families through middle-class eyes—censorious moralists among their contemporaries and critics of mass culture in our own time. To some extent, working-class people gave movie-going their own meaning, something we can only begin to fathom.[50] On the eve of the 1920s, most workers did live in a world of commodity consumption and mass-produced goods. However, there were limits to the extent that mass culture and commercialized leisure shaped their lives. To focus on the new consumption patterns is not necessarily to see the world as contemporaries experienced it. The world of family, neighborhood, ethnic group, and community institutions did much to sustain old meanings for new experiences.

If there was much continuity in patterns of working-class consumption, the old moralist tradition, albeit modified, also continued to inform investigations. The emphasis on prudential values dominated the 1875 MBSL report. Over time, survey takers became less critical of how workers spent their money and more sympathetic to their situation. Yet value judgments remained. Though middle-class survey takers came to appreciate the texture of their subjects' lives, moral categories lingered, often without the edge of an earlier censoriousness. What persisted, to some degree, was suspicion of the communal and expressive aspects of working-class lives, especially when they showed themselves in commercial forms such as saloons, amusement parks, and movies. The middle-class authors hoped that immigrants and workers would turn to "higher" things as their incomes increased. Indeed the published version of the 1918–19 study, printed in 1924, used "Education and Uplift" as the umbrella for newspapers, magazines, books, and music, while movies, plays, concerts, excursions and vacations appeared under "Amusements, Vacations, etc."[51] Similarly, though the studies became less critical of profligacy, economizing remained the principal lesson that both working-class and middle-class studies conveyed. If the focus shifted from how little people could live on to a mimimum level of comfort and decency, antipathy to profligacy and advice on how to economize remained. Carroll D. Wright's 1875 study should have laid to rest the specter of working-class extravagance. Despite evidence to the contrary, that outlook did not die easily.

In addition in a number of areas it is difficult to separate perception and reality in household budget studies carried out between 1875 and 1919. There was considerable persistence in the forms, categories, and assumptions used. Though intact families living in industrial areas, with an employed father, two to five children, and a mother who did not work outside the home, remained the most frequent objects of study, the early-twentieth-century investigations did look at additional groups, especially young working women. The studies of the first two decades of the new century conveyed a lessened sense of the chasm between new and old immigrants, as well as that between unskilled and skilled laborers. The attempt to make ends meet obviously persisted but struggle and uncertainty did not pervade later reports the way they did Carroll D. Wright's 1875 work. Consumption of alcohol remained a tricky problem for which little systematic data were available on the household level. The later reports conveyed a sense of participation in a considerably larger world, mainly through newspapers, transportation, and organizational life. Compared with the 1875 study, the later ones gave a feeling of a greater degree of separation of the worlds of work and leisure. Finally, twentieth-century studies offered a fuller, though still incomplete recognition of the importance of income and outgo that did not involve the exchange of money.

In so many ways, the years surrounding World War I were important in the development of household budget studies and of American attitudes to new patterns of consumption. To a considerable extent, these years, especially after the Armistice, seemed to have reversed or at least halted the process by which middle-class observers were coming to put aside their traditional moralism and accept new standards of living for workers and their families. To an increasing extent, patterns of mass consumption competed with an ethnically based respectability as the benchmarks of social position. More and more, writers and survey takers were coming to elaborate the differences among social groups—between the working class and the middle class, as well as between unskilled and skilled workers. Yet if these were important years, they were also confusing ones. Patriotism and national priorities were uncertain bellwethers for choices among competing values. Inflation and other economic pressures made group relationships more conflictual. Poised between a producer and a consumer economy and reacting to partially understood changes in the nature of work and the family, Americans responded to a period of rapid and intense changes by reasserting a stricter moralism as much as they did by accepting new patterns of living.

Out of the confusion a different way of looking at consumption would emerge in the 1920s. For budget experts, social scientists, and intellectuals, World War I did more to undermine conservative moralism than it did to give it a new lease on life. Well before World War I, new ideas and new economic conditions had begun to weaken traditional moralism. It was more and more difficult for the old middle class to impose its aspirations on others. During the war, traditionalists used nationalism, moralism, and force to regain their influence. In the process, they inadvertently encouraged a new generation of cultural critics to reject old-fashioned values of self-control and genteel Culture.[52] The wartime revival of censoriousness impelled some American intellectuals to seek new, though often moralistic ways of interpreting emerging patterns of consumption. The confusing signals of the war period, when older strains of moralism seemed to regain strength, thus covered up a more major change, the undermining of an ideological approach to consumption that was more than a century old. What emerged in the 1920s was a new vision of the consumer society.

8 Consumers, Budget Experts, and Social Critics in Prosperity and Depression

Until the end of World War I, many Americans thought about personal consumption in predictable ways. Middle-class observers often attacked what they saw as the profligacy of workers and immigrants, a habit that they believed resulted from the abandonment of the prudential virtues of persistence in work and self-restraint in pursuit of pleasures. In the early twentieth century those who began to acknowledge the rising standards of living of the middle class frequently thought about new patterns in old ways, hoping that Culture and affluence went hand in hand.

As observers in the 1920s turned their attention to issues that new kinds of consumption raised, they often offered a different vision, but one not without moralistic elements. The United States had long before begun the transition to a modern consumer society. In the 1920s, an economy built on elaborate advertising campaigns, installment sales, and a plethora of mass-produced consumer goods had arrived for many but hardly all Americans. Movies, radios, automobiles, and home appliances provided millions of people with daily familiarity with widely available commercial goods and experiences.[1] Representatives of the business community greeted the new standard of living with mixed emotions, ranging from celebration and hope to anxiety. In her studies of a variety of social groups, Jessica B. Peixotto, the decade's most important household budget investigator, simultaneouly sanctioned and expressed concern about higher standards of living. Developing a new approach to the culture of consumption, social critics like Helen M. Lynd, Robert S. Lynd, and Stuart Chase worried not about workers and immigrants but about the entire society, especially those between poverty and wealth. In place of profligacy they saw a different set of dangers. What haunted many was the specter of a mass society composed of millions of passive, conforming consumers who struggled in vain against the pressures of a mature capitalism's advertising campaigns. Though the cultivated life was not without its attractions, the more compelling alternative to the dangers of a higher standard of living was the life passionately lived. Opposing alienating work and excessive consumption of mass-produced goods, intellectuals advocated natural and spontaneous experiences.

To a surprising extent, the changed economic circumstances of the 1930s confirmed rather than overturned the patterns of consumption and the responses budget study professionals and intellectuals had offered in the 1920s. During the Depression, a federal investigation revealed that many Americans modified patterns of expenditures so that they could continue to live as they had in more prosperous years. Similarly, the budget guidelines of the Works Progress Administration included expenditures for commercial leisure and recognized the importance to the nation's economy of the worker as consumer. In contrast, Carle C. Zimmerman, in his comprehensive examination of the methods of studying household budgets, celebrated a folk who shunned materialism. Quite different was the perspective of the National Survey of Potential Product Capacity, whose report hailed the possibility that all Americans could live comfortable, cultivated, and distinctive lives. Similarly, the Lynds and Chase hoped that the economic crisis would encourage Americans to seek satisfactions through noncommercialized pursuits. In the same years, Alfred M. Bingham argued that the moment had arrived when all Americans would enjoy a purified, middle-class way of life. Finally, some writers saw American entry into World War II as another opportunity to commit the nation to a less materialistic way of life.

If in the 1920s the business of America was business, how did the business community respond to the arrival of a consumer economy? Advertisers set out to sustain capitalism's power by convincing consumers to find emotional satisfaction in new products. Some who opposed the producer ethic embarked on a crusade to free the middle class from the shackles of puritanical self-restraint.[2] Thus Garet Garrett, a leading advertising publicist in the 1920s, argued that with the problems of production solved, "thrift universally and rigorously practiced" would result in economic disaster. As long as production and consumption stayed "in balance," he continued, "there is no limit to prosperity—to the satisfaction of human wants—this side of satiety."[3] Many representatives of the business community—bankers and advertisers especially—spoke largely in materialistic terms, as if an increased standard of living were justified by itself or by its ability to sustain corporate capitalism through the creation of demand.[4]

Even in the business community, however, the acceptance of new values was far from complete. Some corporate representatives welcomed the new age of consumption because it would reinforce rather than undermine producer values. When he announced the forty-hour week for some of his workers, Henry Ford, though arguing that high wages and leisure were

135

necessary to absorb increased production, nonetheless warned of the danger of putting leisure "before work instead of after work—where it belongs." In fact, though he helped usher in a new age, Ford himself advocated hard work, prudence, and restraint in consumption, especially of alcohol and tobacco.[5] Similarly, an industrial relations counselor in 1927, having suggested that workers might have become more important as consumers than as producers, reasoned that increased consumption would promote discipline in work and savings. Because people came to see luxuries as necessities, he remarked, "existing high standards of living will promote enterprise, energy and stability among all classes." In response to the rhetorical question of whether the United States was coming to a time when "chambers of commerce will be adorned with statues of the Prodigal Son," he stated that a higher standard of living increased individual and corporate savings.[6]

Even more reminiscent of an earlier outlook was the argument that, especially for workers and immigrants, leisure inevitably led to the weakening of civilization.[7] A 1926 National Association of Manufacturers survey of corporate executives revealed a wide range of stances toward the five-day workweek. Many of the opponents argued along economic grounds, taking the position that Ford made his decision because of declining production in the automobile industry. They also stressed that more widespread application of the policy would have adverse economic effects, especially on America's ability to compete with Europe. Others based their opposition on moral and ideological grounds. The president of Westinghouse argued that a reduction in hours would sow "the seed of unrest and dissatisfaction in the structure of our entire industrial machinery." A Philadelphia executive, who saw the United States threatened by the same forces that undermined Rome, asserted that "the men of our country are becoming a race of softies and mollycoddles." The fullest warning along these lines came from the president of Pettibone Mulliken Company, who envisioned workers, especially immigrants, wasting their increased free time "in unnecessary pleasures, if not in vicious habits." Among workers, leisure would create a tendency to "loaf," a desire to purchase "unnecessary" items by going into debt, and a yearning to buy "luxuries and to use the additional holiday for display and injurious amusement."[8]

If some businessmen persisted in seeing a connection between profligacy and ease for immigrants and workers, others continued to hope that a higher standard of living would result in elevated aspirations. In the 1920s Edward A. Filene, the founder of the Boston department store, provided the clearest statement of the position that abundance would turn people's attention to higher things. In the new world of mass production and consumption, he argued, businessmen "must produce customers as well as saleable goods." Filene hailed a future characterized by improved working conditions and trouble-free prosperity. "The modern man" would have true freedom, achieved not by denial but by the "working out of an industrial system that will enable him to get all the necessary comforts and luxuries of life without spending all of his waking hours getting them." "Standardization," he wrote, "does not at all imply that we shall all be as like one another as peas in a pod." "A new competition for beauty and refinement" would prevent standardization from producing ugliness. With basic needs now so easily satisfied, he concluded, "men's minds will inevitably turn to other and higher issues." Like his predecessors who equated more with higher, Filene was not terribly clear about what these "higher issues" were. He argued that affluence for all would undermine interest in socialism and communism. He believed that freedom from want would turn people away from "the sort of useless luxuries that mean only a competition in flashiness." Beyond these goals, he could go no further than to argue that freedom "from the bondage of bread and butter" would instill desires for "better education" that would "in turn give men a better sense of values." Consequently, though Filene argued for more than "mainly material" motives, like those who made similiar arguments before World War I he left it unclear what affluence would bring beyond comfort and luxury.[9] The words of these business representatives thus make it clear that in the 1920s more was going on than the replacement of a nineteenth-century producer ethic with a twentieth-century consumer one.

Similarly the writings of Bruce Barton, the influential author and advertising executive, made apparent the full complexity of competing approaches to the issues raised by new patterns of consumption. Barton was not simply an unabashed apostle of a new age of consumption. The author of *The Man Nobody Knows* (1925) both attacked and promoted the culture of consumption.[10] As with Filene so with Barton, more is involved than the tension between producer and consumer values. In Barton's case an additional tradition persisted, one with its origins in the work of Henry David Thoreau. "We can not all do what Thoreau did," Barton wrote in the early 1920s, "but, at the least, the war helped us to learn the lesson of his example." What Barton learned from Thoreau was "that great lives have almost invariably been simply lived." Doing without, becoming a slave neither to things nor to expanding expectations, living self-sufficiently, and experiencing pleasures that cost nothing—these were the lessons that one of the founders of modern advertising drew from *Walden*. Thus if Barton is at all typical, representatives of American business in the 1920s drew on a variety of contradictory traditions in their response to a consumption-based economy.[11]

In the 1920s the most vivid picture of how Americans reported spending their money appeared in the work of Jessica B. Peixotto (1864–1941). She carried out several highly respected household budget investigations of contrasting social groups, investigations that revealed the degree to which she accepted and yet questioned new patterns of consumption. Born in 1864 into a wealthy and talented family that settled in San Francisco in 1870, following ten years of education by tutors she entered college in her late twenties. From that point in 1891 until her death fifty years later, she spent most of her time at the University of California in Berkeley, where in 1900 she received the second Ph.D. Berkeley granted to a woman. In 1918 she was the first woman in the university to attain the rank of full professor. Dedicated throughout her life to social service, at various times she served on the California Board of Charities and Correction, the U.S. Children's Bureau, the Women's Committee of the Council of National Defense, and the Consumers' Advisory Board of the National Recovery Administration.[12]

What held the center of her scholarly life was social welfare research, especially cost-of-living studies. Her 1917 report on San Francisco workers was a path-breaking effort to establish a minimum comfort standard. For a husband, wife, and three school-age children, she calculated that an annual income of $1320 was necessary to give workers what they insisted was enough: a varied and "palatable" diet, clothing and shelter that "conforms to the traditional idea of the 'decencies,'" as well as funds for education, "relaxation in leisure hours," and provision for sickness and death. With less income, one of three things would happen: the wife or children would have to work, a less than adequate diet would undermine health and industrial efficiency, or the family would have to cut back on sundries and household operation. This last alternative, she warned, made "stupidity, early breakdown, and dependency" probable because "the expression of the more subtle capacities, the capacities for foresight, for generosity, for sociability, depends on having money for 'sundries.'"[13]

In 1921, Peixotto collected the data for her second major study, of typographers' families in San Francisco, though she did not publish the results until 1929. Working with the full cooperation of the Typographical Union, she interviewed eighty-two families. Virtually all of them were English or American in background, with a mean of 1.4 children living at home, and a mean family income of $2818.59, most of it earned by the men who worked at a skilled occupation. The income of the typographers placed them well into the top quartile of individual income earners in the United States and provided funds roughly equivalent, in 1984 dollars, to $16225 a year[14] (family spending in table 14).

Table 14   Expenditures of Families of Typographers, 1921

Item	Average Amount per Family in Dollars	Percentage of Total Expenditures
Food	879.14	31.8
Clothing	313.14	11.4
Shelter	421.56	15.3
Home operation	260.71	9.4
Miscellaneous		
Recreation	167.43	6.1
Vehicles	65.96	2.4
Education	57.96	2.1
Tobacco	41.31	1.5
Church	11.69	0.4
Charity	9.62	0.3
Medical Care	130.47	4.7
Union dues	146.61	5.3
Investments	164.37	6.0
Incidentals	91.45	3.3
Subtotal	886.87	32.1
Total	2761.42	

Source: Jessica B. Peixotto, "How Workers Spend a Living Wage: A Study of the Incomes and Expenditures of Eighty-Two Typographers' Families in San Francisco," in *University of California Publications in Economics* (Berkeley: University of California Press, 1929), 5:185.

Peixotto concluded that this budget represented a "minimum of health and comfort standard," a way of living that was "plain but comfortable." Attacking writers who believed that with higher wages workers would turn to useless luxury goods, she argued that spending patterns corresponded "to the traditions of a careful allocation among the several divisions of household needs." On food, these families spent the same amount as households with twice the income. The subjects of her study lived in comfortable homes, one third of them owned, and usually relied on hired help only for "occasional aid in doing rough housework." With the exception of a childless couple whose wife, aspiring to be a drama critic, spent almost 40 percent of the family's income on clothing, some of it for "display," Peixotto found that the people she studied had "sober ideas" about what they wore. Even their expenditures on miscellaneous items seemed reasonable. Sensible observers, she argued, had to acknowledge the fact of increased expenditures here, however much they might "regret this expansion in the scale of wants." Indeed, she concluded, for almost all the families sundry expenditures "represented 'needs' as well defined and insistent as the 'desires' which dictated the purchase of other wants." The fact that with rising incomes families chose home ownership, telephones, automobiles, and vacations seemed altogether reasonable to her, signaling the pursuit of comfort, "the general tendencies of our time."[15]

Peixotto judged reasonable some things that others would have called into question. As she compared their expenditures with the wartime minimum comfort budgets, she discovered that these families spent a somewhat lower percentage on food, a greatly lower one on clothing, a somewhat lower one on shelter, and a much greater percentage on miscellaneous items. Within this last category, they spent more on recreation, automobiles, education, health care, investments, and union dues. The pattern did not simply involve self-expressiveness and commercial consumption: as incomes rose, these households added both defensive and recreational items.

Nonetheless, their choices would have confirmed a nineteenth-century moralist's fears and help strengthen the judgment that the 1920s marked the arrival of a consumer economy for many Americans. Half of the families took a vacation away from home. The average family contributed less than 1 percent of its expenditures to church and even less to charity, though those figures did not vary significantly from earlier estimates. Only one in seven families belonged to an organization other than a union. Movies commanded the lion's share of recreation expenditures, with one hundred dollars as the "most recurrent estimate" and even the poorest families spending money on this "requisite diversion." Few families attended "the dance, the poolroom," or sports events. Even the fact that one in five families owned an automobile seemed reasonable to Peixotto. In fact, she called cars "instruments of satisfaction." She felt that automobiles, which advertising and "emulation" had transformed into a requisite expenditure, demonstrated how blurred the line was between luxuries and necessities. In making their purchases, automobile owners, evenly distributed over the range of income levels, had not neglected savings and life insurance. As incomes rose, people did not satisfy newer urgings only after taking care of "basics." Some families, she concluded, "can offer a rationale to prove an automobile more necessary than an 'adequate' diet or 'comfortable' housing," while others, like those in her sample, would make such a purchase "by a series of small economies without sacrificing either 'basic needs' or such 'secondary' needs as provision for the future."[16] To a considerable extent, Peixotto was reporting rather than judging what she witnessed. In her hands, the budget studies of workers came close to accepting whatever standard of living a group had chosen.

In 1922, a year after she collected the data on skilled workers, Peixotto turned her attention to a group closer to home, ninety-six Berkeley faculty families. Though her conclusions were mixed, here too she was moving toward a relativistic position. Published in 1927 as *Getting and Spending at the Professional Standard of Living*, this study was the most intensive examination of middle-class budgets done in the United States in the first four decades of the twentieth century. Peixotto's interest in her colleagues' financial situation originated in a debate over the fairness of a new salary scale, announced in 1922 in response to acrimonious protests that compensation had not kept up with rising prices. A group of faculty wives then conducted a survey and concluded that without outside income all but the most highly paid professors could not adequately provide for their families. In such a circumstance, they argued, a faculty wife "cannot expect any material expression in her home of her love of comfort and beauty, or any intellectual or artistic quality in her daily occupations; in fact can expect little but housework."[17]

Peixotto's study confirmed and extended the faculty wives' contentions that to meet their cost of living, the families, with an average of 1.5 children living at home, had to rely heavily on income other than the fathers' salaries. With a mean household income of $5343.50 and a mean salary of $3375.76, the families made up the difference between the two figures in a wide variety of ways but principally from the faculty member's additional professional work, income from investments, and the "helpmate's earnings."[18] The families had mean expenditures of $5511.77, roughly equivalent to $33950.00 in 1984 dollars (see table 15).

To make ends meet, these families held down their expenditures for food, clothing, and household operation so that they would have funds for shelter and miscellaneous. Compared with the sample of skilled workers who had half their income, the academic families spent an average of only fifteen dollars more a year on food. With clothing, on which they spent a greater dollar amount but a smaller percentage than the typographers, they chose a standard of "rigorous simplicity," with the wives pursuing economies that Peixotto judged "startling." Similarly, in household operation the relatively low expenses for help represented a "stern economy"—even the women who worked outside the house for an income "used house servants no more than the group as a whole."[19]

How then did these families spend their income? Academics, Peixotto noted, "will eat the plainest food and spend resignedly a total sum upon clothing that underpaid clerks would rebel against" but felt they must have a house of at least six rooms in a good neighborhood. Partly because they entertained so much, they felt that a "comfortable and presentable" house was a necessity, "a supreme source of 'psychic income.'" The other area where they spent more freely was on miscellaneous items, a term Peixotto

Table 15 Expenditures of Families of Berkeley Professors, 1922

Item	Amount in Dollars	Percentage of Budget
Food	893.73	16.2
Clothing	487.78	8.8
Shelter	871.11	15.8
House operation	746.49	13.5
Miscellaneous		
Investments	722.04	13.1
Automobile	385.82	7.0
Recreation	286.61	5.2
Health	314.17	5.7
Dependents	88.19	1.6
Gifts	126.77	2.3
Education	165.35	3.0
Professional expenses	164.66	3.0
Incidentals	88.19	1.6
Associations	77.16	1.4
Church	33.07	0.6
Charity	38.58	0.7
Tobacco	22.05	0.4
Subtotal	2512.66	45.6
Total	5511.77	

Source: Jessica B. Peixotto, *Getting and Spending at the Professional Standard of Living: A Study of the Costs of Living an Academic Life* (New York: Macmillan Co., 1927), p. 122–24.

characterized as "nondescript," usable only "as an act of mere conformity." Even in this catchall category, academic families made clear choices. They spent small amounts on tobacco, charity, church, associations, professional expenses, and education. Unlike the typographers, the academics spent little on commercial recreation. The word *movies* did not appear in the book and Peixotto noted the group's "bias in favor of types of relaxation that cost nothing, walks, evening reunions, club gatherings, etc." Five items claimed nearly three of every four miscellaneous dollars: insurance and investments (26.3 percent), automobiles (16.9 percent), recreation (10 percent), health (9.9 percent), and dependents (10.2 percent). Noting that this meant that 35 percent of the miscellaneous expenses provided for health and future, Peixotto poked fun at a budget division "euphemistically called 'higher life,' and supposed to represent the field of choice."[20]

Peixotto's judgment of her colleagues' expenditures was complicated, not the least by the fact that they *were* her colleagues. On the one hand, she praised them for their economy, foresight, rationality, and caution. They intelligently sought out and enjoyed "in moderation the 'new known goods.'" In their choices, the families emphasized "what in conservative circles" was called " 'higher life.' " In short, they fulfilled "the ideological spending objectives current in universities, 'plain living and high thinking.' " She noted that bankers, still influenced by Ellen H. Richards, recommended spending more on food and clothing and less on miscellaneous expenses than the faculty families actually did.[21]

Peixotto concluded that the evidence pointed to the emergence of a new professional way of life, "a scale of wants that by formula grows legitimately in volume and intensity," standardized and sanctioned by custom. With an income of less than seven thousand dollars a year, "much energy is deflected from constructive tasks," partly "to be used up by the abstinence attitude so at variance with the dominant thinking of our American life." Below five thousand dollars a year academics would not be able to satisfy needs that were "now socially conceded, desirable and professionally necessary to satisfy." What justified a pattern of spending was its conformity with the custom of a group. Thus, for example, she sanctioned automobiles, which 57 percent of the families owned, because "custom is rapidly ranging in the class of necessities though comfortable conservatives still regard it darkly as a luxury." In all, throughout much of the report, Peixotto characterized the families of university professors as ones that, showing "no desire to make an appearance of material prosperity," organized their expenditures so they could "acquire and give knowledge," as well as "pay for those things that express simply the satisfactions of hospitality, generosity and citizen life."[22]

The report also contained evidence and arguments that were contrary to this favorable evaluation. Elsewhere she pointed out that academics were pinching pennies on an income that exceeded what the great majority of Americans lived on. In this study, Peixotto did not acknowledge the apparent contradiction between her judgment of the families' commitment to knowledge and generosity and the small amount of money they actually spent on education, professional expenses, concerts, and charity. Nor did she see any problem in saying that people who owned automobiles and large houses showed no desire to display their prosperity. She often placed key phrases—such as rational, solid satisfactions, satisfied—in quotation marks, as if to call their authenticity into question. She remained equivocal on key issues, especially whether a high salary was just or whether a greater income provided genuine satisfactions.[23]

Moreover, in the preliminary chapter and occasionally in the body of the study, Peixotto presented an argument that contradicted her conclusions about the caution and reasonableness of the academic way of life and that demonstrated her commitment to a modern version of moralism. At times, she seemed to question the rationality of the decisions academic families made. Yet by arguing that their salaries should be higher, she suggested taking seriously the irrationality of their expenditures. Peixotto saw academic families (and most Americans) caught in the contradictory pulls of prudential virtues and escalating desires. On the one hand, professors gave "formal allegiance" to Ben Franklin's homilies, "loyalty to a creed that ties success in the search for truth with simple living, breeds patience with a scale of living that the successful in the business and professional world about them dub poverty." On the other hand, standards set by advertising and by other professional families impelled them to seek "a generous satisfaction of increasing wants."[24]

By and large, Peixotto believed that escalation had triumphed over thrift. Even academic circles, "possibly the last stand of the 'rational spender,'" had "succumbed to the spender's theory," with much of the "praise of Poor Richard" being "lip service." "The essential characteristic of the American standard of living," Peixotto said, "is not belief in abstinence, but rather this exuberant creed that the scale of wants . . . must and should increase in volume, in variety and in intensity; that expanding and varying wants spell increase of personal happiness and general well-being."[25] If the group best able to resist escalation of desires by keeping to its commitment to higher, nonmaterial things was in fact succumbing to consumer culture, she seemed to be saying, then how could others resist?

Later in the 1920s, when Peixotto directed a study of a different middle-class group, she turned up additional evidence of the power of "emulative display" but not, with the possible exception of the automobile, of the drive to achieve self-realization through experience with new kinds of mass commercial consumption. Her 1927 study of "the professional class" in the San Francisco Bay area concentrated on families with annual expenditures of $6500, an amount then earned by fewer than 10 percent of the individual income recipients in the United States. In 1984 dollars, their income equaled about $38,500. Peixotto took pains to note that the pattern, based on "customary spending," did not necessarily represent "a theory of ideal expenditure" (see table 16 for the expenditures of the average family).

Much like the Berkeley sample, these families placed a high priority on home and household expenses, as well as on savings. To be sure, they owned automobiles, which, the report noted, "present custom in California dictates." There was remarkably little evidence of expenditures for new kinds of mass, commercial consumption. "Social entertainment" was mostly for parties at home. Of the $219.40 for recreation, $76.40 went for "amusements" such as movies and concerts, $125.00 for a vacation "for a brief period" at "a summer hotel," and $18.00 for "phonograph records or radio accessories." Thus, these families balanced traditional expenses such as savings, health care, education, charity, concerts, organizations, and

Table 16 Expenditures of Families of Professionals, 1927

Item	Amount in Dollars	Percentage of Budget
Food	1043.28	16.0
Clothing	893.44	13.7
Housing	1343.30	20.7
House operation	991.98	15.3
Miscellaneous		
Savings, life insurance	620.00	9.6
Automobile	382.48	5.9
Medical care	275.00	4.2
Recreation	219.40	3.4
Education	136.80	2.1
Gifts	125.00	1.9
Social entertainment	123.00	1.9
Charity	60.00	0.9
Incidentals	60.00	0.9
Tobacco	54.00	0.8
Church	50.00	0.8
Barber, cosmetics	46.32	0.7
Carfare	40.00	0.6
Organization dues	36.00	0.6
Subtotal	2228.00	34.3
Total	6500.000	

Source: Jessica B. Peixotto et al., "Quality and Cost Estimate of the Standard of Living of the Professional Class," in *University of California Publications in Economics* (Berkeley: University of California Press, 1928), 5: 133–34.

tobacco with new ones such as automobiles, radios, vacations, and movies.[26] The expenditures of professionals, resting so heavily on non-commercial entertainment, home ownership, savings, and automobiles, demonstrated both the persistence of older patterns of spending and the extent to which a new age of consumption had arrived.

In her 1920s budget studies, Peixotto painted contrasting pictures—skilled workers who lived restrained, plain, and comfortable lives; academics torn between thrift and emulation but spending the vast bulk of their incomes on food, clothing, shelter, health, and welfare; and professionals choosing various kinds of emulation. The studies contained remarkably few references to each other or to the majority of American families that lived on incomes below that of all three groups.[27] In *Getting and Spending* Peixotto referred to Thorstein Veblen's ideas, especially the notion that canons of reputability constantly pushed the standard of living as high (or higher) as income allowed. Of course Peixotto hardly unleashed the power of Veblen's analysis to launch a biting attack on her colleagues. In fact, with the application of economizing and custom as the principal standards by which she made her judgments, the academic families came off well.[28]

Peixotto's studies mark important changes in the ideology of the household budget tradition. In the 1920s, one observer argued that for "self-respecting Anglo-Saxons" taste continued to provide a link between ethnicity and consumer choices. Yet to a considerable extent, Peixotto used consumption patterns, not ethnicity, to define social status. She embraced the notion of different social groups having distinctive expectations, habits, and standards of living. Peixotto's work was part of a larger shift that took place in the budget study tradition in the 1920s. During and after World War I, union leaders, government officials, and business representatives discovered the importance of the worker as a consumer, something Gunton had stressed decades earlier. Experts now emphasized the positive impact higher incomes would have on the nation's economic well-being. To the extent that Peixotto sanctioned whatever patterns of consumption groups of people adopted, she minimized the presence of moral judgments. Yet again and again her ambivalence toward display, excess, and irrationality came up against her tolerance. Unlike her predecessors who worried about immigrants and workers, however, Peixotto kept an anxious eye on the middle class. It was as if just below the surface of her language was an aristocratic disdain for bourgeois striving.[29]

At times, Peixotto believed that patterns of expenditure were acceptable as long as they conformed to group standards and were justified by custom. "Wise men, democrats and perhaps demogogues united in questioning the relation between income, a long scale of wants, and healthful and comfortable modes of existence," Peixotto wrote in 1928. She reported that a country editor "waxed eloquently indignant" about the judgment of families who spent as much on automobiles, tobacco, and recreation as the Berkeley professors did, but, she had to conclude, the editor had "everything in favor of his position, except matter of fact." For Peixotto, what was critical was "the test of custom" of "a specific occupational group." Idealists and moralists might question given standards of living but for Peixotto they were usually just that, a fact that represented what a particular group was accustomed to expect.[30] To the extent that her response is at all typical, budget analysts tended to see the middle class, not workers, as those who had turned their backs on simplicity and self-discipline.

In the foreword to a handbook on household budgets entitled *The Economizer*, Peixotto mentioned the distinction between "real" and "sham satisfactions."[31] However, in her investigations, she did not provide clear guidelines for separating the one from the other. Indeed, when she was not hinting that new patterns of consumption were of dubious value, Peixotto ended up with a relativistic position: a particular group deserved whatever custom made it insist on having. Given the speed of change in custom that she accepted, it was hard to see what, other than a provision for savings, might limit the rise in people's expectations. Strongly identifying with the aspirations of the subjects of her studies (and, ironically, showing distance mainly from those of the academics), Peixotto came close to embracing the assumption that whatever people chose was reasonable, even while she acknowledged the power of advertising and of the wealthy's example. "In standards of living as in spiritual growth," commented a study with which she was connected, "there is always upward striving."[32]

In the 1920s, between persistent poverty and wealth lay a growing number of families who lived comfortable lives.[33] In thinking about the new middle-class standard of living, Peixotto, like consumer economists of the 1920s such as Warren G. Waite, Hazel Kyrk, and Elizabeth E. Hoyt, acknowledged the force of emulation. Like them, Peixotto argued that outside forces were ushering in the new era that paid little more than lip service to prudence and instead encouraged people to chase constantly after pleasures that would remain just beyond their reach. Yet she welcomed her peers' choices, partly because they were colleagues fighting for higher salaries and partly because as an economist she believed in maximizing market-defined satisfactions. Although she hinted at grounds for having reservations, Peixotto seemed to accept new levels of expenditure and new definitions of custom. As she and others sanctioned the way emulation and advertising were reshaping expectations, they left themselves little choice but to accept what new customs and desires dictated.[34]

Nonetheless, doubts remained in Peixotto's mind. Despite the fact that the subjects of all of her studies had to make careful decisions to allow room for new kinds of pleasures, automobile ownership especially, Peixotto saw little on the horizon to prevent emulation from conquering self-restraint and leading to a series of escalating pleasures. The families of Berkeley professors contained a group of " 'spenders' " about whom little was known because they kept no records and refused to answer questions. "These are the consumers," she remarked, "who get what they want when they want it," who borrow as much as they can, and drive up their income "to meet needs that are largely dictated by the traditions of competitive display, the love of ease, of comfort, and of rapid change." Though people who consider themselves thrifty look at high spenders scornfully, she concluded in a way that suggested that self-indulgence was quite prevalent, "consciously or unconsciously, the imagination of most of us plays around that selection of goods and services dear to such as these."[35] Those who worried about the power of a consumer society could take little comfort from *Getting and*

147

Spending at the Professional Level. Though the ninety-six Berkeley families in some ways exemplified "plain living and high thinking," perhaps they were paying lip service to prudential values at the same time that their customs were changing to allow for purchase of automobiles. For society at large, the thrust of Peixotto's general analysis was clear: simplicity, higher things, and plain living were giving way to the pressures of reputability, emulation, advertising, and social ambition.

In the 1920s, the most influential book that explored implications of new patterns of consumption for American life was *Middletown: A Study in Modern American Culture* (1929) by Helen M. Lynd and Robert S. Lynd.[36] With their use of household budgets and concepts of income adequacy, the Lynds brought the budget study tradition into the mainstream of American social thought. Moreover, their book is a central text in the story of how intellectuals concerned with the standard of living shifted their focus from the profligacy of workers to a consumer culture suffusing an entire society. In their classic study of a small Midwestern city, the Lynds argued that in the 1890s Muncie, Indiana, was a nearly ideal place, a simple and inclusive town where Americans led spontaneous, natural, and unalienated lives. Work was the satisfying center of people's worlds, for it provided genuine fellowship and rested on the close connection between the exercise of skill and the manufacture of useful products. Based on folk traditions, leisure involved active participation in informal neighborhood and community groups. Taking the matter of getting a living in stride, in the 1890s Muncie residents had time to be active and informed citizens.[37]

By the 1920s, the Lynds found this idyllic scene upset by the "intrusion" into Muncie of what they saw as a series of outside influences: routinized manufacturing, advertising, movies, radios, the credit system, and automobiles. To them, these forces made alienation a dominant characteristic in the life of the town. They noticed a widening "gap between the things the people do to get a living and the actual needs of living." Installment buying served "as a repressive agent tending to standardize widening sectors of the habits of the business class." Noticeable also was the "decrease in the psychological satisfactions formerly derived from the sense of craftsmanship and in group solidarity" of the working class. Leisure was becoming passive, commercialized, and nonparticipatory.[38] The divisions among people had hardened. Although so many aspects of life were more organized, "contacts" among people seemed "more casual," leaving "the individual somewhat more isolated from the close friends of earlier days."[39]

"Why Do They Work So Hard?" asked a chapter title of *Middletown*. In the 1890s, the Lynds answered, the people appeared "to have lived on a series of plateaus as regards standard of living." In contrast, by the 1920s

148

"the edges of the plateaus have been shaved off, and every one lives on a slope from any point of which desirable things belonging to people all the way to the top are in view." Into the vacuum caused by the decline of satisfaction derived from work had come the values of a "pecuniary" culture that made people seek "some compensatory adjustments" elsewhere, especially through mass, commercial culture. People now worked hard at spending, not working. "Thus this crucial activity of spending one's best energies year in and year out," the Lynds reiterated, "doing things remote from the immediate concerns of living eventuates apparently in the ability to buy somewhat more than formerly." The end result was that people seemed "to be running for dear life in this business of making the money they earn keep pace with the even more rapid growth of their subjective wants."[40]

Outside agencies thus stimulated needs and then provided ways of fulfilling them. Industry, advertising, and the credit system stimulated a desire for a higher standard of living based on mass consumption and commercialized leisure. "It is perhaps impossible," they cautioned, "to overestimate the role of motion pictures, advertising, and other forms of publicity in this rise in subjective standards." Industries were "pooling their strength to ram home a higher standard of living," they argued, replacing matter-of-fact advertising of an earlier age with "a type of copy aiming to make the reader emotionally uneasy, to bludgeon him with the fact that decent people don't live the way he does." Given "these rapidly multiplying accessories to living," people concluded that they could solve their problems "if they can only inch themselves up a notch higher in the amount of money received for their work."[41]

The Lynds felt the inadequacy of a purely pecuniary solution to the problems Middletowners faced. Adopting the notion of cultural lag, the authors noted that differential rates of change in institutions and values had left people bewildered. Perhaps, they concluded, the propensity "for Middletown to link its emotional loyalities together, to vote the good-fellow ticket straight, may probably lie in its increasing sense of strain and perplexity in its rapidly changing world that can be made to hang together and make sense in no other way." Throughout their book, the Lynds suggested that education could solve the problems change had brought to Muncie. Mass culture, they believed, had created "new forms of social illiteracy," a situation that training for consumers would help reverse. At one point, they hinted that if the "pressure of maladjustment" became "acute," local institutions would provide the setting for "specific" solutions. In the meantime, boosterism—the "verbal ornamentation" that made "question marks straighten out into exclamation points"—prevented people from coming to grips with the situation. Although they offered no specific plan of action, in the last sentence of the book they returned to the question of what might compete with the shallow pieties of Main Street. "The foregoing pages," they concluded, "suggest the possible utility of a deeper-cutting procedure that would involve reexamination of the institutions themselves."[42]

The Lynds researched and wrote *Middletown* as if they were anthropologists. Some members of the staff of the Rockefeller-funded Institute of Social and Religious Research (ISRR), which supported their field work and writing from 1923 until 1926, had strenuously objected to the anthropological approach, especially the authors' pose as "naive observers."[43] Though they toned down their use of that persona, the Lynds persisted in speaking of their research as field investigation, acted as participant observers, and organized their book with categories common to anthropological studies. This stance enabled the Lynds to appear as objective observers.[44] Moreover, it enabled Robert Lynd, who was responsible for directing the research and doing most of the writing, to change his approach from a religious to a social science one and shift his career from the Protestant ministry to academic sociology.

Contemporaries applauded the Lynds' anthropological perspective. In a review entitled "Revenge for the Ancients," John Frederick Lewis, Jr., described the Lynds' "Anthropological Expedition" entering into "the wild jungle of Babbitt-land to record the real culture of the American small town." H. L. Mencken, in a review entitled "A City in Moronia," commented that the townspeople "were anatomized precisely as an anthropologist anatomizes a savage tribe."[45] Though most observers saw *Middletown* as anthropology, there was hardly the same degree of agreement on the book's tone. Earlier drafts of the manuscript had drawn varied judgments from the reviewers the ISSR solicited: the Lynds' detractors detected a mixture of fact and opinion and their supporters saw it as "true to life, remorsely realistic."[46] With the publication of the book came a similiar range of judgments of its tone, from Mencken's attempt to align *Middletown* with his own biting judgment of the Boobus Americanus to those who felt the Lynds had simply stated the facts and let others draw the conclusions. However, the Lynds' use of anthropology could hardly hide the fact that they were neither objective, detached, nor outsiders.[47] They both grew up not far from Muncie (Helen Lynd in a small town not unlike Middletown) before going East for education and careers. Robert Lynd's first significant position, as managing editor of *Publishers' Weekly*, put him in close touch with advertising. Marketing metaphors appeared in his religious and autobiographical writings of the early 1920s.[48] The tone of *Middletown* was more restrained and less ironic than that of the writings of many of their generation who had left the Middle West.

Despite their denial of any attempt to criticize, the Lynds had used anthropology to make some value judgments of the American quest for a higher standard of living.[49] The obvious comparison is with *The Theory of the Leisure Class* (1899), whose author, Thorstein Veblen, was the patron saint of the Lynds' work.[50] Though Veblen's classic study spoke more positively of mechanization, *Middletown* shared with its predecessor an affection for unalienated work. Like Veblen, the Lynds used anthropology to try to stand outside their own culture, suggesting that not all peoples valued pecuniary strivings and preferred a continual increase in the amount of material possessions that money could buy. The differences were as important as the similarities. The Lynds wrote with less bitterness than Veblen, using ironic detachment that was more subtle. Veblen worked within the nineteenth-century ideology, attacking the extravagance and profligacy of the rich and seeing it as the source of emulation that influenced all society. The Lynds emphasized the way that key institutions held out goods as compensation for satisfactions that filled the vacuum created by the demise of meaningful work. The Lynds were reshaping Veblen to take account of new circumstances.

Yet however much Veblen influenced them, in fact the Lynds presented an argument that diverged from nineteenth-century moralism and represented the dominant approach to a rising standard of living taken by many intellectuals in the 1920s and 1930s. In describing the transition from the village of unalienated folk of the 1890s to Muncie of the 1920s, the Lynds had implied that mass culture, with all its dangers, characterized twentieth-century America. They exaggerated the appealing qualities of the late-nineteenth-century town and painted an inaccurate picture of the contemporary scene. *Middletown* neglected the very considerable amount of face-to-face and unorganized activity that persisted in the town in the 1920s.[51]

The Lynds' handling of the question of class was problematic. Especially on the issue of automobile use and ownership, they overestimated the deleterious impact of mass culture on working-class lives and assumed that advertisers and manufacturers forced cars on unwilling consumers. Their mathematical miscalculations led them to exaggerate working-class expenditures for automobiles. When they commented on the way the working class was emotionally dependent on the automobile, the Lynds displayed the bias of their own social position. They failed to recognize that workers and their families, like other Americans, used automobiles for practical as well as symbolic reasons.[52] They argued that "the outstanding cleavage in Middletown" was between the "Working Class," whose members "address their activities in getting their living primarily to *things*," and the "Business

Class," composed of people who "address their activities predominantly to *people*." They recognized some of the difficulties of this bipolar division, which had the effect of placing school teachers, clerks, and bookkeepers in the business class.[53] The distinction eliminated from their analysis the category of white collar or middle class, concepts readers for the ISRR had urged them to include.[54] The nature of their class analysis, consistent with their larger ideological strategy, nonetheless meant that they did not join the chorus of those who were arguing that the middle class was the leading victim or culprit in the transformation of America into a mass society.

Middletown, researched in 1924 and 1925 and published in 1929, reflected the way that many American intellectuals were coming to view the arrival of a consumer society in the 1920s. In that decade Stuart Chase was one of the writers who most fully articulated the new attitude toward mass consumption. His recollection of his family's New England past continually suggested to him that there was something more important in life than "buying" a living. His 1914 honeymoon, spent as a participant observer among the unemployed, had taught him to abhor the worst of what he felt his class promoted, a materialistic way of life for itself and a moralistic attack on the profligacy of the working class. His government experience in World War I convinced him that the United States could have a planned economy that would eliminate nonessential industries and excessive spending on luxuries. In the 1920s he wrote about the irrationality of consumption patterns influenced by an economy based on the profit motive and advertising's power. He provided the ideological basis for the organized consumer movement of the next decade by calling for technical experts who would advise people how to be rational consumers. His attack on ill-advised spending combined a moralist's abhorrence of waste, a liberal's commitment to an equitable distribution of goods, and an elitist's sense of taste. In place of a society based on commercialized mass consumption, he preferred hard (but not routinized) work, leisure, tasteful (even luxurious) expenditures, and intense nonmaterialistic pleasures. In advocating passionate, noncommercial experiences, Chase thus broke the tension between increased production and restrained consumption. Yet even he had to admit that when he spoke of a utopia that included playful abandon, his New England heritage "dogs me like an iron shroud."[55]

In the 1920s, other writers joined the Lynds and Chase in expressing concern about the impact of a mass consumer society, especially on the middle class. Waldo Frank bemoaned the enshrinement of comfort as a value and art as a source of sensation rather than understanding. In his novels Sinclair Lewis portrayed America as a nation where standardization had destroyed individualism, taste, and any possibility of pleasures that were authentic, natural, and life giving. Matthew Josephson lamented the way mass society was undermining freedom and individualism. Drawing on Alexis de Tocqueville's *Democracy in America*, he argued that Americans were opting for "the appurtenances of wealth and comfort" as ends in themselves, rather than as means to a liberated life. The result was standardization and regimentation, a world in which advertising played upon the foibles of the "rudderless and helpless" masses. The only hope was that "artists of a heroic mold" might use the mass media "to communicate with and to lead the blind multitudes." Attacking Americans as self-denying Puritans and materialistic, conforming Philistines, writers like Frank, Lewis, and Josephson lamented the middle-class reluctance to pursue goals nobler than the accumulation of possessions.[56]

To a surprising degree, during the Depression consumers, budget experts, and intellectuals followed paths their predecessors had explored in the 1920s.[57] Studies of the poor and working class demonstrated that what most Americans lacked was not self-restraint but adequate incomes. Millions of Americans, by shifting expenditures so they would not have to forgo gains made during prosperous years, made clear their desires for a high standard of living. In the 1930s some budget study experts looked for groups of Americans that displayed what the Lynds admired about Muncie of the 1890s, the commitment to a communal, nonmaterialistic way of life. In a somewhat parallel way, some intellectuals hoped that the Depression would teach Americans the futility of materialism and the desirability of nobler pursuits. Others saw the Depression as an opportunity to bring about fundamental changes in the economy that would turn America into a nation of people with both middle-class comforts and aspirations for higher goals.

The BLS investigation entitled *Family Expenditures in Selected Cities, 1935–1936*, a study of how more than one-third of a million American households spent their money, disclosed the considerable extent to which families wanted to sustain their previous standard of living. The sharp decline in food prices in the early 1930s was among the factors that enabled people to continue to purchase a way of life that would have appeared more than comfortable to earlier generations.[58] Faith M. Williams, the investigation's director, noted that, in comparison with a roughly similar group studied at the end of World War I, the Depression families of employed workers with incomes between $1200 and $1500 had a better diet that included more milk, vegetables, and fruits and lived in quarters that were more likely to have electricity and indoor plumbing. Noting more expenditures for personal appearance and sharply increased automobile ownership, she commented that there had occurred since 1919 "an important change in attitudes toward consumption expenditures . . . among moderate-income urban families."[59]

This study reflected fundamental changes in household expenditures and in the budget study tradition. Indeed it is ironical that during the Depression it became clear to many professionals that new consumption patterns were here to stay. What is less surprising is that in this decade budget experts welcomed changes rather than moralized about them. Reflecting the recognition of the importance of the worker as a consumer, the acting commissioner of the BLS noted that the data "will be of great value to businessmen wishing to estimate the demand" for goods. The summary report of the investigation pointed to "fundamental changes which had taken place in the consumption patterns of the great majority of American families" since the end of World War I. The more widespread use of electricity, radios, automobiles, and synthetic fabrics had brought "within the reach of moderate-income families" goods previously unavailable. The new American standard of living "reflected adjustments to the quickened tempo of post-war American life."[60]

The federal study contained no moral judgments. In fact, the dominant response was to lament the fact that few Americans could afford a decent standard of living. The authors found it hard to distinguish between luxuries and necessities. They noted that spending on items such as rugs and silverware contributed "more to the amenities of living than to comfort in the physical sense of the term." Reflecting a shift from a moral to a sociological explanation, the report commented that people selected restaurant meals and "novelty items of clothing and of homefurnishings" "with an eye to their prestige value." Reading a newspaper, listening to a radio, and attending a movie had become ways of obtaining "information and the relaxation necessary in the tension of city living." Routine work and crowded cities made "desirable some form of relaxation and diversion to maintain bodily and mental health."[61]

If millions of Americans struggled to maintain a materialistic standard of living under adverse conditions, Harvard sociologist Carle C. Zimmerman rejected the equation of more with better and instead emphasized the importance of stability and security achieved by noncommercial activities. In the most comprehensive and analytic treatment of household budgets ever produced in the United States, Zimmerman contrasted two styles of living. On the one hand were patterns he characterized as antisocial, individualistic, and atomistic. Defined as "the American" standard of living and pursued by "the upper classes, the urban groups, and speculators," this path involved " 'egoistic' sensation," "immediate rather than deferred consumption," "direct sensory experience," and selfish "hedonic pleasure." In contrast stood the *gemeinschaft*, groups like the isolated Ozark Highlanders. Involving "non-economic goods and services," social stability, deferred gratification, altruism, and a commitment to community, this was a way of life of "the lower classes, the rural groups, and the conservatives."[62]

In the midst of the Depression, Zimmerman hoped that social forces would begin to bring about a shift from material to non-material pleasures, from an emphasis on change to preservation. He attacked the primacy of "linear progress in the material sense" and denied the equation of happiness with a constantly increasing standard of living. Excessive advancement expenditures, he argued, would lead to "social pathology." Reminiscent of the position of Ellen Richards was his strong preference for budgetary practices that kept people close to home. "The development of extra-family life," he wrote, "tends to have some enervating influences on society." If adults were unwilling to forgo self-centered pleasures, the result might be "race extinction."[63]

If Zimmerman celebrated an antimaterialistic folk, very different assumptions underlay the federal government's effort to define an adequate standard of living for families of employed manual workers. The Works Progress Administration (WPA) calculated that in 1935 a family of four needed $903.27 to live at "the emergency level." To the WPA, this budget involved "certain economies which may be made under depression conditions," especially a diet that could be harmful in the long run [64] (see table 17). Above this, but not as "liberal as that for a 'health and decency' level which the skilled worker may hope to attain" was the "maintenance" budget of $1260.62 per year (see table 18). With that income, the report stated, a family lived in a four- or five-room house or apartment with indoor plumbing, gas, and electricity but could not afford an automobile.[65]

Margaret L. Stecker, the author of the report, made it clear that these budgets were inadequate from a number of standpoints. They did not represent "a desirable standard of living," enable people to achieve "'the abundant life,'" allow "families to enjoy the full fruits of what we have come to call the American standard of living," or provide the "basis for a national volume of consumption sufficient to keep pace with the increasing output of industry." The definition of *adequacy* thus recognized the importance for the nation's economic health of more widespread purchasing power. The author had to admit that both budgets included money for items like "tobacco, 'treats' of various kinds, games, athletic equipment, and a variety of other leisure-time accesories, serving no particular purpose but contributing something to life's more frivolous moments."[66]

In a number of ways, the WPA study demonstrated how far the budget study tradition had come since 1875. Recognition of the importance of

155

Table 17 Budget at Emergency Level, WPA, 1935

Item	Amount in Dollars	Percentage of Budget
Food	339.63	37.6
Clothing, upkeep, personal care	128.26	14.2
Housing	168.01	18.6
Household operation	121.94	13.5
Miscellaneous		
Medical care	47.26	5.1
Transportation	44.94	5.0
School attendance	6.84	0.8
Motion picture theater admissions	7.85	0.9
Newspapers	0.00	0.0
Organizations	0.00	0.0
Tobacco and toys	4.80	0.5
Life insurance	20.80	2.3
Church contributions and other contributions	10.47	1.2
Taxes (not including sales)	2.47	0.3
Subtotal	145.43	16.1

Source: Margaret L. Stecker, "Intercity Differences in Cost of Living in March 1935, 59 Cities," Works Progress Administration, Division of Social Research, Research Monograph no. 12 (Washington, D.C.: GPO, 1937), pp. 6 and 68.

workers as consumers, the economic conditions of the Depression, and the professionalization of the investigators helped cause a virtual end to moralism within the budget study tradition. What workers should spend was not a question of character but of the nation's economic health. Stecker did not chastise those she studied for their spending habits, something that is not surprising given the economic conditions and political climate of the period. "Frivolous" connoted playfulness more than sinfulness. Both budgets included allotments for items missing from Carroll D. Wright's study of sixty years before: funds for transportation, medical care, insurance, toys, taxes, and school attendence. Particularly striking are the different dollar amounts the two levels allowed for recreation, especially the inclusion of funds in the emergency level for movies but none for organizational life or newspapers. Both budgets thus showed the impact of new patterns of consumption. For the "standard of health and decency," the Bureau of Labor Statistics in 1919 had recommended "moving pictures once in a while." Now, the WPA mentioned enough funds for each member of a family to see a movie once a week on a maintenance budget and about once a month on an emergency one.[67]

If the WPA study confirmed these shifts in the notion of adequacy for workers and their families, the discussion of middle-class expenditures also

Table 18 Budget at Maintenance Level, WPA, 1935

Item	Amount in Dollars	Percentage of Budget
Food	449.38	35.6
Clothing, upkeep, and personal care	184.05	14.6
Housing	222.28	17.6
Household operation	153.80	12.2
Miscellaneous		
Medical care	51.98	4.1
Transportation	53.74	4.3
School attendance	6.78	0.5
Motion picture theater admissions	33.65	2.7
Newspapers	10.80	0.9
Organizations	9.54	0.8
Tobacco and toys	20.84	1.7
Life insurance	45.95	3.6
Church contributions and other contributions	15.32	1.2
Taxes (not including sales)	2.51	0.2
Subtotal	251.11	20.0

Source: Margaret L. Stecker, "Intercity Differences in Costs of Living in March 1935, 59 Cities," Works Progress Administration, Division of Social Research, Research Monograph no. 12 (Washington, D.C.: GPO, 1937), pp. 6 and 68.

showed both change and continuity. The clearest vision of a budgetary ideal for middle-class living emerged during the Depression in the work of National Survey of Potential Product Capacity. Building on the ground laid by an earlier Brookings Institution study, sponsored by the Civil Works Administration, and published in 1935, the report argued that basic changes in the American economic system would make it possible to provide an annual income, at 1929 prices, of more than four thousand dollars for the average family. As Stuart Chase wrote in the foreword to one version of the deliberations, the work of the survey would give "the lie to the scarcity men, the hucksters, gamblers, and financial jugglers who once promised the end of poverty, and who now, their system in reverse, foretell an America of industrial serfs, peasants, and belt-tighteners, into a bleak and undated future."[68]

The project director Harold Loeb confidently asserted that "modern technology has abolished the necessity of witholding from consumption most items of the human budget." Using 1929 figures, he argued that the nation could produce enough to provide $4370 for a family of four, an amount Chase saw as "not affluent . . . but looks like paradise to most" American families [69] (see table 19). The report emphasized the comforts and refinement such a standard of living provided. Loeb believed that after a

Table 19 Budget of National Survey of Potential Product Capacity

Item	Amount in Dollars	Percentage of Budget
Food	990	22.65
Wearing apparel	540	12.38
Housing, etc.	958	21.91
Transportation	467	10.69
Personal	290	6.63
Health	165	3.77
Education	407	9.30
Recreation	393	8.99
Social	65	1.50
Civil	13	0.30
Savings	36	0.83
Taxes	46	1.05

Source: Harold Loeb et al., *The Chart of Plenty: A Study of America's Product Capacity Based on the Findings of the National Survey of Potential Product Capacity* (New York: Viking Press, 1935), p. 118.

long period of scarcity Americans were ready to express their natural acquisitiveness. There was no reason, he asserted, for "frustrating" the "reasonable desires" of the population. "No virtue resides in witholding desired goods" when it was possible to supply them. Once basic needs were taken care of, noted a popularized version of the report, people could "appreciate or enjoy literature, politics, music, or art." Similarly, Loeb constrasted the pecuniary standard of living of the present economic system with a more varied and elevating one. "Vendibility" and commercialization had "perverted" the "artistic appreciation" of the very few and "cheapened" "the play of the multitudes." Freed of the necessity to produce a profit, the economy would give all people "the same opportunity for aesthetic, emotional, and intellectual development which formerly only the more fortunate members of society enjoyed." With "material plenty and economic security" assured, people might devote themselves to "such so-called humble objectives as baking angel cake or growing exotic vegetables" or fulfill "the so-called higher faculties by painting pictures, writing poetry, or inventing a new style of hat."[70]

The budget studies reflected a variety of responses to the Depression, including the desires to maintain a standard of living established during more prosperous times, to emphasize nonmaterial satisfactions, and to spread the benefits of comfort and refinement. The writings of intellectuals paralleled these reactions. Stuart Chase, the Lynds, and Alfred M. Bingham responded to the national economic crisis by hoping that Americans would turn their backs on what they saw as debased kinds of commercialized consumption. For Chase the Depression raised the hope that Americans would reconsider their commitments to capitalism, acquisitiveness, profligate spending, and mass consumption. When he reviewed *Middletown* in early 1929, he had commented that the Lynds approached their subject "with the same detachment . . . that a good anthropologist devotes to the habits of the natives in the New Hebrides." Muncie tried to live, Chase observed, but "failing life, it drops to the level of existence."[71]

Chase soon went south of the border to find a culture where people really "lived" and in 1931 published *Mexico: A Study of Two Americas*. The second America in the subtitle was Middletown and at the end of his book Chase offered his advice to citizens of the United States. Consider regional self-sufficiency as a solution to the problem of unemployment, he wrote, return to the genuine pleasures of folk play, balance mass production with crafts and small-scale efforts. Echoing the Lynds, Chase concluded his book with a question for Americans. "Have you time to live as you gulp your coffee and rush to the station, or to the garage, and back again?"[72]

Calling himself a "thrifty Yankee," in the 1930s Chase hoped a cultivated elite would promote an abundance that involved a rejection of commercialized consumption and leisure.[73] To Chase and many other American intellectuals, the Depression provided an opportune moment when the failure of the economic system would purge the society of its materialistic excesses. New economic conditions would show Americans the wisdom of learning the value of craft work and passionate experiences from less-developed times and places. In ways essentially different from Zimmerman, Chase during the Depression thus emphasized the transcience of materialism and pointed instead to a world where spiritual pleasures dominated.

For Alfred M. Bingham, the economic crisis opened up the possibility of a utopia where all Americans could lead a middle-class life marked by comforts and by consumption that was rational, efficient, and noncommercialized. At the age of fifteen, in 1920, Bingham received an allowance roughly equivalent to the minimum comfort budget experts advised for a working-class family. Even so, his father inculcated in him the importance of puritanical values and moral righteousness. In his twenties, he was chagrined that Americans aspired not to Culture but to routine jobs, comforts, movies, dance halls, and pleasures of a "tabloid civilization." To taste "real" life, Bingham spent several summers working as a laborer. When he traveled around the United States in the late 1920s as a magazine salesman, he abhorred the fact that "every house interior in Oklahoma City was exactly like every house interior in Pittsburgh, a cheap imitation of the furnishings depicted in the garish advertisements in the magazines" he was selling. In the 1930s, in books and in the pages of *Common Sense*, the magazine he founded and edited, Bingham promoted the idea that all Americans should enjoy the "'good life,' for I have had the opportunity to live it virtually dumped in my lap. I know that health and happiness and creative living depend in no small degree on the level of material well-being which economic arrangements might make possible for each of us."[74]

Drawing on the writings of Edward Bellamy, Thorstein Veblen, and Howard Loeb, Bingham advocated replacing capitalism with an economic system based on planning, efficiency, and production for use, one that would take full advantage of America's potential productive capacity. The result would be affluence without advertising, a world "washed clean of the misery and falsity of commercialism," where there was "no mass of drably similar automatons." "With a new moral health that comes from the ending of greed," people would no longer pursue false pleasures. Americans would turn instead to an appreciation of the good things of life: creativity and Culture, not entertainment; collectivism in meaningful work and *"the fullest opportunity for individualism apart from it"*; and the universal striving for beauty. "With the wide margin for errors and experimentation that becomes possible under conditions of plenty," he concluded, "the widest conceivable range for expression of individual choice, or idiosyncrasy, or even idle whim, becomes possible."[75]

To people like Chase and Bingham who hoped that the Depression would make Americans retire from the pursuit of excess goods and lead a more balanced life, the Lynds' *Middletown in Transition: A Study in Cultural Conflicts*, researched in 1935 and published two years later, was not very encouraging. Like the government investigation of household expenditures, the study of Muncie in the 1930s found evidence that the Depression did not change habits and beliefs as much as the Lynds had expected. "It is conceivable," they wrote in a revealing passage, "that Middletown families are emerging from the pit of the depression into a scene in which the cultural demands upon the individual family for pretentious living have lessened." Then, perhaps realizing that they were speaking of their own expectations and not of Muncie's experiences, they concluded "there are no evidences of this."[76] The fact that Americans had not reoriented themselves convinced the Lynds that they were wrong to expect that the Depression would teach people to appreciate the benefits of the way of life Chase had witnessed in Mexico or Bingham advocated for the United States. "The depression," they had to conclude, "has operated not as a call to adventure in developing new fruitful ways of 'living.'"[77]

Partly because of what they discovered when they returned to Muncie, during the 1930s the Lynds' analysis of the origins of America's chase after a higher standard of living became more thoroughgoing and critical. They now explained the pursuit of a higher standard of living as something intrinsic in American life. The United States, they wrote at a critical juncture in the second book, was a "culture hypnotized by the gorged stream of new things to buy," a nation where businesses tempt people in "every waking moment with adroitly phrased invitations to apply the solvent remedy of more and newer possessions and socially distinguishing goods and comforts to all the ills that flesh is heir to—to loneliness, insecurity, deferred hope, frustration."[78]

In the 1930s, the consumer became the central figure in Robert Lynd's writings and political activity. He recognized that most people were caught between "the lingering Puritan tradition of abstinence" and "the increasing secularization of spending and the growing pleasure basis of living." By and large, he had to conclude, big business had triumphed over cherished values, creating "the new citizenship, which makes it a civic duty to spend to make the wheels of industry turn." People no longer tailored their expenditures to match their income; rather, they had learned that it was necessary to spend money in order to earn it. In the 1930s, Robert Lynd worked to redress the imbalance between what he saw as organized, powerful producers and isolated, weak, and irrational consumers. He lost whatever confidence he had earlier in the ability of common people to use reason to resist the force of salesmanship and advertising. He therefore worked on New Deal efforts to educate and organize consumers, hoping this would lead to a "fundamental reconstruction of the traditional vested interests and procedures of business." Disillusioned with the results of this strategy, by the end of the decade he envisioned the creation of a group of social science experts that would decide what producers would produce and consumers would consume. The aim, Lynd wrote in 1939, was not to bring forth a "dull, methodical culture," but "to create a cultural situation which, by minimizing occasions for wasteful mistakes, would free energy and resources for the vital creativities of living." Among other things, that would make possible an "opportunity for creative, spontaneous expression of emotion."[79]

The work of Robert S. Lynd, Helen M. Lynd, Stuart Chase, Alfred M. Bingham, and others points to a fundamental shift in how American social critics responded to changing patterns of consumption. Throughout the nineteenth and into the early twentieth centuries moralists had focused on the danger of working-class and immigrant profligacy. To them, excessive drinking and expressive ethnic customs made apparent the flawed character of people who could not restrain their impulses. Against these harmful tendencies of the dangerous classes stood hard work, restrained living, and the pursuit of "higher wants," principally Culture.

In contrast, in the 1920s and 1930s emerged a newer view, that might appropriately be labeled *modern moralism*, for which *Middletown* was in most respects a key text. Those who worried about the impact of mass culture were moralists because they hoped less materialistic patterns of consumption would serve moral goals. Moreover, they believed that both primitive and sophisticated ways of life were superior to those the middle class led. Modern moralists assumed the nobility of folk who lived in natural communities.[80] What undermined that possibility were the corrosive forces of capitalists' greed and mass society's sameness. Inspired by a need to create markets for its abundant production and playing on the weaknesses of ordinary Americans, the argument went, an expansive economic system devised new institutions like advertising and the installment plan to convince or force people to chase after an ever-elusive good life defined in materialistic terms. The result was a mass society in which consumer culture destroyed genuine working-class life and elevated to a position of prominence the homogeneous and vacuous lives of the middle class, suffused by commercialism. Writers in the 1920s and 1930s focused on the emergence of the middle class and mass consumption as the central elements in their concern about the effects of affluence on society. To a greater or lesser extent, this analysis assumed that by nature people had limited needs and that consumers were victims who accepted commercial goods and experiences on the terms on which the economic system and advertisements offered them. In the minds of modern moralists, people rarely derived genuine pleasure from modern kinds of consumption.

Intellectuals of the 1920s and 1930s argued that the purchase of mass-produced goods was much less worthwhile than the enjoyment of exciting and enriching experiences. They stood against puritanical self-restraint, alienating work, and commercial leisure. What intellectuals preferred varied somewhat but usually centered on lives passionately lived, in which restraint obtained for material goods and commercial experiences but not for expressive, communal, or sexual aspects of life. In some cases, their vision of higher goals, though still carrying with it a sense of superiority, was more playful and challenging than that of people, like the Bruères, who emphasized genteel respectability and refinement. Modern moralists contrasted the conforming, passive consumer with the plain people whose folk traditions modernization bypassed or with the solitary artist and intellectual who struggled to maintain a cultivated and dignified life in a materialistic world. During the 1920s and 1930s American intellectuals spelled out a variety of positions that followed this general line of argument, mixing romantic and technical, conservative, liberal, and radical, political and cultural analyses into different combinations.

What accounts for the shift from the older moralism of Francis Wayland, Carroll D. Wright, and Simon N. Patten to the modern moralism of people like the Lynds, Chase, and Bingham? To some extent, of course, writers were responding to new patterns of consumption. However, given America's long experience with mass commercial consumption, other forces had to be at work. To some extent it was not the rise of mass consumption but its spread to new groups that stood behind modern moralism. It is possible that changes in the nature of budget expertise were at work, though the similarity of outlook of professional investigators and social critics suggests one limitation to such an explanation.

To a very considerable extent, the shift from old to new moralism stemmed from long-term changes in middle-class culture and the position of intellectuals in American life. Especially in the years between 1910 and 1920, as gentility lost whatever hold it still had on a new generation of American writers, the older moralism weakened. Traditional middle-class culture had long provided native-born, small town people of substance and cultivation with the obligation to uplift those they considered their inferiors. As genteel culture tried to strengthen its hold, an effort that intensified during World War I, its shrillness undermined its integrity. The new moralists developed a new stance, one that disdained bourgeois values and called for the emergence of a vital liberating American culture. Writers spoke of a poetic vision, one that rejected bourgeois self-control and celebrated passion. They hoped to make Culture exciting and innovative, not genteel. They saw themselves as outsiders to the mainstream of American life, something reflected in their admiration for the disenfranchised. Against what they saw as the uniformity and tastelessness of American life, the younger generation hoped that immigrant culture might revitalize the nation. To their chagrin, they found themselves witnessing the birth of a new mass culture that had its own drive to control. The fact that immigrants and workers had helped shape the new commercial leisure provided an added irony for a younger generation that expected something different from the folk.[81]

For many American intellectuals, the experience of World War I shattered a genteel culture that was already beyond repair. Although during the conflict government policy opened the possibility that planning would eliminate waste and hasten the arrival of an efficient society that lacked invidious distinctions, the war also provided an example of the dangers of mass propaganda.[82] The postwar disillusionment and the Depression made some intellectuals question the desirability of material progress and the viability of the capitalist economic system. Wartime and postwar changes in patterns of consumption and class relationships spoke to the social condi-

163

tion of the new moralists, who often represented an elite that now saw social groups—upwardly mobile immigrants, the newly rich, and successful executives—who seemed to be grasping after new goods and experiences. The response of modern moralists is not, however, another example of a status revolution—a social elite displaced by parvenus. The social position of the critics enabled them to sense that something fundamental was happening. Nor was class the only dimension that defined their location, for it is precisely their sense of themselves as outside society that was so central to them.

The lives of Robert Lynd, Alfred Bingham, and Stuart Chase demonstrate how these and other factors worked to produce the new view of a consumer society. Growing up in comfortable to upper-class backgrounds, these three men understood the pleasures that material comforts could and could not bring. Brought up in homes that emphasized puritanical virtues and Culture, they inherited a sense of righteousness. However, commitments stemming from formative experiences with the poor and workers made it harder for them to direct their moralism to the traditional recipients of accusations about the lack of self-restraint. Instead, they turned their moralism in another direction. Their backgrounds gave them a sense of superiority that encouraged them to see middle-class consumers as lacking in taste and honor, people whose self-control capitalism and advertising had eroded. Modern moralists articulated one variant of the ethnocentric cultural perspective of twentieth-century upper-middle-class intellectuals when they observed that some of those below them were partaking in a debased mass culture. Lynd, Chase, and Bingham saw in preindustrial villages, Mexico, and utopian towns what they actually achieved or hoped to achieve in their own lives—the conditions for meaningful work and authentic pleasures without what they felt were the worst corruptions of commercialized consumption.[83]

In the late 1930s, as the Depression looked like it might last for more than a decade, people like the Lynds, Chase, and Bingham could hardly foresee that they were living at the beginning of a sustained period of economic and social change that would fulfill their worst expectations about American as a mass consumer society. Nor could they understand how the pent-up consumer demands of the 1930s would be among the factors that would feed the consumer culture of the postwar period.[84] Indeed, for some writers the approach of World War II signaled the arrival of yet another crisis that would turn Americans away from commercialized consumption. As the nation debated whether to enter World War II, some writers called for a renewed commitment to "love, poetry, disinterested thought, the free use of the imagination, the pursuit of non-utilitarian activities, the production of non-profitmaking goods, the enjoyment of non-consumable wealth" as "the sustaining values of a living culture." "Fruitful and refined leisure," vivid experiences, personal growth, meaningful manual labor, the restoration of public life would enable Americans to turn away from consumption and leisure that only stimulated or sedated. As with budget study professionals and intellectuals of the late nineteenth and early twentieth centuries, intellectuals of the 1920s and 1930s believed the wrong kind of affluence was corrupting. Earlier generations had hoped that poverty, World War I, and aspirations for the finer things in life would teach Americans a lesson in the value of self-restraint. Now World War II might also provide an opportunity to learn importance of seeking satisfactions "outside the market" and in "refined leisure," not in amusement parks or department stores.[85]

Epilogue

The differences between traditional and modern moralism are fundamental but there are also important similarities. Social critics of the period beginning in the 1920s replaced a nineteenth-century conservative moralism with a twentieth-century moralism. Both the nineteenth-century writers who feared the profligacy of the workers and their successors who worried about the dangers of mass society believed in the superiority of lives led in opposition to materialism and commerce. They shared a hostility to commercial recreation and hoped that with affluence people would pursue "higher" goals. Similarly, both groups of thinkers assumed that worldly goods were compensatory: in the earlier version, alcohol rushed in to fill the vacuum created by a loss of virtue; in the later one, mass culture became the refuge for people destroyed by alienating work. In effect both versions wrote jeremiads calling on the individual and society to change their ways or face the demise of civilization.[1] Both argued that chasing after false gods undermined the value of the community and the vitality of public life. Moreover, traditional and modern moralism both had a puritanical preference for self-control: the earlier group when it came to production and profligate consumption; the later one when it came to mass commercial consumption. What nineteenth-century observers had feared in the working class, their successors tended to see in the middle class—the pursuit of transitory happiness, the absence of self-control in consumption, the risk of corruption, and the failure to aspire to higher things. For both sets of observers, the danger was that people selected escape, not renewal; false pleasures, not true ones.

By associating modern moralism with its more traditional and conservative counterpart, I do not wish to minimize the very considerable differences between the two. Their political commitments were usually worlds apart. Though Thorstein Veblen transformed the nineteenth-century version into a radical critique of American society, conservative moralism remained in most basic ways just that, conservative. People like Francis Wayland and Carroll D. Wright had no basic reservations about the justice and efficacy of the economic system—their questions had to do with the values of workers and immigrants, not the value of capitalism. In contrast, at the heart of most versions of modern moralism is a critique, sometimes radical and always adversarial, of the economy. For people like Stuart Chase, Helen M. Lynd, Robert S. Lynd, or Alfred M. Bingham, exploitation, competition, and wastefulness turned innocent if gullible people into the victims of an inhumane economic system. Moreover, the two versions of moralism treated Culture differently. In the earlier one, books and concerts provided sentimental uplift; in the later, they offered the potential for liberation. In addition, there is a significant distinction between refinement and passion, the goals of the respective visions of a higher life. Bourgeois respectability is not the same as bohemian eccentricity.

The parallels, however, are striking enough to suggest continuities in the ways that Americans (and not just Americans) have understood consumption. In a different context, a scholar has reminded us of the American "tendency to account for any evil which threatened the garden empire by ascribing it to alien intrusion. Since the evil could not conceivably originate within the walls of the garden, it must by logical necessity come from without."[2] American writers have responded to machines, cities, and immigrants in this way. The process of pointing to intrusions of evil from the outside has been a dominant and, in exaggerated form, overly simple explanation that social critics have offered of the pursuit of a higher standard of living and mass culture.

There is obviously a considerable amount of truth to the argument that changes in the standard of living have harmed the nation and its people. Yet critics have constructed reality in specific and patterned ways. Many twentieth-century social theorists have defined consumption as a key problem. Commercialized pleasures, the loss of self-control, and the chase after the satisfactions of an ever-elusive higher standard of living may have posed threats to capitalism and have had baneful effects on consumers, but as values they troubled social critics as well. Affluence helped cause some of the problems ordinary Americans faced, but it also made problematic the position of intellectuals. With millions of Americans making apparent their commitments to values other than Culture and social concern, critics and budget professionals have used consumption as a way of defining their relationship to central but shifting aspects of American life—to immigrant and working-class culture in the nineteenth and early twentieth centuries and to bourgeois life later in the twentieth.

Above all, writers used a common language to talk about consumption. Corruption, decadence, self-control, higher aspirations have remained the central terms of discourse. There are very real differences in the nature and thrust of these conversations over time. Nonetheless, it is still possible to recognize that there are common and persistent ways Americans have thought about the consequences of consumption.[3] Just as stories about what they purchase provide common experiences for millions of consumers, so too discussion about what other people buy forms one of the essential elements of how writers talk to one another. Denouncing other people for their profligacy and lack of Culture is a way of reaffirming one's own commitments. Consumer culture hardly exists only in the minds of scholars, critics, and budget investigators, but it is striking how writers formulate that as a problem.

In saying this, I do not wish to call into question all aspects of the explanatory power of modern moralism. Rather, I am suggesting that moralist reactions have a history. Moreover, better than most observers, modern moralists have understood some of the factors that impelled Americans to celebrate consumption in words and deeds. They comprehend the force and consequences of consumption. At its best this mode of analysis is powerful and convincing. Although it does not necessarily explain the meaning ordinary people have given to new goods and experiences, it presents a reasonably convincing analysis of the economic system's attempt to control from above.

If modern moralism is a less than perfect explanation, what alternatives are there? One possibility is a more reciprocal model, one that emphasizes the power of the economic system and elites to set the framework of consumer culture but does not forget the ability of people, within limits, to shape the meaning of their consumption patterns. A fuller explanation of the emergence and impact of consumer society must take into account several important pieces of data that seem to contradict, but may be reconcilable with, modern moralism. Alexis de Tocqueville, Henry David Thoreau, the new social historians of consumption, and others recognized that Americans sought happiness through commercial goods and experiences before the arrival of advertising or corporate capitalism. Writers as diverse as Richard Hoggart, Herbert J. Gans, James Agee, Lee Rainwater, and Kai T. Erickson have explored the ways that people actually use what capitalism and advertising proffers.[4] In household budget studies, several ways of perceiving commercial consumption have persisted over time. In some cases, demand for new goods has outstripped supply.[5] The culture of a wide range of groups has endured despite the effort of capitalism to shape people's lives through mass consumption. Anthropologists have argued that we can understand consumption as a form of symbolic exchange.[6] Evidence from the Soviet Union suggests that people living in a noncapitalist economy still chase after an ever-elusive higher standard of living.[7] No one has yet pulled these scattered pieces of evidence and different modes of interpretation into a coherent counterargument, but recognition of their significance would help enrich the modern moralist position and suggest the possibility of alternative visions.

If both budget professionals and social critics offered a moralist reaction to consumer culture, what do the data themselves tell us? Of course, there are many things such data cannot measure, especially the relationship between aspiration and achievement of an indulgent or self-expressive standard of living. This study suggests two additional criteria to measure the arrival and impact of consumer culture: the information in household budgets and the writings of budget experts. The budgets themselves present a mixed picture. On the one hand, between 1875 and the late 1930s there was a considerable increase in the amount and percentage of money available for items other than food, clothing, and shelter. Many of the households in the WPA investigation of 1935 had a standard of living unavailable to all but a few in Carroll D. Wright's report sixty years earlier. In addition, generations of budget studies made clear the direction of change toward the day when more and more Americans would experience mass commercial culture in all aspects of their lives, on a daily basis, and to a significant degree. On the other hand, for millions of families living before 1940— perhaps a majority of Americans—discretionary expenditures for nondefensive purposes remained relatively small. Too many people lived too close to poverty to make comfort, affluence, or easy sufficiency sure and predominant expectations.

The writings of budget professionals present a similarly mixed picture. By the 1930s, experts had come to sanction expenditures that were unthinkable or even unacceptable to Carroll D. Wright. Censoriousness had all but died and what had taken its place was the recognition of the importance of consumer spending to the health of the economy. Yet many of those who studied household budgets still hoped that Americans would turn their eyes to higher things and avoid the hollow pleasures of consumer culture.

The story of the fascination of social critics with consumer culture does not end with 1940, although this book does. After World War II, writers continued to elaborate on twentieth-century moralism. For many intellectuals and social scientists of the 1950s and 1960s, the American standard of living became a central issue. They offered quite varied analyses, most of which saw new patterns of middle-class consumption as a key social problem. John Kenneth Galbraith's *The Affluent Society* (1958) described "the entire modern range of sensuous, edifying, and lethal desires" and argued for a greater commitment to public good.[8] In *The Lonely Crowd* (1950), David Riesman discussed the emergence of the upper-middle-class "other-directed" personality, a phenomenon that represented the demise of frugality and hard work and the rise of luxurious consumption.[9] In *Eros and Civilization* (1955), Herbert Marcuse brought the Lynds' theory up to date when he called for reducing the commitment to alienating work and attacked the materialism of a mass society. Accept a lessened standard of living, Marcuse and other cultural radicals argued, in exchange for an intensification of erotic life.[10]

The economic difficulties of the years since 1973 strengthened the hold of modern moralism and encouraged a return to ideas reminiscent of the dominant nineteenth-century approach to consumption. Politicians and economists tried to devise policies to restore the work ethic, encourage savings, and lessen what they saw as unproductive consumption. Some observers seemed to welcome the economic crises of the 1970s, much as previous generations had looked to war to cleanse the society of materialism and selfishness.[11] Social scientists worried about the dangers of profligate spending, both of the middle class and of those below. In *The Culture of Narcissism* (1978), Christopher Lasch argued that mass consumption helped foster a new and dangerous self-indulgence. Daniel Bell in *The Cultural Contradictions of Capitalism* (1976) described a society coming apart because of the decline of the work ethic and the rise of self-indulgence. He sounded like writers one hundred years ago in his attack on a sense of entitlement, in his hope that religion would promote self-restraint, and in his call for a renewed sense of the public good.[12]

It is possible to discern in recent years the emergence of an ideology that either reshapes modern moralism in basic ways or moves beyond it. In *New Rules* (1981), Daniel Yankelovich describes an emerging American ethic that turns against self-denial and toward self-fulfillment. He argues that some Americans who recognized that additional material goods did not make them happy sought deeper satisfactions in meaningful work, human relationships, leisure, community, and autonomy.[13] In the work of Marshall Sahlins, Mary Douglas, and Baron Isherwood there has emerged an anthropology of consumption that refuses to see commodities as things foisted on ordinary people. Similarly, the work of Albert O. Hirschman offers an analysis of consumption free of the hold of the old and new moralism. Concentrating on the shift from the passions to the interests, he has explored the personal and political economy of consumption.[14] The sociologist Herbert J. Gans has studied the ways that people actually use items of mass culture and consumption as distinct from the ways capitalists and moralists think they use them. From a variety of perspectives this new approach criticizes neither the middle class nor the working class for what others have seen as profligacy and self-indulgence. It tends to minimize the power of elites and the economic system to shape the lives of ordinary people. It accepts modern mass consumption as something with which individuals and groups construct meaning in their lives. Without blaming capitalism for the drive to a higher standard of living, it calls for a renewed commitment to public life and nonmaterial satisfactions. It is still too early to tell where these formulations will lead. However, they promise a rethinking of the moral tradition that has shaped the way American social critics have understood consumption and the American standard of living.

Appendix A
Expenditures Reported in Selected Budget Studies, 1875–1981

The more than sixty years beginning with the MBSL's collection of data in 1874 comprise an important period in the history of household budget studies in the United States and of the development of patterns of working-class and middle-class consumption. Public and private agencies undertook several hundred surveys, some of them monumental in scale, most of them relatively rigorous in their standards, and all of them providing a significant body of material that reveals how millions of families spent their money. Although the beliefs of the investigators shaped the studies, the material they presented is the best we have. Used cautiously, it can help us begin to answer questions about the history of the American standard of living. An analysis of household data collected between 1874 and 1935 makes it possible to look at the major changes in patterns of expenditure.

For American families, but especially for those within the working class, the most important change reflected in these investigations is the way a declining proportion of expenditures for food made possible an increasing percentage and amount of spending on things other than food, clothing, and shelter. For the sake of comparison, I have included figures on the BLS budgets at the "lower," "intermediate," and "higher" levels for a family of four in the autumn of 1981. Presentation of the division of expenditures in a series of landmark studies reveals something of the direction of changes in patterns of consumption (see table A–1).

Table A-1 Changes in Family Expenditures, 1875–1981

Survey and Range	Price Index[1]	Percentage for Food	Percentage for Shelter	Percentage for Clothing	Percentage for Miscellaneous
1875 MBSL	137				
$300–450		64.0	26.0	7.0	3.0
$450–600		63.0	21.5	10.5	5.0
$600–750		60.0	20.0	14.0	6.0
$750–1200		56.0	23.0	15.0	6.0
$1200 +		51.0	20.0	19.0	10.0[2]
1907 Chapin	113				
$400–499		40.8	32.4	13.0	13.8
$800–899		44.3	25.7	14.0	16.0
$900–999		44.7	24.1	14.6	16.6
$1100–1199		45.6	20.0	14.9	19.5
$1500–1599		36.8	20.4	16.8	26.0[3]
1912 Bruère	114–17				
under $1000		27.65	9.51	9.05	46.19
$1000–2000		24.99	18.99	10.99	44.97
$2000–3000		19.99	15.99	9.99	53.97
$3000–4000		14.84	12.16	14.19	58.79
$4000–5000		12.65	11.55	9.28	66.49[4]
1918 WLB	180				
$1386		44.37	17.46	16.88	21.28
$1760.50		35.50	16.76	17.81	29.93[5]
1918–19 BLS	180				
under $900		44.1	21.3	13.2	21.4
$900–1199		42.4	19.9	14.5	23.1
$1200–1499		39.6	19.4	15.9	25.0
$1500–1799		37.2	18.7	16.7	27.3
$1800–2099		35.7	18.2	17.5	28.5
$2100–2499		34.6	16.6	18.7	30.0
$2500 + above		34.9	14.7	20.4	30.1[6]
1919 BLS	207				
$2015.56		35.52	19.75	22.94	21.80
$2262.47		34.21	18.92	22.71	24.17[7]
1921 Typographers	214				
$2761.42		31.8	15.3	11.4	41.5[8]
1922 Berkeley faculty	200				
$5511.77		16.2	15.8	8.8	59.1[9]
1927 Professionals	208				
$6500		16.0	20.7	13.7	49.6[10]
1935 WPA	164				
$903.27		37.6	27.6	12.9	21.9
$1260.62		35.6	25.5	13.6	25.3[11]
1934–46 BLS	160–66				
$500–600		38.4	30.0	7.5	24.1
$600–900		37.0	28.8	8.7	25.5
$900–1200		35.8	27.8	9.1	27.3
$1200–1500		34.4	25.6	9.9	30.1
$1500–1800		33.3	24.3	10.3	32.1
$1800–2100		31.9	22.7	11.0	34.4

$2100–2400		31.7	21.3	11.9	35.1
$2400–2700		31.4	19.7	12.8	36.1
$2700–3000		31.0	18.5	14.4	36.1
$3000 + above		31.4	17.2	14.5	36.9[12]
1935 NSPPC	205				
$4370		22.65	21.91	12.38	43.06[13]
1981 BLS	1117				
$15323		29.7	18.4	6.1	45.8
$25407		23.0	21.9	5.2	49.9
$38060		19.4	22.1	5.1	53.4[14]

1. The consumer prices are for the year the data were collected. The price index is from Peter A. David and Peter Solar, "A Bicentenary Contribution to the History of the Cost of Living in America," in Research in Economic History: An Annual Compilation of Research, ed. Paul Uselding (Greenwich, Conn.: JAI, 1977), 2:16–17. For a discussion of the problems of comparing household budget data from studies carried out over a long period of time, see U.S., Department of Labor, Bureau of Labor Statistics, How American Buying Habits Change (Washington, D.C.: GPO [1959]), pp. 217–42.

2. Massachusetts, Bureau of Statistics of Labor, Sixth Annual Report (Boston: Wright and Potter, 1875), p. 441. Unless otherwise noted, in this and the following studies, Shelter includes fuel and light and Miscellaneous includes transportation, furnishings, and items of household operation other than fuel and light.

3. Robert C. Chapin, The Standard of Living Among Workingmen's Families in New York City (New York: Charities Publication Committee, 1909), p. 70.

4. Martha B. Bruère and Robert W. Bruère, Increasing Home Efficiency (New York: Macmillan Co., 1912), p. 315. In this case, in Miscellaneous I had to include fuel and light. This makes Miscellaneous somewhat higher and rent correspondingly lower. For the Bruères' study, the following are the average incomes at different levels: $959.93 at $1000 and under; $1510.09 at $1000–2000; $2552.62 at $2000–3000; $3623.88 at $3000–4000; and $4524.56 at $4000–5000. Below $1000 there was a deficit of 7.6 percent. There were very small deficits (0.03 percent and 0.01 percent respectively) at the $1000–2000 and $2000–3000 levels.

5. U.S., National War Labor Board, Memorandum on the Minimum Wage and Increased Cost of Living (Washington, D.C.: GPO, 1918), pp. 10 and 14.

6. U.S., Department of Labor, Bureau of Labor Statistics, Cost of Living in the United States, Bulletin of the Bureau of Labor Statistics, no. 357 (Washington, D.C.: GPO, 1924), p. 5.

7. "Tentative Quantity-Cost Budget Necessary to Maintain Family of Five in Washington, D.C.," Monthly Labor Review 9 (December 1919): 28.

8. Jessica B. Peixotto, "How Workers Spend a Living Wage: A Study of the Incomes and Expenditures of Eighty-two Typographers' Families in San Francisco," in University of California Publications in Economics (Berkeley: University of California Press, 1929), 5:185. In this case, Miscellaneous includes light, heat, and fuel.

9. Jessica B. Peixotto, Getting and Spending at the Professional Standard of Living: A Study of the Costs of Living an Academic Life (New York: Macmillan Co., 1927), p. 124. Here Miscellaneous includes light, heat, fuel, and ice.

10. Jessica B. Peixotto et al., "Quantity and Cost Estimate of the Standard of Living of the Professional Class," in University of California Publications in Economics (Berkeley: University of California Press, 1928), 5:133–34. Miscellaneous includes fuel, electricity, and ice.

11. Margaret L. Stecker, "Intercity Differences in Costs of Living in March 1935, 59 Cities,"

Appendix A

Works Progress Administration, Division of Social Research, *Research Monograph* no. 12 (Washington, D.C.: GPO, 1937), p. 6. Miscellaneous includes the cost of clothing upkeep.

12. Faith M. Williams and Alice C. Hanson, "Expenditure Habits of Wage Earners and Clerical Workers," *Monthly Labor Review* 49 (December 1939): 1314.

13. Harold Loeb et al., *The Chart of Plenty: A Study of America's Product Capacity Based on the Findings of the National Survey of Potential Product Capacity* (New York: Viking Press, 1935), p. 118. Miscellaneous includes transportation. The NSPPC based its calculations on 1929 figures.

14. U.S., Department of Labor, Bureau of Labor Statistics, "Autumn 1981 Urban Family Budgets and Comparative Indexes for Selected Urban Areas," news release, 16 April 1982, p. 2. (Mimeographed.)

Appendix B
A Note on Miscellaneous Expenditures, 1918–1919

The expenditures in the 1918–19 Bureau of Labor Statistics study illuminate the nature of spending patterns (see table B-1). The report listed forty-seven miscellaneous items for which families in the $1200.00 to $1499.99 income range spent an average of $262.40. What follows are two tables. The first ranks items by the frequency with which families reported them; the second, by the dollar amount spent.

These two different ways of looking at the statistics reveal that most working-class families spent most of their miscellaneous money on organizational life, maintenance of home and clothes, transportation to work, protection of health and life, and the traditional "indulgences" of liquor and tobacco. The average family in this income range spent a relatively small percentage of the miscellaneous portion of the budget in ways that involved new kinds of mass commercial consumption such as movies, excursions, vacations, and vehicles. Only by concentrating on items on which most of the families at this income level paid little or a few families used a lot is it possible to see a pattern different from a largely defensive one. At this income level, the 75.8 percent who spent an average of $7.76 on movies, the 24.7 percent who allocated $15.07 to telephones, the 13 percent who used $66.20 for automobiles, motorcycles, or bicycles, the 23.5 percent who paid $22.34 for vacations, the 9 percent who spent $17.11 on travel, and the 13.9 percent who allotted $18.78 to household help point to an emerging pattern of personal comforts and commercial pleasures already more widely available to the middle class.

If the working poor, those with family incomes between $1200.00 and $1499.99, had clear limitations to their experiences with comforts, commercial recreation, and mass culture, what were patterns of consumption like at higher income levels? Examination of the 1918–19 manuscript schedules for Fall River, Massachusetts, an old New England industrial city where George Gunton worked as a union organizer and where Carroll D. Wright's office collected statistics in 1874, allows a closer look at how the families of

Table B-1 Miscellaneous Expenditures, 1918–1919

Item	Percentage	Amount
Cleaning supplies, soap, etc.	99.9	$11.86
Life insurance	86.3	$41.92
Medicine	91.7	$10.38
Physician, surgeon, occulist	86.0	$35.32
Tobacco	79.8	$18.82
Church	71.7	$12.10
Laundry sent out	69.2	$14.70
Streetcar fares to work	55.5	$28.42
Gifts	52.5	$11.21
Dentist	44.7	$15.53
Labor organizations	31.2	$13.83
Liquor	30.2	$22.28
Lodges, clubs, societies, etc.	27.6	$11.17
Telephones	24.7	$15.07
Vacations	23.5	$22.34
Moving	18.5	$ 9.34
Accident and health insurance	18.3	$14.95
Servant and day wages	13.9	$18.78
Automobiles, motor cycles, bicycles	13.0	$66.00
Nurse	12.9	$21.26
Hospital	10.2	$41.57

Note: Families with incomes of $1200–1499. Purchases of items with an average family family expenditure above $9.00, purchased by more than 12 percent of families. Ranked by percentage of family making a purchase.

Item	Percentage	Amount
Automobiles, motorcycles, bicycles	13.0	$66.00
Undertaker	2.6	$57.71
Life insurance	86.3	$41.92
Hospital	10.2	$41.57
Physician, surgeon, occulist	86.0	$35.32
Streetcar fares to work	55.5	$28.42
Vacations	23.5	$22.34
Liquor	30.2	$22.28
Nurse	12.9	$21.26
Tobacco	79.8	$18.82
Servant and day wages	13.9	$18.78
Music	11.4	$17.57
Travel	9.0	$17.11
Cemetery	1.9	$16.98
Dentist	44.7	$15.53
Telephone	24.7	$15.07
Accident and health insurance	18.3	$14.95
Laundry sent out	69.2	$14.70
Labor organizations	31.2	$13.83
Life insurance, nonfamily members	5.5	$13.41

Note: Families with incomes of $1200–1499, purchasing all items above $12.25. Ranked by amount.

Source: U.S., Department of Labor, Bureau of Labor Statistics, *Cost of Living in the United States,* Bulletin of the Bureau of Labor Statistics, no. 357 (Washington, D.C.: GPO, 1924), pp. 447–55.

workers made their expenditures for items other than food, clothing, and shelter.[1] Some Fall River households, especially those with grown children who brought in relatively large amounts of income, spent a considerable amount on furnishings and miscellaneous items. However, even these cases show the limits to the working-class experience with elements of a new standard of living.

In the entire sample of 158 families, 11, with incomes ranging from $1041.50 to $2972.00, paid more than $150.00 for furnishings and furniture.[2] All but 2 of these households had lower miscellaneous expenses than the average for their income group.[3] Two of the 11 were just starting a family, while 7 had four or more children, at least two of whom earned money.[4] The occupations of the principal breadwinner varied, with six as workers in textile mills (loom fixer, weaver, cleaner, second hand, card grinder, and fireman), one a carpenter, one a waterworks pumping engineer, one a window trimmer in a department store, and two—a city fireman and a federal post office clerk—civil servants.

The family that allocated the most money to furniture and furnishings, a loom fixer in a cotton mill with seven children (including three teenagers who also worked in the mills), spent $409.60 of a $2754.00 income on furniture and furnishings. In the miscellaneous category, its only above-average expenditures were $88.73 for 699 movie admissions and $20.10 for music lessons. What keeps the very considerable amount allocated to movies and household goods in perspective is the nature of their other choices. They paid much less than the average of their income group for miscellaneous items and they saved $300.00 in the year. Thus with remarkably few exceptions, those who made large expenditures for furniture and furnishings were outfitting a new home or using the earnings of grown children to furnish an already established one.[5]

A close look at those Fall River budgets with large miscellaneous expenses also demonstrates the nature of consumption decisions. Nine families reported allocating more than $400 *and* more than 25 percent of their income to miscellaneous items. The incomes of the fathers ranged from $560 to $2000. Although the contributions of the children were often considerable, compared with national figures the earnings of three of the fathers were in the lowest quartile of individual incomes and two each were in the second, third, and fourth quartile.[6] This pattern underscores the importance for many families of the contribution of additional income earners to the economic well-being of the household, something that may have been more important in 1918–19 than earlier.

Five of these nine families had high miscellaneous figures largely because of health costs and other defensive expenses. One household allocated

Appendix B

almost 75 percent of its extra expenditures for health care, while $24.60 for a vacation out of the city was the only hint of choice, comfort, or possibly commercial recreation.[7] A city fireman, his wife, and two young children spent almost two-thirds of their $410.26 miscellaneous money on insurance, support of an elderly mother, health care, and church and only 7 percent of their miscellaneous expenditures on movies ($1.00), concerts ($1.00), photographs ($2.00), and a vacation ($25.00).[8] A machinist, his wife, and their young child allocated over 80 percent of their miscellaneous amount to insurance, church, medical bills, and funeral expenses.[9] A weaver, his wife, and their three children spent 72 percent of the miscellaneous funds for medical expenses, most of that on the sixteen-week hospitalization of a twenty-year-old son.[10] The family of a loom fixer used 61 percent of its miscellaneous allotment for the illness and burial of a young son.[11]

In contrast with these five families were three whose expenditure patterns were both defensive and acquisitive or modern. One family—a railroad trainman, his wife, and three children, who had white-collar jobs—saved $248.82 and paid $703.13 for miscellaneous items, almost 84 percent of that going for medical expenses, commuting to work, insurance, church, tobacco, and laundry. Several items in its entire budget that pointed to new patterns of consumption were the $626.26 for clothing (explicable in large measure by the presence of three grown and unmarried children), $193.60 for the daughter's transportation to work in another city, $47.50 for phonograph records, $27.00 for telephone, and $3.36 for movies.[12] A joiner at a shipyard, his wife, and three young children spent $385.00 of their $543.93 miscellaneous funds for an automobile but also allocated money for insurance, church, labor organizations, and tobacco.[13] Another family—with the father and four children bringing in an annual income of $2972.00—showed a similarly mixed pattern. On the one hand, they spent 52 percent of their $837.81 of miscellaneous money on insurance, religious and labor organizations, health, and tobacco. On the other hand, they allocated $49.50 for 450 movie tickets; $44.50 for 160 admissions to plays, concerts, and lectures; $140.00 for two weeks of vacations for the mother and two children; and $27.00 for excursions.[14]

Finally, there was the unique case of a family composed of a child of two, a wife of forty-two, and a husband two years older, who was a stationary engineer in a cotton mill. With only $10.83 going for furniture and furnishings, they used 77.8 percent of their $2000.00 income for four items: 23.4 percent for food, 20.2 percent for the purchase of a home, 5.4 percent for savings, and 28.7 percent for the purchase of a car. The fact that parents were forming a family relatively late in their lives shaped this spending pattern. In their forties and with one young child, this couple held back on

180

most expenses but in one year used almost half of its income to purchase a home and automobile with cash. Even so, they seem far from unequivocally modern or middle class in their choices—less than a dollar for movies; nothing for plays, concerts, magazines, books, or excursions; and relatively little on service or personal care.[15]

An analysis of the families that paid a considerable amount of money for movies further clarifies patterns of expenditure. In the entire Fall River sample, only 16 of the 158 families spent more than $20.00 a year on movies: 7 high attending families who used between $20.68 and $24.96 (104 to 360 admissions) and 9 very high attending families who allocated $34.00 to $88.73 (235 to 676 admissions).[16] The annual expenses of the households in these groups ranged from $1193.30 to $3468.01. Some of fathers held skilled, white-collar, and service jobs, although mill workers headed 4 of the 9 very high attending families. Though most families in both groups (and the very high attenders especially) saved less than the average for their income level, almost all spent a below-average percentage of their income on miscellaneous items.

Two things distinguish both groups from their peers. First, in almost every instance, they tended to spend a less than average amount on organizations (churches, unions, lodges), on newly available consumer goods and experiences (telephones, vehicles, and vacations), and on liquor. The only exception is the very high movie attenders, who used a greater than average amount for religious organizations and were more likely to contribute to labor organizations than their peers in the national sample. The second distinguishing characteristic is that, compared with the high attenders, the very high attenders were more likely to have larger families, more employed children, and children whose income together equaled or exceeded that of the fathers. It therefore looks as if very high movie attendance occurred when a family had older children who earned a good deal of money.

What works against this as an explanation is a comparison of the nine very high attenders with five Fall River families of roughly similar income and composition that spent relatively little on movies.[17] What then distinguishes the very high attending from these low attending families? In terms of savings, ethnicity, and occupation, there were no marked differences, though the average income of the fathers of the low attenders was lower than the average earnings of the heads of both the high and the very high attending families.[18] The parents of the low attending families were several years older, their families somewhat smaller, and the children older. The most important differences were in spending patterns. The low attenders generally paid less for organizational life, vacations, and excursions but more for telephones, housing, and health care. Besides movies, the very high attenders spent more than the low attenders for religion, labor organization membership, and patriotic contributions. The very high attenders were more likely to make gifts, sometimes large ones, to people outside the family.

Though the pattern is not always consistent, the very high attenders, who had more discretionary income, tended to spend on things that helped them participate in the world outside the home—movies, organizational life, and contributions. The parents of the very high attenders were younger than those of the low attenders and therefore perhaps less settled in older cultural patterns. The very high moviegoers, with children in greater number and of a wider age range, had more family members for whom the movie was an alternative to a crowded home. In general, the very high attenders were more oriented outside the house, something for which movie going was but one example. [19]

Another way of gauging the changes in how workers' families spent their money also demonstrates that the arrival of commercial recreation may not have been the only or most significant shift in consumption patterns. In 1881, the MBSL asked of several hundred workers, "What disposition would be made of more leisure?" The dominant response involved home and family-related activities.[20] Almost a third of a century later, George E. Bevans' study of how workers used their "spare time" revealed that laborers spent most (40.8 percent to 45.8 percent) of it with family. Next in order were newspapers (13.8 percent to 16.7 percent) and friends (6.0 percent to 7.6 percent). Then, clustered together at lower percentages were movies, clubs, and cards. Though 55 percent to 64 percent of the workers surveyed reported going to a movie, it was an activity on which they spent only 3.7 percent to 5.1 percent of their extra time and it often commanded less of the households' budgets than liquor, tobacco, or life insurance. Thus even as late as 1913 workers remained home-centered and movies were but one of the ways that they entered the world outside. In some ways, movie attendance was an extension of a world of friends, saloons, and lodges.[21]

Appendix C
Sample Budget, BLS, 1918–1919: Budget 5. Fall River, Massachusetts

U. S. DEPARTMENT OF LABOR—Bureau of Labor Statistics—Washington

COST OF LIVING IN THE YEAR ENDING *Aug. 31, 1918.*

REQUIREMENTS.—1. The family must be that of a wage-earner or salaried worker, but not of a person in business for himself. The families taken should represent proportionally the wage-earners and the low or medium salaried families of the locality, both as between these two occupational classes and as between income groups. Take no family of a salaried worker earning above $2000: there is no limit as to a wage earner. 2. The family must have as a minimum both a husband and wife and at least one child who is not a boarder or lodger. 3. The family must have *kept house* in the locality for the entire year covered. 4. At least seventy-five per cent of the family income must come from the principal breadwinner or others who contribute all earnings to family fund. 5. All items of income or expenditure of members other than those living as boarders or lodgers must be obtainable. 6. The family may not have over three boarders or lodgers, either outsiders or children living as such. 7. The family must have no subrental other than furnished rooms for lodgers. 8. Do not take slum or charity families or non-English speaking families who have been less than five years in the United States. Also see instructions.

1. Name

2. City and State *Fall River, Mass.*

3. Street

4. White or colored (a)

5. Family, relation to husband.	6. Sex.	7. Age.	8. Wks. in home.	9. Industry and occupation, or status.	10. Mls. day.	11. Paid for B. & L.	12. Wks. empd.	13. Rate of wages.	14. Earnings.
1.-0 a. Husband.	M	41	52	*Loom fixer cotton mill*	3		52	2450	1274.00
.90 b. Wife	F	32	52	"	3				
.90 c. Eldest child	F	15	62	*Weaver, cotton mill*	3		52	7	364.00
.90 d. Next child	M	14	52		3				
.90 e. Next child	M	13	52		3				
.90 f. Next child	M	11	52		3				
.75 g. "	F	9	52		3				
.75 h. "	F	7	62		3				
.15 i. "	M	3	52		3				
.15 j. "	F	3	52		3				1638.00
.01	M	3 wks.	52		3				

7.31

15. Summary of income:

a. Earnings of family	$1638.00	
b. Board and lodging	—	
c. Net from garden, chickens, etc. (a)	—	
d. Gifts: money, food, clothing, etc. (a)	2.00	
e. Net from rents, interest, etc. (a)	—	
f. Fuel picked up	—	
g. Other (specify) *Medicine*	1.50	
h. Total	$1641.50	

16. Summary of expenses:

a. Food	$803.31
b. Clothing	284.93
c. Housing—rent	161.00
d. Do. —on owned home	—
e. Fuel and light	59.22
f. Furniture and furnishings	60.08
g. Miscellaneous	222.96
h. Total	$1591.50

17. Amount of surplus or deficit (a) 50.00

18. If surplus, how used. If deficit, how met. *Liberty Bond.* 1641.50

NOTE.—Every person living in the house any part of the year should be shown on the schedule. State age at birthday in year covered. Fill all columns except 11 for all persons contributing entire earnings, if any, and getting all support from the family fund. For children, parents or others living as boarders or lodgers fill 5, 6, 7, 8, 10 and 11, and in 9 enter only B. & L., or B. or L. with inclusive dates of the period in the family. If any person occupies more than one status during the year, report for each condition by interlining above and bracketing. If any wage earner has two or more occupations report only the major occupation and industry in 9, but in 12 and 14 report for all occupations combined. If only one rate enter it in 13, but if more than one rate give approximate average. Items 12 and 13 must be approximately consistent with 14.

(a) Place check over item.

Items.	Cost.	Items.	Cost.
	$	445. School, all expenses of children away	$ 107.91
Insurance:		446. Sickness, physician, surgeon, oculist	17.00
412. Life, Old line. Persons ...... Amt. ......(a)		447. do. medicine	1.50
413. do. Indus. Persons 2 Amt. 340 (a)	13.00	448. do. nurse	
414. do. Frat. Persons ...... Amt. ......(a)		449. do. hospital	
415. do. Estab. Persons ...... Amt. ......(a)		450. do. dentist	30.00
416. do. Persons ...... Amt. ......(a)		451. do. eyeglasses	
417. Accident ...... Persons ...... Amt.		452. do.	
418. Health ...... Persons ...... Amt.		453. Death, undertaker (f)	
419. Personal property		454. do. cemetery (f)	
420. Life, persons not in economic family (b)		455. Liquors, in or out of house	
421. Church and other religious organizations	3.00	456. Tobacco	15.00
422. Labor organizations	13.00	457. Personal property and poll tax	
423. Lodges, clubs, societies (c)		458. Income tax	
424. Charity		459. Tools	
425. Patriotic contributions (d)	3.00	460. Laundry work sent out	30.00
426. Gifts outside family (e)		461. Cleaning supplies, soap	6.00
427. Street car fare, rides to work		462. do. soap powder and liquid	
428. do. do. to school		463. do. others Washing Soda	2.60
429. do. do. other		464. Barber work	4.95
430. Movies (number of tickets 540	52.00	465. Toilet articles (g)	1.00
431. Plays, concerts, lectures (number of tickets......)		466. do. preparations (h)	1.00
432. Dances		467. Telephone	
433. Pool		468. Moving	7.00
434. Other amusements		469. Vehicles, bicycles (i)	
435. Excursions		470. do. motor cycles (i)	
436. Vacation (out of city)		471. do. automobiles (i)	
437. Travel (not vacation)		472. Servant and day work wages	
438. Newspapers (daily 1 weekly ...... other ......)	12.51	473. Other miscellaneous:	
439. Magazines and periodicals	5.46	(j)	
440. Books		(j)	
441. Postage	6.00		
442. School, tuition, children			
443. do. books, do.		474. Total	$ 222.96
444. do. other expenses	107.91		

(a) Also, if obtainable, note kind of policy.
(b) Children living as boarders and lodgers are not in the economic family.
(c) An organization whose object is mainly insurance should be counted insurance.
(d) War bonds and savings stamps are not expenses, but counted as money in hand for investment.
(e) Gifts inside economic family are counted as ordinary family expense. More or less forced contributions outside family are considered gifts.
(f) Show date of death in Column 9. Enter expenses for death outside family in 473.
(g) Brushes, combs, mirrors, tooth brushes, curling iron, manicure sets, razors and blades, etc.
(h) Toilet soap, tooth powder, cosmetics, shoe polish, etc.
(i) Including also supplies, repairs and license.
(j) Specify items above $5.

Source: Industrial and Social Branch, Civil Archives Division, National Archives, Washington, D.C.

Suggested Readings

What follows is a discussion of secondary literature that indicates some of my debts to scholars and points where others might start. In general, these sources do not duplicate the references in the footnotes; therefore, the reader should begin by carefully mining the notes. Moreover, given the vastness of the scholarship on many topics, what ensues does not provide a comprehensive guide to all the relevant subjects and sources. Rather, this essay highlights some of the more important issues in the history of consumption.

Like the rise of the middle class, the emergence of a consumer society seems to have happened in every era. Not very long ago there was a widely shared consensus that the 1920s was the key decade. More recently, the general tendency of scholarship has been to push back to earlier and earlier periods the origins and development of key elements of consumer culture.

The question of the emergence of modern patterns of consumption is part of a larger debate that has focused on the issues of when and how Western Europe and America became "modern." It is possible to locate the origins of consumer culture at least as early as the Middle Ages. Carlo M. Cipolla, *Before the Industrial Revolution: European Society and Economy, 1000–1700*, 2d ed. (New York: W.W. Norton and Co., 1980), pp. 5–63 and 204–47, and Harry A. Miskimin, *The Economy of Early Renaissance Europe, 1300–1460* (Cambridge: Cambridge University Press, 1975), pp. 86–138, discuss important changes in the consumer economy of Medieval and Renaissance Europe. Keith Thomas, "Work and Leisure in Pre-Industrial Society," *Past and Present*, no. 29 (December 1964), pp. 50–62, considers changes in the view of work and leisure. Among the historians who have written on emergence of a modern society in the West in the seventeenth and eighteenth centuries, Joyce O. Appleby has published work especially helpful in understanding the history of consumer culture. In "The Social Origins of American Revolutionary Ideology," *Journal of American History* 64 (March 1978): 935–58; *Economic Thought and Ideology in Seventeenth-Century England*

(Princeton: Princeton University Press, 1978), pp. 14–15, 52, 72, and 275–78; and "Ideology and Theory: The Tension between Political and Economic Liberalism in Seventeenth-Century England," *American Historical Review* 81 (June 1976): 499–515, Appleby has demonstrated that within the Anglo-American world it is possible to find toward the end of the seventeenth century the origins of components of a vision that emphasized the positive qualities of a free market, acquisitiveness, and a rising standard of living. Though this new ideology was not triumphant at the time of the American Revolution, by then the balance had begun to shift to the worldly, individual, and economic as explanations of and sanctions for people's behavior.

Much of the scholarly debate over when the United States became modern had tended to focus on the the decline of self-sufficient agriculture, the rise of its commercial counterpart, and the emergence of a significant number of people who were calculating, individualistic, and oriented to the market and the future. Hardly in agreement on the timing and nature of this transformation, scholars have come to recognize the complexity of the changes involved and the necessity to see the simultaneous existence of contradictory forces and values. Carole Shammas, "How Self-Sufficient Was Early America?" *Journal of Interdisciplinary History* 13 (Autumn 1982): 247–72, questions the notion of household and local self-sufficiency and shows instead a very considerable participation in the world of commercial consumption. Joseph T. Ellis, "Culture and Capitalism in Pre-Revolutionary America," *American Quarterly* 31 (Summer 1979): 169–86—a summary of research on the late colonial period—finds the persistence of traditional, communal values as well as the basis for ideas and economic forces essential in the growth of a capitalist economy. James T. Lemon, *The Best Poor Man's Country: A Geographical Study of Early Southeastern Pennsylvania* (Baltimore: Johns Hopkins University Press, 1972), emphasizes the goal of individual freedom and materialism among farmers in one region in the years before the American Revolution. J. E. Crowley, *This Sheba, Self: The Conceptualization of Economic Life in Eighteenth-Century America* (Baltimore: Johns Hopkins University Press, 1974), shows that in the eighteenth century ethical and social impulses, rather than economic and individual ones, replaced religion as the main justification of economic activity.

With "Families and Farms: *Mentalité* in Pre-Industrial America," *William and Mary Quarterly*, 3d ser., 35 (January 1978): 1–32; *The Evolution of American Society, 1700–1815: An Interdisciplinary Analysis* (Lexington, Mass.: D.C. Heath and Co., 1973), pp. 7, 8, 21, 41, 98–99, and 143–45; and "The Study of Social Mobility: Ideological Assumptions and Conceptual Bias," *Labor History* 18 (Spring 1977): 165–78, James A. Henretta has emerged as the most forceful proponent of the view that at least into the early-nineteenth-century family and communal values struggled to hold their own against those that centered on market orientation, individualism, and social mobility. In *Modernization: The Transformation of American Life, 1600–1865* (New York: Hill and Wang, 1976), Richard D. Brown has suggested the multiple dimensions of the emergence of the United States as a modern society in the early nineteenth century. Christopher Clark, "Household Economy, Market Exchange and the Rise of Capitalism in the Connecticut Valley, 1800–1860," *Journal of Social History* 13 (Winter 1979): 169–89, argues that a new capitalist economic order grew out of the older household economy. John G. Cawelti, *Apostles of the Self-Made Man* (Chicago: University of Chicago Press, 1965), pp. 46–55, 71–75, 102, and 168–71, stresses the persistence into the nineteenth century of reservations about the value of ambition, individualism, materialism, and acquisitiveness. John Bodnar, "Immigration and Modernization: The Case of Slavic Peasants in Industrial America," *Journal of Social History* 10 (Fall 1976): 44–71, calls into question the dichotomy between traditional and modern characteristics and convincingly demonstrates the ability of twentieth-century people to synthesize the two.

British historians have done some of the most important work on the origins of consumer culture before the end of the eighteenth century. The clearest statement of this new social history of consumption is Neil McKendrick, John Brewer, and J. H. Plumb, *The Birth of a Consumer Society: The Commercialization of Eighteenth-Century England* (London: Europa Publications, 1982). By emphasizing the commercialization of leisure, politics, and fashion; the development of advertising; and the widespread use of new goods, they suggest that a consumer revolution arrived much earlier than most historians have usually assumed. It is not easy to reconcile their picture with the one that emerges in Fernand Braudel, *Civilization and Capitalism: 15th–18th Century*, vol. 1: *The Structures of Everyday Life: The Limits of the Possible*, trans. Siân Reynolds (New York: Harper & Row, 1981), pp. 183–333. Compared with the British scholars, the French historian paints a bleaker and less changing picture of the standard of living in Europe in the eighteenth century and makes a sharper distinction between the conditions of rich and poor.

Given some of the stronger claims of McKendrick, Plumb, and Brewer, it is not always easy to know in what ways the consumer revolution was incomplete by 1800, what fundamental elements remained to be invented and diffused. It is still unclear what will emerge from a fuller comparison of the changes discovered for the eighteenth century and those that scholars of the American standard of living have documented for other periods, especially the late nineteenth century, the 1920s, and years since World War II.

When innovations came, how thoroughly their use spread through society, and how they conflicted with older ways of living and thinking—these are some of the issues that call for further research and analysis.

For the emergence of America as a consumer society in the seventeenth and eighteenth centuries, there is no scholarship on consumption as comprehensive and provocative as the work of British scholars. However, studies are beginning to appear. Consequently, although there is some evidence of common trans-Atlantic experiences with consumption, it is not yet possible to compare with enough precision what happened in England and America. Gloria L. Main, *Tobacco Colony: Life in Early Maryland, 1650–1720* (Princeton: Princeton University Press, 1982), pp. 140–266, tells of a low and relatively unchanging pattern of consumption for one colony from the middle of the seventeenth to the early eighteenth century. It is possible that this situation changed dramatically shortly thereafter. For example, in "Urban Amenities and Rural Sufficiency: Living Standards and Consumer Behavior in the Colonial Chesapeake, 1643–1777," *Journal of Economic History* 43 (March 1983): 109–17, Lorena S. Walsh shows that by the middle of the eighteenth century more and more white households in the Chesapeake were defining new consumer goods as essential to their comfort and convenience. Jan Lewis, *The Pursuit of Happiness: Family and Values in Jefferson's Virginia* (Cambridge: Cambridge University Press, 1983), pp. 106–68, explores the patterns and codes of behavior among Virgina planters in the late eighteenth and early nineteenth centuries.

For reasons that are not readily apparent, the half century before the Civil War remains the period least explored in the recent writings on the history of consumption in the United States. British historians have led the way in demonstrating the complexity and significance of the changes in these years. Hugh Cunningham, *Leisure in the Industrial Revolution: c. 1780–c. 1880* (London: Croom Helm, 1980); Geoffrey Best, *Mid-Victorian Britain, 1851–1875* (London: Weidenfeld and Nicolson, 1971), pp. 149–227; and Peter Bailey, *Leisure and Class in Victorian England: Rational Recreation and the Contest for Control, 1830–1885* (London: Routledge and Kegan Paul, 1978), provide detailed and comprehensive pictures of the development of popular and commercial leisure in the years from the late eighteenth to the late nineteenth century. For the United States no studies are as helpful and detailed as two books by John Burnett: *Plenty and Want: A Social History of Diet in England from 1815 to the Present Day* [1966], rev. ed. (London: Scolar Press, 1979), and *A Social History of Housing, 1815–1970* (Newton Abbot, Devon: David and Charles, 1978).

Given the importance of the antebellum years in the history of mass culture in the United States, we need more studies that will build bridges between the scholarship of the eighteenth and of the late nineteenth centuries. For the years before the Civil War in the United States, there are some suggestive beginnings. Ann Douglas, *The Feminization of American Culture* (New York: Alfred A. Knopf, 1977), explores the role of male clergymen and female writers in the growth of a middle-class mass culture. In "The Egalitarian Myth and the American Social Reality: Wealth, Mobility, and Equality in the 'Era of the Common Man,'" *American Historical Review* 76 (October 1971): 1000, Edward Pessen offers a trans-Atlantic comparison that makes clear the similarity of the styles of life of the wealthy in Europe and United States. Edward Pessen, *Riches, Class, and Power Before the Civil War* (Lexington, Mass.: D.C. Heath and Co., 1973), examines the distribution of wealth. Nonetheless, after more than forty years, Edgar S. Martin, *The Standard of Living in 1860: American Consumption Levels on the Eve of the Civil War* (Chicago: University of Chicago Press, 1942), still provides the most comprehensive picture of the American situation in the period. Though American governments did not begin to collect household budget data until the 1870s, information is available. Ezra C. Seaman, *Essays on the Progress of Nations* (New York: Charles Scribner, 1852), pp. 272–99 and Matthew Carey, *Appeal to the Wealthy of the Land* (Philadelphia: L. Johnson, 1833), contain useful data on expenditures. Chase G. Woodhouse, "The Standard of Living at the Professional Level, 1816–17 and 1926–27," *Journal of Political Economy* 37 (October 1929): 552–72, unearthed one household budget from the early nineteenth century and compared it with another from a later period. Donald R. Adams, Jr., "The Standard of Living During American Industrialization: Evidence from the Brandywine Region, 1800–1860," *Journal of Economic History* 42 (December 1982): 903–17, uses company records to document the standard of living. Dorothy S. Brady, "Consumption and the Style of Life," in *American Economic Growth: An Economist's History of the United States*, Lance E. Davis et al. (New York: Harper & Row, 1972), pp. 61–89, looks at household expenditures in the 1830s.

If British historians have discovered a consumer revolution in the eighteenth century, the dominant approach among Americanists has been to stress the changes in the late nineteenth and early twentieth centuries. Peter E. Samson, "The Emergence of a Consumer Interest in America, 1870–1930" (Ph.D. dissertation, University of Chicago, 1980), and John E. Hollitz, "The Challenge of Abundance: Reactions to the Development of a Consumer Economy, 1890–1920" (Ph.D. dissertation, University of Wisconsin-Madison, 1981), provide detailed and well-argued discussions of the growing awareness of consumption and affluence. The contributors to Richard W. Fox and T. J. Jackson Lears, ed., *The Culture of Consumption:*

Critical Essays in American History, 1880-1980 (New York: Pantheon Books, 1983), state the major themes that are coming to shape the scholarship of the history of consumer culture: the role of experts in developing the world of commercialized experiences and goods, the tendency of opponents to consumerism to end up fostering what they claimed they opposed, the critical nature of the four decades beginning in 1880, and the growth of a culture of therapeutic self-realization in which elites and the economic system promoted false pleasures, rather than real ones.

This analysis stands in opposition to the picture of "democratic," "vague," "evanescent," "open," "invisible," and "nonideological" "consumption communities" that Daniel J. Boorstin described in *The Americans: The Democratic Experience* (New York: Random House, 1973), pp. 89–164. Especially in the newer scholarship of leisure, historians have emphasized how conflict suffused the pursuit and definition of styles of life. Roy Rosenzweig, *Eight Hours for What We Will: Workers and Leisure in an Industrial City, 1870-1930* (Cambridge: Cambridge University Press, 1983), is the first community study of the working class that takes recreation as its central focus. In telling the story of the struggles over leisure in Worcester, Massachusetts, Rosenzweig chronicles the changes and continuities in working-class life. Francis Couvares, "The Triumph of Commerce: Class Culture and Mass Culture in Pittsburgh," in *Working-Class America: Essays on Labor, Community, and American Society*, ed. Michael Frisch and Daniel J. Walkowitz (Urbana: University of Illinois Press, 1983), pp. 123–52, explores the influence of entertainment entrepreneurs and the nature of cultural and class conflict over new forms of commercial entertainment. Lary May, *Screening Out the Past: The Birth of Mass Culture and the Motion Picture Industry* (New York: Oxford University Press, 1980), especially pp. 43–59, examines the attempts by Progressives to control movies. In "Cheap Amusements: Gender Relations and the Use of Leisure Time in New York City, 1880 to 1920" (Ph.D. dissertation, Brown University, 1982), Kathy L. Peiss offers the first community study that focuses on the history of women's leisure. David Glassberg, "Public Ritual and Cultural Hierarchy: Philadelphia's Civic Celebrations at the Turn of the Twentieth Century," *Pennsylvania Magazine of History and Biography* 107 (July 1983): 421–48, documents the disagreements over approaches to public rituals. Robert M. Lewis, "Rational Recreation: The Ideology of Recreation in the Northern United States in the Nineteenth Century" (Ph.D. dissertation, Johns Hopkins University, 1980), and Dominick Cavallo, *Muscles and Morals: Organized Playgrounds and Urban Reform, 1880-1920* (Philadelphia: University of Pennsylvania Press, 1981), demonstrate how moralistic reformers tried to shape the leisure activities of the families of workers and immigrants. Robert

L. Goldman, "Meanings of Leisure in Corporate America, 1890-1930" (Ph.D. dissertation, Duke University, 1977), uses critical theory and popular magazine articles to analyze the disciplining of leisure. For a study that brings the story closer to the present, see Marlou Belyea, "The Joy Ride and the Silver Screen: Commercial Leisure, Delinquency and Play Reform in Los Angeles, 1900-1980" (Ph.D. dissertation, Boston University, 1983).

Central to the history of leisure in the nineteenth and early twentieth centuries is a series of changes in institutional arrangements, group relationships, and definitions of culture. Neil Harris, "Four Stages of Cultural Growth: The American City," in Arthur Mann, Neil Harris, and Sam B. Warner, Jr., *History and the Role of the City in American Life* (Indianapolis: Indiana Historical Society, 1972), pp. 25-49, provides a framework for interpreting the development of urban cultural institutions. Helen L. Horowitz, *Culture and the City: Cultural Philanthropy in Chicago from the 1880s to 1917* (Lexington: University Press of Kentucky, 1975) remains the best treatment of elite institutions. Gunther Barth, *City People: The Rise of Modern City Culture in Nineteenth-Century America* (New York: Oxford University Press, 1980), tells the story of department stores, newspapers, ball parks, and vaudeville houses. William R. Leach, "Transformations in a Culture of Consumption: Women and Department Stores, 1890-1925," *Journal of American History* 71 (September 1984): 319-342 and Susan B. Porter, "Palace of Consumption and Machine for Selling: The American Department Store, 1880-1940," *Radical History Review* 21 (Fall 1979): 199-221, analyze important changes in retailing. Lewis A. Erenberg, *Steppin' Out: New York Nightlife and the Transformation of American Culture, 1890-1930* (Westport: Greenwood, 1981), describes the blurring of gender, ethnic, and class barriers in the realm of leisure after the turn of the century. John F. Kasson, *Amusing the Million: Coney Island at the Turn of the Century* (New York: Hill and Wang, 1978), analyzes one new form of commercial entertainment in a way that suggests broader cultural changes. Among those who are providing a much-needed history of immigrant and working-class cultural institutions are Jon M. Kingsdale, "The 'Poor Man's Club': Social Functions of the Urban Working-Class Saloon," *American Quarterly* 25 (October 1973): 472-89; Oliver M. Carsten, "Work and the Lodge: Working-Class Sociability in Meriden and New Britain, Connecticut, 1850-1940" (Ph.D. dissertation, University of Michigan, 1981).

A number of scholars have demonstrated the diversity of sources and approaches available in writing the history of changes in American patterns of living. In "The Commercial Amusement Audience in Early 20th-Century American Cities," *Journal of American Culture* 5 (Spring 1982): 1-19, Alan Havig examines fifteen surveys carried out between 1910 and 1920 and points to the very considerable extent to which family members participated together in new forms of commercial entertainment. Lizabeth A. Cohen, "Embellishing a Life of Labor: An Interpretation of the Material Culture of American Working-Class Homes, 1885–1915," *Journal of American Culture* 3 (Winter 1980): 752–75, uses the evidence of material culture to draw constrasting visions of working-class and middle-class residences and values. Warren J. Belasco, *Americans on the Road: From Auto Camp to Motel, 1910–1914* (Cambridge: MIT Press, 1979), uses material culture to suggest changing vacation patterns. Michael Spindler, "Youth, Class, and Consumerism in Dreiser's *An American Tragedy,*" *Journal of American Studies* 12 (April 1978): 63–79, and Daniel L. Bratton, "Conspicuous Consumption and Conspicuous Leisure in the Novels of Edith Wharton" (Ph.D. dissertation, University of Toronto, 1983), use literary sources to analyze aspects of consumer culture.

Historians have offered a variety of perspectives on the history of advertising. Daniel Pope, *The Making of Modern Advertising* (New York: Basic Books, 1983), focuses on the contribution of business needs and institutional developments in shaping the industry. Stephen Fox, *The Mirror Makers: A History of American Advertising and Its Creators* (New York: William Morrow and Co., 1984), explores the interplay between advertising and social change. T. J. Jackson Lears, "The Rise of American Advertising," *Wilson Quarterly* 7 (Winter 1983): 156–67, discusses fundamental shifts in assumptions and strategies. Michael Schudson, *Advertising, the Uneasy Persuasion: Its Dubious Impact on American Society* (New York: Basic Books, 1984), evaluates advertising's effectiveness and its place in American life.

In telling the story of the emergence of consumer culture in America, many writers have emphasized how the economic system, industrialists, and professionals have wielded power in the effort to strengthen capitalism by transforming Americans into compliant consumers. Among the many who have offered one or another variant of this theme are Paul A. Baran and Paul M. Sweezy, *Monopoly Capitalism: An Essay on the American Economic and Social Order* [1966] (New York: Monthly Review Press, 1968), pp. 127–31; Stuart Ewen, *Captains of Consciousness: Advertising and the Social Roots of the Consumer Culture* (New York: McGraw-Hill Book Co., 1976); Stuart Ewen and Elizabeth Ewen, *Channels of Desire: Mass Images and the Shaping of American Consciousness* (New York: McGraw-Hill Book Co., 1982); John Alt, "Beyond Class: The Decline of Industrial Labor and I eisure," *Telos* 28 (Summer 1976): 55–80; Charles F. Owen, "Consumerism and Neocapitalism: The Politics of Producing Consumption" (Ph.D. dissertation, University of Minnesota, 1976); Vance O. Packard, *Hidden Per-*

suaders (New York: David McKay Co., 1957); and John Kenneth Galbraith, *The New Industrial State* [1967] (New York: New American Library, 1968), especially pp. 208–20 and 281–82.

In *The Dialectical Imagination: A History of the Frankfurt School and the Institute of Social Research, 1923–1950* (Boston: Little, Brown and Co., 1973), p. 180, Martin Jay comments on how one influential group of neo-Marxists saw in consumption the potential for genuine happiness, the possibility of social cohesion, and a way of rejecting asceticism. Similarly, some historians have drawn a picture that emphasizes the ability of ordinary people to struggle to resist what the economic system offers and use what they consume for their own purposes. Rather than concentrating on how elites hope to control the consciousness of consumers, these scholars demonstrate how people consume on their own terms, terms often influenced by bonds of kin, community, ethnicity, region, and social class. Rosenzweig, *Eight Hours for What We Will*, pp. 171–221, shows how ethnic traditions shaped immigrant and working-class experience with movies. Joan M. Seidl, "Consumers' Choices: A Study of Household Furnishing, 1880–1920," *Minnesota History* 48 (Spring 1983): 183–97, describes how archival sources offer a picture of the influence of media campaigns very different from what the published self-promotions of advertising publicists claim. Using family correspondence, she argues that when husbands and wives set about to decorate a house, they relied not on advertising but on the experiences of friends and relatives. Fox, "Epitaph," p. 125, suggests that Middletown consumers were not "innocent, unwilling victims." Joseph Interrante, "You Can't Go to Town in a Bathtub: Automobile Movement and the Reorganization of Rural American Space, 1900–1930," *Radical History Review* 21 (Fall 1979): 151–68, and Joseph Interrante and Carol Lasser, "Victims of the Very Songs They Sing: A Critique of Recent Work on Patriarchial Culture and the Social Construction of Gender," *Radical History Review* 20 (Spring–Summer 1979): 25–40, criticize the approach that emphasizes power from above, victimization, and false needs in the explanation of consumer culture. They suggest a more interactive model, one that shows how, within a framework established by capitalism, consumers use what they purchased. Among other scholars who stress "agency"—the capacity of people to shape their world under circumstances over which they have limited control—are Leach, "Transformations," pp. 319–42; Schudson, *Advertising*; Couvares, "Triumph of Commerce," p. 147; Stephen Hardy and Alan G. Ingham, "Games, Structures, and Agency: Historians of the American Play Movement," *Journal of Social History* 17 (Winter 1983): 285–301. Neil Harris, *Humbug: The Art of P. T. Barnum* (Boston: Little, Brown and Co., 1973), p.

77, suggests that those in the audience of at least one nineteenth-century commercial amusement were self-conscious and eager participants in the trickery of a skilled entertainment entrepreneur.

Because politics and work have been the dominant concerns of social historians, consumption has received relatively little focused attention. One notable exception is Peter R. Shergold, *Working-Class Life: The "American Standard" in Comparative Perspective, 1899-1913* (Pittsburgh: University of Pittsburgh Press, 1982). Exploring the differences between the purchasing power of workers in Pittsburgh, Pennsylvania, and Birmingham, England, and between that for skilled and unskilled workers in both countries, Shergold demonstrates that the nonimmigrant, American skilled laborers had standards of living dramatically higher than their English counterparts or than immigrant, unskilled American workers.

Other social, women's, and labor historians have shed light on the data and judgments offered in household budget studies. Daniel J. Walkowitz, *Worker City, Company Town: Iron and Cotton-Worker Protest in Troy and Cohoes, New York, 1855-84* (Urbana: University of Illinois Press, 1978), pp. 101-10, discusses the standard of living and the emergence of an ethnic middle class in the late nineteenth century. The lack of money for transportation in the MBSL's 1874 sample contrasts with the picture drawn in Theodore Hershberg, Harold E. Cox, Dale Light, Jr., and Richard R. Greenfield, "The 'Journey-to-Work': An Empirical Investigation of Work, Residence and Transportation, Philadelphia, 1850 and 1880," in *Philadelphia: Work, Space, Family, and Group Experience in the Nineteenth Century: Essays Toward an Interdisciplinary History of the City,* ed. Theodore Hershberg (New York: Oxford University Press, 1981), pp. 128-73. Viviana A. R. Zelizer, *Morals and Markets: The Development of Life Insurance in the United States* (New York: Columbia University Press, 1979), pp. xi-xiii, 27, 64-65, and 150-53, considers the tension between life insurance and cultural traditions. John E. Bodnar, "A Culture of Sharing: Family and Community in Pennsylvania's Anthracite Region, 1900-1940," *Pennsylvania Heritage* 9 (Summer 1983): 13-17, uses oral history to explore one kind of nonmarket exchange. Lewis Hyde, *The Gift: Imagination and the Erotic Life of Property* (New York: Vintage Books, 1983) examines the nature of market and nonmarket exchanges. For some suggestions on the relationship between social class and the standard of living, see Clyde Griffin, "Occupational Mobility in Nineteenth-Century America: Problems and Possibilities," *Journal of Social History* 5 (Spring 1972): 325-27. For treatment of the issue of respectability in class relationships, see Robert Q. Gray, *The Labour Aristocracy in Victorian Edinburgh* (Oxford: Oxford University Press, 1976), pp. 2-5, 91, 95, 98-102, 110, 115, 121, 124-25, 130, and 136-43.

Among those who have considered the connection between ethnicity and home ownership are Carolyn T. Kirk and Gordon W. Kirk, Jr., "The Impact of the City on Home Ownership: A Comparison of Immigrants and Native Whites at the Turn of the Century," *Journal of Urban History* 7 (August 1981): 471–98, and John Bodnar, Roger Simon, and Michael P. Weber, *Lives of Their Own: Blacks, Italians, and Poles in Pittsburgh, 1900–1960* (Urbana: University of Illinois Press, 1982), pp. 153–54, 160, and 255.

A number of historians have touched on the relationship between the family and consumption. Frances H. Early, "The French-Canadian Family Economy and Standard of Living in Lowell, Massachusetts, 1870," *Journal of Family History* 7 (Summer 1982): 180–99, uses Carroll D. Wright's study to explore the nature of the family economy. For the ideology of the family economy in the nineteenth and early twentieth centuries, see Martha May, "The Historical Problem of the Family Wage: The Ford Motor Company and the Five Dollar Day," *Feminist Studies* 8 (Summer 1982): 399–424 and "The 'Good Managers': Married Working Class Women and Family Budget Studies, 1895–1915," *Labor History* 25 (Summer 1984): 351–72. On women's centrality in the family economy, see Joan W. Scott and Louise A. Tilly, "Women's Work and the Family in Nineteenth-Century Europe," *Comparative Studies in Society and History* 17 (January 1975): 36–64. Leslie W. Tentler, *Wage-Earning Women: Industrial Work and Family Life in the United States, 1900–1930* (New York: Oxford University Press, 1979), pp. 15 and 140–42, examines the budgetary contribution of working women. Claudia Goldin, "Household and Market Production of Families in a Late Nineteenth Century American City," *Explorations in Economic History*, 2d ser., 16 (April 1979): 111–31, looks at patterns of child labor in Philadelphia in 1880. On the relation between youth and consumer culture in the 1920s, see Paula S. Fass, *The Damned and the Beautiful: American Youth in the 1920s* (New York: Oxford University Press, 1977), pp. 219–21, 230–34, and 257–58.

For analyses of the changing nature of the poverty level, see Michael R. Haines, "Poverty, Economic Stress, and the Family in a Late Nineteenth-Century American City: Whites in Philadelphia, 1880," in *Philadelphia*, ed. Hershberg, pp. 240–76; Steven Dubnoff, "A Method for Estimating the Economic Welfare of American Families of Any Composition: 1860–1909," *Historical Methods* 13 (Summer 1980): 171–80; Eudice Glassberg, "Work, Wages, and the Cost of Living, Ethnic Differences and the Poverty Line, Philadelphia, 1880," *Pennsylvania History* 46 (January 1979): 17–58.

On the history of the effort to reduce the working day, see David R. Roediger, "The Movement for a Shorter Working Day in the United States before 1866" (Ph.D. dissertation, Northwestern University, 1980); Thomas Dublin, "A Personal Perspective on the Ten Hour Movement in New

England," *Labor History* 24 (Summer 1983): 398–403; Hyman Kuritz, "Ira Steward and the Eight Hour Day," *Science and Society* 20 (Spring 1956): 118–34; Irwin Yellowitz, "Shorter Hours as a Response to Industrialization," *Amerikastudien* 26 (1981): 431–45; Kenneth Fones-Wolfe, "Boston Eight Hour Men, New York Marxists, and the Emergence of the International Labor Union: Prelude to the AFL," *Historical Journal of Massachusetts* 9 (June 1981): 47–59; Benjamin K. Hunnicutt, "Monsignor John A. Ryan and the Shorter Hours of Labor: A Forgotten Vision of 'Genuine' Progress," *Catholic Historical Review* 69 (July 1983): 384–402; and Benjamin K. Hunnicutt, "The End of Shorter Hours," *Labor History* 25 (Summer 1984): 373–404.

Fall River, Massachusetts, has been the focus of a number of studies, including Teresa A. Murphy, "Labor, Religion and Moral Reform in Fall River, Massachusetts, 1800–1845" (Ph.D. dissertation, Yale University, 1982); Philip T. Silvia, Jr., "The Spindle City: Labor, Politics, and Religion in Fall River, Massachusetts, 1870–1905" (Ph.D. dissertation, Fordham University, 1973); Philip T. Silvia, Jr., "The Position of Workers in a Textile Community: Fall River in the Early 1880s," *Labor History* 16 (Spring 1975): 230–48; and Anthony Coelho, "A Row of Nationalities: Life in a Working Class Community: The Irish, English, and French Canadians of Fall River, Massachusetts, 1850–1890" (Ph.D. dissertation, Brown University, 1980).

In "Intellectual History and the New Social History," in *New Directions in American Intellectual History*, ed. John Higham and Paul K. Conkin (Baltimore: Johns Hopkins University Press, 1979), pp. 3–26, Laurence Veysey calls on intellectual historians to respond to the challenges of social history. In demonstrating the biases built into the data social historians use, Margo A. Conk has offered one way to proceed: see "Social Mobility in Historical Perspective," *Marxist Perspectives*, 1 (Fall 1978), 52–69; "Occupational Classification in the United States Census: 1870–1940," *Journal of Interdisciplinary History* 9 (Summer 1978): 111–30; and "Labor Statistics in the American and English Census: Making Some Invidious Comparisons," *Journal of Social History* 16 (Summer 1983): 83–102.

Two books show other ways that cultural and intellectual historians might approach the questions and data social historians usually use. Gertrude Himmelfarb, *The Idea of Poverty: England in the Early Industrial Age* (New York: Alfred A. Knopf, 1984), examines how social investigators interpreted the facts of poverty. Rosalind H. Williams, *Dream Worlds: Mass Consumption in Late Nineteenth-Century France* (Berkeley: University of California Press, 1982), treats the emergence of styles and institutions of consumption and the ways intellectuals responded to new standards of living.

The following works are among those that discuss the nature of class relationships, including the distinction between old and new middle classes:

198

Anthony Giddens, *The Class Structure of the Advanced Societies* (New York: Harper & Row, 1973); Erik O. Wright, *Class Structure and Income Determination* (New York: Academic Press, 1979); Giorgio Gagliani, "How Many Working Classes?" *American Journal of Sociology* 87 (September 1981): 259–85; Stuart M. Blumin, "Black Coats to White Collars: Economic Change, Nonmanual Work, and the Social Structure of Industrializing America," in *Small Business in American Life*, ed. Stuart W. Bruchey (New York: Columbia University Press, 1980), pp. 100–121; and R. S. Neal, *Class and Ideology in the Nineteenth Century* (London: Routledge and Kegan Paul, 1972). Among American historians and sociologists, there is a long tradition of distinguishing between new and old middle class. See, for example, C. Wright Mills, *White Collar: The American Middle Classes* [1951] (New York: Oxford University Press 1956); David Riesman, *The Lonely Crowd: A Study of the Changing American Character* (New Haven: Yale University Press, 1950), pp. 21 and 47–48; Samuel P. Hays, *The Response to Industrialism: 1885–1914* (Chicago: University of Chicago Press, 1957), pp. 73–74; and Robert H. Wiebe, *The Search for Order, 1877–1920* (New York: Hill and Wang, 1967), pp. 111–32.

Although most of the new social history concentrates on the working class, there is a growing body of material on the middle class. Mary P. Ryan, *Cradle of the Middle Class: The Family in Oneida County, New York, 1790–1865* (Cambridge: Cambridge University Press, 1981), looks at the situation from the perspective of one community. Karen Halttunen, *Confidence Men and Painted Women: A Study of Middle-Class Culture in America, 1830–1870* (New Haven: Yale University Press, 1982), argues for the emergence of distinctive middle-class cultural styles. Burton J. Bledstein, *The Culture of Professionalism: The Middle Class and the Development of Higher Education in America* (New York: W. W. Norton and Co., 1976), analyzes one component of the new middle class and another is the subject of Cindy S. Aron, " 'To Barter Their Souls for Gold': Female Clerks in Federal Government Offices, 1862–1890," *Journal of American History* 67 (March 1981): 835–53. John S. Gilkenson, Jr., "A City of Joiners: Voluntary Associations and the Formation of the Middle Class in Providence, 1830–1920" (Ph.D. dissertation, Brown University, 1981), is a community study that focuses on important aspects of middle-class life. Joan S. Rubin, " 'Information, Please!': Culture and Expertise in the Interwar Period," *American Quarterly* 35 (Winter 1983): 499–517, examines the packaging and consumption of genteel culture.

Without denying that women are responsible for market and nonmarket production, a number of historians have looked at the ways in which women also act as consumers. Bonnie G. Smith, *Ladies of the Leisure Class: The Bourgeoises of Northern France in the Nineteenth Century* (Princeton:

Princeton University Press, 1981), examines the style of life of one group of European women. Mary P. Ryan, *Womanhood in America: From Colonial Times to the Present* [1975], 2d ed. (New York: Franklin Watts, 1979), pp. 124–29, 151–82 and 196–97, surveys some aspects of women's lives as consumers. In history of women as consumers, housework has received the most concentrated attention. Ruth Schwartz Cowan, *More Work for Mother: The Ironies of Household Technology from the Open Hearth to the Microwave* (New York: Basic Books, 1983); Susan Strasser, *Never Done: A History of American Housework* (New York: Pantheon Books, 1982); and Heidi I. Hartmann, "Capitalism and Women's Work in the Home, 1900–1930" (Ph.D. dissertation, Yale University, 1974), analyze ways housewives have spent time and money. On household help, one aspect of domestic production and consumption, see Daniel E. Sutherland, *Americans and Their Servants: Domestic Service in the United States from 1800 to 1920* (Baton Rouge: Louisiana State University Press, 1981); David M. Katzman, *Seven Days a Week: Women and Domestic Service in Industrializing America* (New York: Oxford University Press, 1978); and Fay E. Dudden, *Serving Women: Household Service in Nineteenth-Century America* (Middletown: Wesleyan University Press, 1983).

For dimensions of changes in middle-class styles of living in the late nineteenth and early twentieth centuries, see Gwendolyn Wright, *Moralism and the Model Home: Domestic Architecture and Cultural Conflict in Chicago, 1873–1913* (Chicago: University of Chicago Press, 1980). Lois Scharf, *To Work and To Wed: Female Employment, Feminism, and the Great Depression* (Westport: Greenwood, 1980), pp. 39–41 and 147–53, examines aspects of women as consumers in the 1930s. Lois Banner, *American Beauty* (New York: Alfred A. Knopf, 1983), looks at changing aesthetic and commercial patterns in fashions. Sarah Stage, *Female Complaints: Lydia Pinkham and the Business of Women's Medicine* (New York: W.W. Norton and Co., 1979), considers issues in the history women's health care.

We are only beginning to have the work we need on women's activity as consumers outside the home. Emma S. Weigley, "It Might Have Been Euthenics: The Lake Placid Conferences and the Home Economics Movement," *American Quarterly* 26 (March 1974), 79–96, treats one kind of women's leadership in efforts to educate consumers. For an example of the way that women have extended their activity as consumers into the political arena, see Allis R. Wolfe, "Women, Consumerism, and the National Consumers' League in the Progressive Era, 1900–1923," *Labor History* 16 (Summer 1975): 378–92. Judith E. Smith, "Our Own Kind: Family and Community Networks," *Radical History Review* 17 (Spring 1978): 114–15 and Paula E. Hyman, "Immigrant Women and Consumer Protest: The New York City

Kosher Meat Boycott of 1902," *American Jewish History* 70 (September 1980): 91–105 deal with collective action by women as consumers.

In *The Age of Reform, From Bryan to F.D.R.* (New York: Alfred A. Knopf, 1955), pp. 168–69, Richard Hofstadter suggested the relationship between inflation and Progressivism, a connection that generally remains unexplored. Among the few historians who have recognized the importance of rising prices in the early twentieth century are Shergold, *"American Standard,"* pp. 92–115; Hollitz, "Challenge of Abundance," pp. 103–47; Samson, "Consumer Interest," pp. 112–83; and Daniel Pope, "American Economists and the High Cost of Living: The Late Progressive Era," *Journal of the History of the Behavioral Sciences* 17 (January 1981): 75–87.

Notes

Introduction

1. Daniel Bell, *The Cultural Contradictions of Capitalism* (New York: Basic Books, 1976), pp. xi–xii and 70; Christopher Lasch, *The Culture of Narcissism: American Life in an Age of Diminishing Expectations* (New York: W.W. Norton and Co., 1978), p. 72.

2. For recent treatments of aspects of a moralist tradition, see Daniel T. Rodgers, *The Work Ethic in Industrial America, 1850–1920* (Chicago: University of Chicago Press, 1978), pp. xv and 15–16; Gwendolyn Wright, *Moralism and the Model Home: Domestic Architecture and Cultural Conflict in Chicago, 1873–1913* (Chicago: University of Chicago Press, 1980), pp. 1–2 and 5; Paul Boyer, *Urban Masses and Moral Order in America, 1820–1920* (Cambridge: Harvard University Press, 1978), pp. viii–ix.

3. In their Introduction to *The Culture of Consumption: Critical Essays in American History, 1880–1980*, ed. Richard W. Fox and T. J. Jackson Lears (New York: Pantheon Books, 1983), pp. x–xi, Fox and Lears recently stated that "the best way to proceed in investigating American consumer culture is not to focus on patterns of consumption themselves, nor to examine the lives of ordinary consumers." In contrast, most of those social historians and historical economists who have considered the American standard of living have tended to treat information in household budgets as facts, without fully acknowledging how moral and cultural perspectives influenced those who collected, categorized, and presented the information: see John Modell, "Patterns of Consumption, Acculturation, and Family Income Strategies in Late Nineteenth-Century America," in *Family and Population in Nineteenth-Century America*, ed. Tamara K. Hareven and Maris Vinovskis (Princeton: Princeton University Press, 1978), pp. 206–40; Jeffrey G. Williamson, "Consumer Behavior in the Nineteenth Century: Carroll D. Wright's Massachusetts Workers in 1875," *Explorations in Entrepreneurial History*, 2d ser., 4 (Winter 1967): 98–135. Modell acknowledges

how students of budgets offered "verbal formulation of norms" (p. 206) and Williamson notes the emphasis on "Puritan virtue" in the 1875 report (fn. 34, p. 131).

4. In Suggested Readings, I indicate the sources on which the following lengthy summary relies.

5. Among the most important studies of work are E. P. Thompson, "Time, Work-Discipline, and Industrial Capitalism," *Past and Present*, no. 38 (December 1967), pp. 56–97; Herbert G. Gutman, "Work, Culture, and Society in Industrializing America, 1815–1919," *American Historical Review* 78 (June 1973): 531–87; Rodgers, *Work Ethic*; James B. Gilbert, *Work Without Salvation: America's Intellectuals and Industrial Alienation, 1880–1910* (Baltimore: Johns Hopkins University Press, 1977).

6. Joan Thirsk, *Economic Policy and Projects: The Development of a Consumer Society in Early Modern England* (Oxford: Oxford University Press, 1978), p. 8.

7. J. H. Plumb, *The Commercialisation of Leisure in Eighteenth-Century England* (Reading, Berks.: University of Reading, 1973), p. 19.

8. Carole Shammas, "The Domestic Environment in Early Modern England and America," *Journal of Social History* 14 (Fall 1980): 17–18; Carole Shammas, "Consumer Behavior in Colonial America," *Social Science History* 6 (Winter 1982): 74.

9. Alice H. Jones, *Wealth of a Nation to Be: The American Colonies on the Eve of the Revolution* (New York: Columbia University Press, 1980), p. 300; Lois G. Carr and Lorena S. Walsh, "Changing Life Styles in Colonial St. Mary's County," *Working Papers from the Regional Economic History Research Center* 1 (1978): 110; Lois G. Carr and Lorena S. Walsh, "Inventories and the Analysis of Wealth and Consumption Patterns in St. Mary's County, Maryland, 1658–1777," *Historical Methods* 13 (Spring 1980): 96.

10. Neil McKendrick, Introduction, in Neil McKendrick, John Brewer, and J. H. Plumb, *The Birth of a Consumer Society: The Commercialization of Eighteenth-Century England* (London: Europa Publications, 1982), p. 1; Neil McKendrick, "The Consumer Revolution in Eighteenth-Century England," in ibid., pp. 9 and 11; J. H. Plumb, "The Acceptance of Modernity," in ibid., p. 316; Neil McKendrick, "Home Demand and Economic Growth: A New View of the Role of Women and Children in the Industrial Revolution," in *Historical Perspectives: Studies in English Thought and Society, in Honour of J. H. Plumb*, ed. Neil McKendrick (London: Europa Publications, 1974), p. 172.

11. Faye E. Dudden, " 'Getting Started' in Commodity Consumption," paper presented at the Seventy-fifth Annual Meeting of the Organization of American Historians, Philadelphia, 2 April 1982, p. 2.

12. The summary in this and the following paragraph relies on Lasch, *Culture of Narcissism*, pp. 7, 32, 48, and 68–74; Philip Rieff, *The Triumph of the Therapeutic: Uses of Faith After Freud* (New York: Harper & Row, 1966), pp. 2–27, 49–50, 54, and 236–49; Warren I. Susman, " 'Personality' and the Making of Twentieth-Century Culture," in *New Directions in American Intellectual History*, ed. John Higham and Paul K. Conkin (Baltimore: Johns Hopkins University Press, 1979), pp. 214–22; Elaine T. May, *Great Expectations: Marriage and Divorce in Post-Victorian America* (Chicago: University of Chicago Press, 1980), p. 58; Lary May, *Screening Out the Past: The Birth of Mass Culture and the Motion Picture Industry* (New York: Oxford University Press, 1980), pp. 98–99; T. J. Jackson Lears, *No Place of Grace: Antimodernism and the Transformation of American Culture, 1880–1920* (New York: Pantheon Books, 1981), pp. xiii–xvii, 37, 54–56, and 301–6; Fox and Lears, *Culture of Consumption*, pp. ix–xvii.

13. Fox and Lears, *Culture of Consumption*, p. xiii; Lasch, *Culture of Narcissism*, p. 7; Rieff, *Triumph of the Therapeutic*, p. 241.

14. Frank Stricker, "Affluence for Whom?—Another Look at Prosperity and the Working Classes in the 1920s," *Labor History* 24 (Winter 1983): 32.

15. Laurence Veysey, "A Postmortem on Daniel Bell's Postindustrialism," *American Quarterly* 34 (Spring 1982): 67, describes some ways in which an age of affluence did not arrive until after World War II; Winifred D. Wandersee, *Women's Work and Family Values, 1920–1940* (Cambridge: Harvard University Press, 1981), pp. 25–26, notes how new consumption patterns reinforced or made apparent traditional family values; Don S. Kirschner, *City and Country: Rural Responses to Urbanization in the 1920s* (Westport: Greenwood, 1970), pp. 232–33, and Blaine A. Brownell, "A Symbol of Modernity: Attitudes toward the Automobile in Southern Cities in the 1920s," *American Quarterly* 24 (March 1972): 44, demonstrate that in Southern, Protestant, small town and rural areas people may have been materialists in their behavior but not in their beliefs.

16. Lasch, *Culture of Narcissism*, p. 115, suggests some similar qualifications.

17. Lears, *No Place of Grace*, p. 37.

18. Ibid., p. 304; Rieff, *Triumph of the Therapeutic*, p. 249; Lasch, *Culture of Narcissism*, pp. 73–74.

Chapter 1

1. Francis Wayland, *The Elements of Political Economy* (New York: Leavitt, Lord and Co., 1837), pp. 414–15 and 431–39.

2. Ibid., pp. 415 and 436–38.

3. Ibid., p. 439.

4. Francis Wayland, *Sermons to the Churches* (New York: Sheldon, Blackman, and Co., 1858), pp. 206, 207, and 211.

5. Henry David Thoreau, *Walden; or, Life in the Woods* [1854] (New York: Modern Library, 1937), pp. 10, 63, 83, and 178. In " 'The Most Estimable Place in All the World': A Debate on Progress in Nineteenth-Century Concord," *Studies in the American Renaissance* 2 (1978): 1–15, and "Culture and Cultivation: Agriculture and Society in Thoreau's Concord," *Journal of American History* 69 (June 1982): 42–61, Robert A. Gross places Thoreau's writings in context. For an analysis of Thoreau's view of work, see John P. Diggins, "Thoreau, Marx, and the 'Riddle' of Alienation," *Social Research* 39 (Winter 1972): 571–98.

6. Thoreau, *Walden*, pp. 7, 14, and 69.

7. Ibid., pp. 4–5 and 81.

8. Ibid., p. 11; Wayland, *Political Economy*, pp. 436–37.

9. Ibid., pp. 104–05 and 439; Wayland, *Sermons*, pp. 207 and 211. I use *puritan* here to refer not to the religious group dominant in New England in the seventeenth century but to people who advocate prudential values and self-control.

10. Thoreau, *Walden*, p. 46.

11. Horace Bushnell, "Work and Play" [1848], *Work and Play; or Literary Varieties* (New York: Charles Scribner, 1864), pp. 13–15 and 38–42; Daniel W. Howe, "The Social Science of Horace Bushnell," *Journal of American History* 70 (September 1983): 309–10.

12. Alexis de Tocqueville, *Democracy in America* [1835, 1840], ed. Phillips Bradley (New York: Vintage Books, 1954), 2:136–38, 140, 144, and 145.

13. Ibid., 2:137, 140, 141, 149–51, and 154.

14. Ibid., 2:154 and 159.

15. Lyman Beecher, "Sermon LIV: The Gospel the Only Security For Eminent and Abiding National Prosperity," *National Preacher* 3 (March 1829): 147.

16. Daniel Webster, "Lecture Before the Society for the Diffusion of Useful Knowledge" [1836], *Writings and Speeches of Daniel Webster* (Boston: Little, Brown and Co., 1903), 13:66 and 74; Rush Welter, *The Mind of America, 1820–1860* (New York: Columbia University Press, 1975), pp. 113–17.

17. Tocqueville, *Democracy*, 2:140.

18. Edgar W. Martin, *The Standard of Living in 1860: American Consumption Levels on the Eve of the Civil War* (Chicago: University of Chicago Press, 1942), pp. 400–402. In Suggested Readings, I discuss other works on antebellum spending patterns.

19. Ibid., pp. 393 and 401. Prices in 1984 ranged from about six to twelve times those in the 1860s. Throughout the book, for prices between 1774 and 1967 I use Paul A. David and Peter Solar, "A Bicentenary Contribution to the History of the Cost of Living in America," in *Research in Economic History: An Annual Compilation of Research*, ed. Paul Uselding (Greenwich, Conn.: JAI, 1977), 2:16–17. For the years since 1967, I use the Consumer Price Index of the Bureau of Labor Statistics. Because long-term indexes do not easily allow for substitutions of new, less expensive items, because over time market purchases became a more significant element in budgets, and because the relation between wages and prices is so complicated, estimates of long-term price changes are only very rough approximations of reality.

20. Henry Ward Beecher, *Lectures to Young Men, on Various Important Subjects* (Salem, Mass.: John P. Jewett, 1846), p. 24; Clifford E. Clark, Jr., *Henry Ward Beecher: Spokesman for a Middle-Class America* (Urbana: University of Illinois Press, 1978), pp. 108–09.

21. Daniel W. Howe, *The Political Culture of the American Whigs* (Chicago: University of Chicago Press, 1979), p. 300; Daniel W. Howe, *The Unitarian Conscience: Harvard Moral Philosophy, 1805–1861* (Cambridge: Harvard University Press, 1970), p. 159.

Chapter 2

1. Massachusetts, Bureau of Statistics of Labor (MBSL), *Sixth Annual Report* (hereafter 6 AR) (Boston: Wright and Potter, 1875), p. 202; Jeffrey G. Williamson, "Consumer Behavior in the Nineteenth Century: Carroll D. Wright's Massachusetts Workers in 1875," *Explorations in Entrepreneurial History*, 2d ser., 4 (Winter 1967): 103. James Leiby's *Carroll Wright and Labor Reform: The Origin of Labor Statistics* (Cambridge: Harvard University Press, 1960) is an excellent biography of Wright. The Inter-university Consortium for Political and Social Research (ICPSR) has made available the data of this MBSL study in computer readable form: ICPSR #9032. ICPSR #7711 presents the statistics, originally collected by the U.S. Department of Labor between 1888 and 1890, on household budgets of 8,544 families in the United States and several Western European nations. Faith M. Williams and Carle C. Zimmerman, *Studies of Family Living in the United States and Other Countries: An Analysis of Material and Method*, U.S., Department of Agriculture, Miscellaneous Publication no. 223 (Washington, D.C.: GPO, 1935), contains summaries of 458 U.S. studies.

2. MBSL, 6 AR, p. 359.

3. Ibid., p. 441. The 1981 figures are from the U.S., Department of Labor,

Bureau of Labor Statistics, "Autumn 1981 Urban Family Budgets and Comparative Indexes for Selected Urban Areas," news release, 16 April 1982, p. 2. (Mimeographed.)

4. MBSL, 6 AR, pp. 438 and 441–45.

5. Ibid., pp. 384–85 and 435.

6. Ibid., pp. 305, 323, 434, 435, and 443.

7. Ibid., pp. 445–46.

8. For rough estimates of the distribution of family incomes in the late nineteenth century, see Charles B. Spahr, *An Essay on the Present Distribution of Wealth in the United States* (New York: Thomas Y. Crowell and Co., 1896), p. 128.

9. MBSL, 6 AR, p. 360.

10. Ibid., pp. 442 and 446–48.

11. Massachusetts, Bureau of Statistics of Labor, *Second Annual Report* (Boston: Wright and Potter, 1871), p. 549.

12. MBSL, 6 AR, pp. 447–48.

13. Roy Rosenzweig, *Eight Hours for What We Will: Workers and Leisure in an Industrial City, 1870–1920* (Cambridge: Cambridge University Press, 1983), p. 42.

14. MBSL, 6 AR, p. 434.

15. A. E. Dingle, "Drink and Working-Class Living Standards in Britain, 1870–1914," *Economic History Review*, 2d ser., 25 (November 1972): 611–12; W. J. Rorabaugh, *The Alcoholic Republic: An American Tradition* (New York: Oxford University Press, 1979), p. 233.

16. MBSL, 6 AR, pp. 434–35.

17. Massachusetts, Bureau of Statistics of Labor, *Tenth Annual Report* (Boston: Rand, Avery, and Co., 1879), p. 167; MBSL, 6 AR, p. 261; Carroll D. Wright, "Practical Elements of the Labor Question," *International Review* 12 (1882): 25–26; New Jersey, Bureau of Statistics of Labor and Industries, *First Annual Report* (Trenton: Naar, Day, and Naar, Printers, 1878), p. 47; Illinois, Bureau of Labor Statistics, *Third Biennial Report* (Springfield: H. W. Roker, 1884), p. 379.

18. U.S., Commissioner of Labor, *Sixth Annual Report* [1890] (Washington, D.C.: GPO, 1891), p. 613; Carroll D. Wright, *Outline of Practical Sociology with Special Reference to American Conditions* [1899], 2d ed., rev. (New York: Longmans, Green, and Co., 1899), p. 390; Raymond Calkins, *Substitutes for the Saloon* (Boston: Houghton Mifflin and Co., 1901), p. 25. Wright served on the Sub-Committee on the Economic Aspects of the Liquor Problem of the Committee of Fifty for the Investigation of the Liquor Problem.

19. Carroll D. Wright, "The Growth and Purposes of Bureaus of Statistics of Labor," *Journal of Social Science*, no. 25 (December 1888), p. 8.

20. For criticisms of Wright's work for lack of sympathy for those he studied, see National Convention of Officers of Bureaus of Labor Statistics in the United States, *Proceedings* (Topeka: Hall and O'Donald Litho. Co., 1891), pp. 36–37 and 45; Leiby, *Wright*, pp. 132–33; Florence Kelly Wischnewetzky, "A Decade of Retrogression," *Arena* 4 (August 1891): 368–69.

21. John Modell, "Changing Risks, Changing Adaptations: American Families in the Nineteenth and Twentieth Centuries," in *Kin and Communities: Families in America*, ed. Allan J. Lichtman and Joan R. Challinor (Washington, D.C.: Smithsonian Institution Press, 1979), p. 128.

22. John Modell, "Patterns of Consumption, Acculturation, and Family Income Strategies in Late Nineteenth-Century America," in *Family and Population in Nineteenth-Century America*, ed. Tamara K. Hareven and Maris Vinovskis (Princeton: Princeton University Press, 1978), p. 211.

23. There is no mention of expenditures for commuting or excursions; #252 reported a vacation that may not have cost money; #27 and #365 mentioned "two weeks' recreation."

24. #78, #248, #252, and #302.

25. #93, #147, #154, #166, #171, and #268.

26. #104, #131, #147, #205, #258, and #365.

27. #200; see also #259.

28. The quote is from #63; for other examples, see #41, #105, #106, #136, #256, #357, and #369.

29. #19, #136, and #143.

30. For examples, see #58 and #80.

31. #65, #68, #78, and #80.

32. #170, #235, #240, #242, #247, #251, #295, #307, #310, #311, #319, #322, #329, and #341.

33. #388.

34. #83, #92, #164, #241, #242, #246, #309, #311, #329, #345, #350, and #363. For information on the data collectors, see James Leiby, letter to author, July 1980.

35. #92.

36. #164, #194, #212, #221, #248, #284, and #308.

37. #221.

38. #171, #303, and #357.

39. #63, #136, and #257.

40. H. Gregg Lewis and Paul H. Douglas, "Studies in Consumer Expenditures (1901, 1918–19, 1922–24)," in University of Chicago, *Studies in Busi-*

ness Administration 17 (October 1947): 8–9; S. J. Prais and H. S. Houthakker, *The Analysis of Family Budgets* [1955], 2d ed., abridged (Cambridge: Cambridge University Press, 1971), pp. 36–42; Robert B. Pearl, *Methodology of Consumer Expenditure Surveys*, U.S., Bureau of Census, Working Paper no. 27 (1968), pp. 4–5 and 10–13.

41. #351; the cases are #212, #341, and #345.

42. Carroll D. Wright, "The Factory as an Element in Social Life," New England Cotton Manufacturers' Association, *Transactions*, no. 69 (October 1900), p. 82; U.S., Congress, Senate, *Report on the Chicago Strike of June–July 1894 by the United States Strike Commission*, S. Exec. Doc. 7, 53d Cong., 3d sess., 1895, pp. xix and xlviii; Carroll D. Wright, *Some Ethical Phases of the Labor Question* (Boston: American Unitarian Association, 1902), pp. 151 and 153–54; Massachusetts, Bureau of Statistics of Labor, *Eighth Annual Report* (Boston: Albert J. Wright, 1877), pp. vi–vii; Daniel Horowitz, "Genteel Observers: New England Economic Writers and Industrialization," *New England Quarterly* 48 (March 1875): 65–83.

43. Carroll D. Wright, *The Relation of Political Economy to the Labor Question* (Boston: A. Williams and Co., 1882), p. 18; Wright, *Outline of Practical Sociology*, pp. 233–34, 334, and 348; Leiby, *Wright*, p. 199.

44. U.S., Commissioner of Labor, 6 AR, pp. 688–90.

45. Modell, "Changing Risks," p. 128.

46. Cf. #53 and #306.

47. MBSL, 6 AR, p. 356.

48. Ibid., pp. 355–56 and 433; Leiby, *Wright*, p. 198.

49. Wright, *Outline of Practical Sociology*, p. 312.

50. MBSL, 6 AR, p. 202.

51. Illinois, BLS, *Third Biennial Report*; Missouri, Bureau of Labor Statistics, *Eleventh Annual Report* (Jefferson City: Tribune Printing Co., 1889).

52. For examples of reports with no descriptive comments and few evaluative ones, see U.S., Commissioner of Labor, *Seventh Annual Report* (Washington, D.C.: GPO, 1892), and U.S., Commissioner of Labor, *Eighteenth Annual Report* (Washington, D.C.: GPO, 1904).

Chapter 3

In a somewhat different form, this chapter appeared as "Consumption and Its Discontents: Simon N. Patten, Thorstein Veblen, and George Gunton," *Journal of American History* 67 (September 1980).

1. John L. Thomas, "Utopia for An Urban Age: Henry George, Henry Demarest Lloyd, and Edward Bellamy," *Perspectives in American History* 6

(1972): 136–39, 145, 148, and 152–53. For Bellamy's concerns, expressed in the 1870s, about the corrupting power of wealth, see Arthur Lipow, *Authoritarian Socialism in America: Edward Bellamy and the Nationalist Movement* (Berkeley: University of California Press, 1982), p. 41.

2. The best source of information on Patten's life is Daniel M. Fox, *The Discovery of Abundance: Simon N. Patten and the Transformation of Social Theory* (Ithaca: Cornell University Press, 1967).

3. Rexford G. Tugwell, "Notes on the Life and Work of Simon Nelson Patten," *Journal of Political Economy* 31 (April 1923): 166. Among those who see Patten's emphasis on abundance but not on restraint are T. J. Jackson Lears, *No Place of Grace: Antimodernism and the Transformation of American Culture, 1880–1920* (New York: Pantheon Books, 1981), p. 54, and Daniel T. Rodgers, *The Work Ethic in Industrial America 1850–1920* (Chicago: University of Chicago Press, 1978), p. 121. Fox, *Discovery*, p. 1, and John E. Hollitz, "The Challenge of Abundance: Reactions to the Development of a Consumer Economy, 1890–1920" (Ph.D. dissertation, University of Wisconsin-Madison, 1981), pp. 159–71, note Patten's ambivalence.

4. Simon N. Patten, *The New Basis of Civilization* (New York: Macmillan Co., 1907), pp. 155–56.

5. Simon N. Patten, *The Theory of Dynamic Economics*, University of Pennsylvania, Political Economy and Public Law Series, 3 (1892): 129–31.

6. Richard T. Ely, *An Introduction to Political Economy* (New York: Chautauqua Press, 1889), p. 154; Edward Bellamy, *Looking Backward, 2000–1887* [1888] (New York: New American Library, 1960), p. 165; Ignatius Donnelly, *Caesar's Column: A Story of the Twentieth Century* [1890] (Chicago: F.J. Schulte and Co., 1891), pp. 132 and 364; Laurence Gronlund, *The Cooperative Commonwealth in Its Outlines. An Exposition of Modern Socialism* [1884], ed. Stow Persons (Cambridge: Harvard University Press, 1965), p. 102.

7. Simon N. Patten, *The Premises of Political Economy; Being a Re-examination of Certain Fundamental Principles of Economic Science* (Philadelphia: J.B. Lippincott Co., 1885), p. 11; Patten, *Dynamic Economics*, pp. 83–84; Simon N. Patten, "Over-Nutrition and Its Social Consequences," American Academy of Political and Social Science, *Annals* 10 (July 1897): 45 and 50–51; Simon N. Patten, *The Development of English Thought: A Study in the Economic Interpretation of History* (New York: Macmillan Co., 1899), p. 382.

8. Simon N. Patten, *Heredity and Social Progress* (New York: Macmillan Co., 1903), pp. 131–39 and 205; Patten, *Dynamic Economics*, p. 153; Simon N. Patten, *The Theory of Social Forces* (Philadelphia: American Academy of Political and Social Science, 1896), pp. 84–98; Patten, "Over-Nutrition," pp. 43–51.

9. Patten, *New Basis*, pp. 4 and 9–10.

10. Ibid., pp. 43–44, 211, 213, and 215.

11. Ibid., pp. 125–38, 141, and 156.

12. Fox, *Discovery of Abundance*, pp. 105–6. I have tried to uncover evidence for a clearer picture of the connection between Patten's life and writing in this period, but to no avail: Scott Nearing, letter to author, September 1974; Rexford G. Tugwell, letter to author, 4 October 1974; and Daniel M. Fox, letter to author, 8 February 1973; *Hartford Times*, 27 May 1909.

13. Simon N. Patten, *Product and Climax* (New York: B.W. Huebsch, 1909), pp. 22, 25, 29, 52, and 58–59. "Climax" did not have a sexual meaning until 1918: R. W. Burchfield, ed., *A Supplement to the Oxford English Dictionary* (Oxford: Oxford University Press, 1972), 1:545.

14. Patten, *Product and Climax*, pp. 42–53.

15. Ibid., p. 43. For the relation between Nearing and Patten, see Stephen J. Whitfield, *Scott Nearing: Apostle of American Radicalism* (New York: Columbia University Press, 1974), pp. 8–9; Scott Nearing, *Educational Frontiers: A Book About Simon Nelson Patten and Other Teachers* (New York: Thomas Seltzer, 1925), pp. x and 7–56; Scott Nearing, *The Making of a Radical: A Political Autobiography* (New York: Harper & Row, 1972), pp. 19–26. For the Nearings' reliance on Thoreau, see Helen Nearing and Scott Nearing, *Living the Good Life: How to Live Sanely and Safely in a Troubled World* [1954] (New York: Schocken Books, 1970), pp. 46 and 108.

16. Patten, *Product and Climax*, pp. 23–24, 30, and 137.

17. Ibid., p. 13.

18. Rodgers, *Work Ethic*, p. 99.

19. Simon N. Patten, *The Reconstruction of Economic Theory* (Philadelphia: American Academy of Political and Social Science, 1912), p. 94; Simon N. Patten, "Extravagance as a Virtue," *Current Opinion* 54 (January 1913): 51–52; Simon N. Patten, *Mud Hollow; From Dust to Soul* (Philadelphia: Dorrance, 1922), p. 382.

20. Most observers see Veblen as a critic of traditional economics without also noticing the ways in which he used its terms to attack it. For important exceptions, see T. W. Adorno, "Veblen's Attack on Culture: Remarks Occasioned by the Theory of the Leisure Class," *Studies in Philosophy and Social Science* 9 (1941): 389–413; Hollitz, "Challenge of Abundance," pp. 15–16; Lears, *No Place of Grace*, p. 28. For information on Veblen's life and thought, see Joseph Dorfman, *Thorstein Veblen and His America* (New York: Viking Press, 1934); David Riesman, *Thorstein Veblen: A Critical Interpretation* (New York: Charles Scribner's Sons, 1953); and John P. Diggins, *The Bard of Savagery: Thorstein Veblen and Modern Social Theory* (New York: Seabury Press, 1978).

21. Thorstein Veblen, *The Theory of the Leisure Class: An Economic Study in the Evolution of Institutions* [1899] (New York: New American Library, 1953), p. 208.

22. Ibid., pp. 41–60; Thorstein Veblen, "Industrial and Pecuniary Employments" [1900], *The Place of Science in Modern Civilisation and Other Essays* (New York: B.W. Huebsch, 1919), pp. 318–19 and 321.

23. Veblen, *Leisure Class*, pp. 134 and 141.

24. Ibid., pp. 35, 46, 86, 106, and 216–34; Thorstein Veblen, *The Theory of Business Enterprise* [1904] (New York: New American Library, 1958), pp. 122 and 179; Thorstein Veblen, *Imperial Germany and the Industrial Revolution* (New York: Macmillan Co., 1915), p. 236.

25. Arthur K. Davis, "Veblen on the Decline of the Protestant Ethic," *Social Forces* 22 (March 1944): 282–86.

26. Veblen, *Leisure Class*, p. 29; Thorstein Veblen, *The Instinct of Workmanship and the State of the Industrial Arts* [1914] (New York: Augustus M. Kelley, Bookseller, 1964), p. 228.

27. Veblen, *Leisure Class*, p. 85; Thorstein Veblen, *The Engineers and the Price System* [1921] (New York: Viking, 1934), p. 121.

28. Veblen, *Engineers*, pp. 134 and 142; Thorstein Veblen, "Some Neglected Points in the Theory of Socialism" [1892], *Place*, p. 399. Thorstein Veblen, *The Higher Learning in America: A Memorandum on the Conduct of Universities by Business Men* [1918] (New York: Sagamore Press, 1957), pp. 2–3, did hold out for activities that, if untainted, were admirable.

29. Veblen, *Leisure Class*, pp. 149–52, 154, and 217; Thorstein Veblen, "Christian Morals and the Competitive System" [1910], *Essays in Our Changing Order* [1934], ed. Leon Ardzrooni (New York: Augustus M. Kelley, Bookseller, 1964), pp. 214–18; Veblen, *Business Enterprise*, pp. 154 and 176; Veblen, *Instinct*, pp. 318–20.

30. Riesman, *Veblen*, pp. 22, 145, and 179–82; Isador Lubin, "Reflections on Veblen," in *Thorstein Veblen: The Carleton College Veblen Seminar Essays*, ed. Carlton C. Qualey (New York: Columbia University Press, 1968), p. 133.

31. [George Gunton], review of "The Economic Causes of Moral Progress," by Simon N. Patten, in *Social Economist* 4 (January 1893): 56; [George Gunton], review of *Theory of Social Forces*, by Simon N. Patten, in *Gunton's Magazine* 10 (March 1896): 203; [George Gunton], review of "Some Neglected Points in the Theory of Socialism," by Thorstein Veblen, in *Social Economist* 2 (November 1891): 62. I have attributed unsigned articles in *Gunton's Magazine* and *Social Economist* to Gunton because of their style and content. For confirmation of this judgment, see [George Gunton],

"Position of Gunton's Magazine," *Gunton's Magazine* 13 (November 1897): 362–66.

32. Ira Steward, untitled fragment, Ira Steward Papers, State Historical Society of Wisconsin; Ira Steward, "Economy and Extravagance," Steward Papers, p. 10. Pagination and titles of items from the Steward Papers refer to typescript copies. For a brief biography, see Dorothy W. Douglas, "Ira Steward," *DAB*, 18:1–2.

33. John T. Cumbler, *Working-Class Community in Industrial America: Work, Leisure, and Struggle in Two Industrial Cities, 1880–1930* (Westport: Greenwood, 1979), p. 151. For information on Gunton's life, see Davis R. Dewey, "George Gunton," *DAB*, 8:55–56; Daniel C. Weary, "George Gunton: Advocate of Labor, Defender of Trusts, Social Darwinian" (unpublished honors thesis, Harvard University, 1949).

34. George Gunton to Edwin R. A. Seligman, 8 December 1886 and 11 March 1889, Seligman Papers, Low Library, Columbia University; Allan Nevins, *John D. Rockefeller: The Heroic Age of American Enterprise* (New York: Charles Scribner's Sons, 1940), 2:141–42 and 340; Weary, "Gunton," pp. 33–34 and appendix A (unbound clippings).

35. George Gunton to Parke Godwin, 2 September 1885 and 19 September 1885, Bryant-Godwin Collection, Rare Books and Manuscripts Division, New York Public Library, Astor, Lenox and Tilden Foundations; George Gunton, *Wealth and Progress: A Critical Examination of the Labor Problem* (New York: D. Appleton and Co., 1887), dedication; John R. Wennersten, "Parke Godwin, Utopian Socialism, and the Politics of Antislavery," *New-York Historical Society Quarterly* 60 (July–October 1976): 107–27.

36. George Gunton to Theodore Roosevelt, 1 April 1901, Roosevelt Papers, Library of Congress.

37. Gunton, *Wealth*, pp. 30, 33, 88–89, and 93.

38. Ibid., pp. 94, 189, 201–02, 232–34, 260, 366, 374, and 375; George Gunton, *Principles of Social Economics, Inductively Considered and Practically Applied, with Criticisms on Current Theories* (New York: G.P. Putnam's Sons, 1891), pp. 213–14; George Gunton, *The Economic and Social Importance of the Eight-Hour Movement* (New York: American Federation of Labor, 1889), pp. 22–24.

39. Gunton, *Economic and Social Importance*, pp. 3, 5, and 11–12; Gunton, *Principles*, p. 21; [George Gunton], "Individualism," *Social Economist* 1 (April 1891): 77.

40. Ira Steward, "Less Hours," Steward Papers, p. 9; Ira Steward, "Poverty," in Massachusetts, Bureau of Statistics of Labor, *Fourth Annual Report*

(Boston: Wright and Potter, 1873), pp. 425–26; Ira Steward, "The Eight-Hour Movement," *Labor Standard*, 19 May 1887, p. 2.

41. [George Gunton], "The Opening of Biltmore," *Gunton's Magazine* 10 (January 1896): 34–35; Gunton, *Principles*, pp. 31 and 44; [George Gunton], "Public Effect of Great Fortunes," *Social Economist* 8 (May 1895): 276–77; [George Gunton], "Philosophy of Immigration," *Social Economist* 4 (April 1893): 199.

42. *New York Times*, 13 September 1919, p. 11.

43. For information on others like Gunton, see Charlotte Erickson, *Invisible Immigrants* (Coral Gables: University of Miami Press, 1972), pp. 236–39.

44. Rowland T. Berthoff, *British Immigrants in Industrial America* (Cambridge: Harvard University Press, 1953), pp. 97, 105–6, and 125–28; Gerald N. Grob, *Workers and Utopia: A Study of Ideological Conflict in the American Labor Movement, 1865–1900* (Evanston: Northwestern University Press, 1961), pp. vii and 188; David Montgomery, *Beyond Equality: Labor and the Radical Republicans, 1862–1872* (New York: Alfred A. Knopf, 1967), pp. 208, 215, and 228.

45. Paul Faler, "Cultural Aspects of the Industrial Revolution: Lynn, Massachusetts, Shoemakers and Industrial Morality, 1826–1860," *Labor History* 15 (Summer 1974): 391–94; Bruce Laurie, " 'Nothing on Compulsion': Life Styles of Philadelphia Artisans, 1820–1850," *Labor History* 15 (Summer 1974): 354–66.

46. Rodgers, *Work Ethic*, p. 155; E. P. Thompson, "Time, Work-Discipline, and Industrial Capitalism," *Past and Present*, no. 38 (December 1967), p. 85; I am grateful to Steven Ross for showing me a copy of "Preamble and Declaration of Principles of the [Cincinatti] Central Labor Councils," *Chronicle* 1 (February 1892): 2, which provides evidence of labor's shift in interest from production to consumption.

47. Irwin Yellowitz, *Industrialization and the American Labor Movement, 1850–1900* (Port Washington, N.Y.: Kennikat Press, 1977), pp. 7, 37, and 42.

48. [Gunton], "Individualism," p. 77; Gunton, *Principles*, p. 322; Emerson P. Harris, "The Economics of Advertising," *Social Economist* 4 (March 1893): 171–74.

49. For a discussion of Gunton's lack of influence, see Daniel Horowitz, "Consumption and Its Discontents: Simon N. Patten, Thorstein Veblen, and George Gunton," *Journal of American History* 67 (September 1980): 315–16. On Patten's impact, see Fox, *Discovery of Abundance*, pp. 154–78; Martin Meyerson and Dilys P. Winegrad, *Gladly Learn and Gladly Teach: Franklin and His Heirs at the University of Pennsylvania, 1740–1976* (Philadel-

phia: University of Pennsylvania Press, 1978), pp. 145–55; Rexford G. Tugwell, *To the Lesser Heights of Morningside: A Memoir* (Philadelphia: University of Pennsylvania Press, 1982), pp. 43–45, 47–49, 130–38, 154–55, and 157.

50. For an attempt to understand the implications of Veblen's argument for advertising, see Adorno, "Veblen's Attack," pp. 393–94. Thorstein Veblen, *Absentee Ownership and Business Enterprise in Recent Times: The Case of America* (New York: B.W. Huebsch, 1923), pp. 284–325, discusses advertising.

Chapter 4

1. For reviews of Chapin's book, see T. I. Riley in *American Journal of Sociology* 15 (September 1909): 268–74; Henry R. Mussey in *Survey* 22 (24 April 1909): 147–48; William B. Bailey in *Yale Review* 18 (November 1909): 325–29; Marian Talbott in *Journal of Political Economy* 17 (October 1909): 541–43. Chapin's study remained a respected and standard work for some time: see U.S., National War Labor Board, *Memorandum on the Minimum Wage and Increased Cost of Living* (Washington, D.C.: GPO, 1918), p. 10. For biographical information, see Edward D. Eaton, "Aaron Lucius Chapin," *DAB*, 4:12–13; *Who Was Who in America* (Chicago: Marquis—Who's Who, 1966), 1:212.

2. Robert C. Chapin, *The Standard of Living Among Workingmen's Families in New York City* (New York: Charities Publication Committee, 1909), pp. 28–29.

3. Ibid., pp. 40, 44–52, and 55.

4. Ibid., pp. 55–58.

5. Ibid., pp. 70, 75–84, 111, 123, 125, 127, and 168.

6. Ibid., pp. 70, 185, 193, 194, and 197.

7. Ibid., pp. 199–201 and 206–8.

8. Ibid., pp. 210–11.

9. Ibid., pp. 211–15.

10. Ibid., pp. 219–22.

11. Ibid., pp. 31, 133–34, 198, and 221.

12. Ibid., p. 198.

13. Ibid., pp. 229–32 and 247.

14. Ibid., pp. 232, 234, 240, and 246.

15. Ibid., pp. 248–49.

16. Ibid., p. xiii.

17. George E. Bevans, *How Workingmen Spend Their Spare Time* (New

York: n.p., 1913), pp. 5 and 10–11. John C. Kennedy et al., *Wages and Family Budgets in the Chicago Stockyards District, with Wage Statistics From Other Industries Employing Unskilled Labor* (Chicago: University of Chicago Press, 1914) was one of the first studies to rely on members of the group under consideration to do the interviewing. John McClymer, *War and Welfare: Social Engineering in America, 1890–1925* (Westport: Greenwood, 1980), pp. 50–64, notes the tension between sponsors and experts in one investigation.

18. Bevans, *How Workingmen Spend*, p. 10. Chapin, *Standard of Living*, p. xiii, lists the people who oversaw his work.

19. Frank Tucker, "Report of the Committee on Standard of Living," in Chapin, *Standard of Living*, p. 261; John A. Ryan, *A Living Wage: Its Ethical and Economic Aspects* (New York: Macmillan Co., 1906), pp. 117, 123, and 132; Chapin, *Standard of Living*, pp. 54–60 and 229–39. On changes in definition of poverty levels, see Oscar Ornati, *Poverty Amid Affluence* (New York: Twentieth Century Fund, 1966), pp. 11–13.

20. Sue A. Clark and Edith Wyatt, *Making Both Ends Meet: The Income and Outlay of New York City Working Girls* (New York: Macmillan Co., 1911), p. 23.

21. Robert Hunter, *Poverty* [1904], ed. Peter d'A. Jones (New York: Harper & Row, 1965), p. 7; Robert C. Chapin, "Wages and the Cost of Living," *Survey* 24 (3 September 1910): 810; Talbot, review, p. 542.

22. Naomi Aronson, "Social Definitions of Entitlement: Food Needs, 1885–1920," *Media, Culture and Society* 4 (January 1982): 54–56. In *Poverty*, Hunter tried to determine what percentage of families reached a given standard but this was not an issue generally pursued before 1917. In "Pay Envelope and Market Basket," *Survey* 30 (26 July 1913): 544–45, Scott Nearing, one of the few radicals to work on household budgets, juxtaposed cost of living and income distribution figures for Fall River, Massachusetts.

23. Margaret F. Byington, "Some Unconsidered Elements in Household Expenditures," American Academy of Political and Social Science, *Annals* 48 (July 1913): 112. There are some important exceptions to the lack of consideration of the effects of a low income on successive generations: see, for example, Hunter, *Poverty*, p. xxv.

24. Chapin, *Standard of Living*, pp. 211 and 222.

25. Louise B. More, *Wage-Earners' Budgets: A Study of Standards and Cost of Living in New York City* (New York: Henry Holt and Co., 1907), pp. 168, 170, 171, and 175–80.

26. Charles P. Neill, "The Standard of Living," *Charities* 14 (22 July 1905): 942; Frank A. Streightoff, *The Standard of Living Among the Industrial People of America* (Boston: Houghton Mifflin Co., 1911), p. 113.

27. Kennedy, *Wage and Family Budgets*, p. 76; Margaret F. Byington,

Homestead: The Households of a Mill Town (New York: Charities Publication Committee, 1910), p. 106; Clark and Wyatt, *Making Both Ends Meet*, p. 10.

28. More, *Wage-Earners' Budgets*, p. 46.

29. Clark and Wyatt, *Making Both Ends Meet*, p. 21; picture in Byington, *Homestead*, facing p. 22; Hunter, *Poverty*, pp. 194 and 220; Lawrence A. Finfer, "Leisure and Social Work in the Urban Community: The Progressive Recreation Movement, 1890–1920" (Ph.D. dissertation, Michigan State University, 1974), p. 104.

30. Mary K. Simkhovitch, *The City Worker's World in America* (New York: Macmillan Co., 1917), pp. 52 and 109–10; Peter Roberts, "Immigrant Wage-Earners," in *Wage-Earning Pittsburgh*, ed. Paul U. Kellogg (New York: Survey Associates, 1914), p. 50.

31. The quote is from Simkhovitch, *City Worker's World*, p. 111. For other reactions to movies, see ibid., pp. 110–11 and 122–24; Byington, *Homestead*, pp. 111–12; Roberts, "Immigrant Wage-Earners," p. 50; Chapin, *Standard of Living*, p. 211; Louise M. Bosworth, *The Living Wage of Women Workers: A Study of Incomes and Expenditures of Four Hundred and Fifty Women Workers in the City of Boston* (Philadelphia: American Academy of Political and Social Science, 1911), pp. 85–87; Elizabeth B. Butler, *Women and the Trades: Pittsburgh, 1907–1908* (New York: Charities Publication Committee, 1909), p. 333.

32. Robert Sklar, *Movie-Made America: A Cultural History of American Movies* (New York: Random House, 1975), pp. 18–19.

33. Bosworth, *Living Wage of Women Workers*, p. 85; Bevans, *How Workingmen Spend*, p. 11. For one of the few pictures of the striving consumer, see Streightoff, *Standard of Living*, pp. 2–4.

34. Butler, *Women and the Trades*, p. 333; Robert C. Chapin, "The Influence of Income on Standards of Life," *American Journal of Sociology* 14 (March 1909): 647; Chapin, *Standard of Living*, p. 198; Streightoff, *Standard of Living*, pp. 5, 6, 8, 164, and 177.

35. Chapin, *Standard of Living*, p. 198; Byington, *Homestead*, pp. 149 and 151.

36. Simkhovitch, *City Worker's World*, pp. 108, 112, 118, 119, and 123–24.

37. Ibid., pp. 112–15.

38. More, *Wage-Earners' Budgets*, p. 66; Scott Nearing, "Wages and Salaries in Organized Industry," *Popular Science Monthly* 86 (May 1915): 503; Byington, *Homestead*, p. 106; Mussey, review, p. 148.

39. Bosworth, *Living Wage of Women Workers*, pp. 66 and 87.

40. Paul Boyer, *Urban Masses and Moral Order in America, 1820–1920* (Cambridge: Harvard University Press, 1978), p. 61.

Chapter 5

1. F. P. Dunne, "Mr. Dooley on the Cost of Living," *American Magazine* 69 (January 1910): 327.

2. Paul A. David and Peter Solar, "A Bicentenary Contribution to the History of the Cost of Living in America," in *Research in Economic History: An Annual Compilation of Research*, ed. Paul Uselding (Greenwich, Conn.: JAI, 1977), 2:16.

3. Jeffrey G. Williamson, "The Sources of American Inequality, 1896–1948," *Review of Economics and Statistics* 58 (November 1976): 387–89; Jeffrey G. Williamson, "American Prices and Urban Inequality Since 1820," *Journal of Economic History* 36 (June 1976): 321; Paul H. Douglas, *Real Wages in the United States, 1890–1926* (Boston: Houghton Mifflin Co., 1930), pp. 191–203 and 358–88; Albert Rees, *Real Wages in Manufacturing, 1890–1914* (Princeton: Princeton University Press, 1961), p. 121; Stanley Lebergott, *Manpower in Economic Growth: The American Record Since 1800* (New York: McGraw-Hill Book Co., 1964), p. 524.

4. See Suggested Readings for the sources on which this discussion of class draws.

5. "The Rise in the Cost of Living," *American Magazine* 64 (September 1907): 554–56.

6. Elaine T. May, *Great Expectations: Marriage and Divorce in Post-Victorian America* (Chicago: University of Chicago Press, 1980), pp. 137–55.

7. A University Professor, "The Cost of Living to a University Professor," *World To-Day* 21 (September 1911): 1073.

8. Nellie M. S. Nearing and Scott Nearing, "Four Great Things a Woman Does at Home That Make Her the Greatest Power in America Today," *Ladies' Home Journal* 29 (May 1912): 12; "What Companion Readers Think About the Cost of Living," *Woman's Home Companion* 38 (September 1911): 4; Wesley C. Mitchell, "The Backward Art of Spending Money," *American Economic Review* 2 (June 1912): 271, 272, and 279.

9. The best example of these impulses is the Housewives League: Mrs. Julian Heath, "Work of the Housewives League," American Academy of Political and Social Science, *Annals* 48 (July 1913): 122; Anna S. Richardson, " 'You Seem to Know:' The Story of a Woman Who Started Things," *Woman's Home Companion* 40 (February 1913): 4.

10. Williamson, "Sources," pp. 387–97; Williamson, "American Prices," pp. 303–33; and Jeffrey G. Williamson, " 'Strategic' Wage Goods, Prices, and Inequality," *American Economic Review* 67 (March 1977): 29–41; Jeffrey G. Williamson and Peter H. Lindert, *American Inequality: A Macroeconomic History* (New York: Academic Press, 1980), pp. 77, 78, 81, and 132.

11. The Man, "The Most for My Money," *Good Housekeeping* 50 (February 1910): 247. John M. Leeds, *The Household Budget: With a Special Inquiry into the Amount and Value of Household Work* (Philadelphia: John B. Leeds, 1917), applied to middle-class budgets the techniques normally used for working-class ones.

12. Martha B. Bruère, "Experiments in Spending: The Budgets of a California School-Teacher and a Massachusetts Clergyman," *Woman's Home Companion* 38 (November 1911): 14.

13. Maria Parola, "How We Live on $1,000 a Year or Less," *Ladies' Home Journal* 21 (November 1904): 34.

14. "The Increase in Household Expenditures," *Harper's Bazar* 40 (August 1906): 754 and 40 (October 1906): 954.

15. "The Slighting of the Middle Class," *Harper's Weekly* 46 (15 February 1902): 197.

16. Elizabeth Hewes, "Some Dangers From High Prices: A Document on the Cost of Living," *American Magazine* 69 (January 1910): 346–47; Simon N. Patten, "The Crisis in American Home Life," *Independent* 68 (17 February 1910): 344.

17. "A Concrete Illustration Showing How the Cost of Living Greatly Exceeds the Increase of Wages," *Arena* 37 (May 1907): 534.

18. Walter G. Clark, "Why Should the Cost of Living Increase? A Survey and Analysis of the Assigned Causes," *American Review of Reviews* 41 (February 1910): 183–89; Irving Fisher, "An International Commission on the Cost of Living," *American Economic Review Supplement* 2 (March 1912): 92–101.

19. Byron Holt, "The Tariff and the Cost of Living," *Independent* 61 (24 February 1910): 392–95; George D. Mumford, "When Will the High Cost of Living Reach Its Climax?" *New York Times*, 9 February 1913, sec. 6, p. 12; Fisher, "International Commission," pp. 92–101; J. Laurence Laughlin, "The Increased Cost of Living," *Scribner's Monthly* 47 (May 1910): 539–50; "Symposium: The Problem of Subsistence," *Cosmopolitan* 49 (June 1910): 21–42; "Symposium: Pinching the Pocketbook," *Cosmopolitan* 49 (July 1910): 165–72; David S. Jordan, "Taxing the Cost of Living," *World's Work* 25 (January 1913): 302–10.

20. Frederic C. Howe, *The High Cost of Living* (New York: Charles Scribner's Sons, 1917), pp. 13 and 157; "Making War on the Middleman and the High Cost of Living," *Current Literature* 52 (March 1912): 289–92; Hutchins Hapgood, "The Real Underdog," *Cosmopolitan* 49 (July 1910): 165–67.

21. Peter Crispell, "The Cost of Advertising," *Independent* 68 (14 April 1910): 799; Herbert W. Hess, "Advertising and the High Cost of Living,"

American Academy of Political and Social Science, *Annals* 48 (July 1913): 239.

22. S. R. Guggenheim, "Extravagance the Real Cause," *Cosmopolitan* 49 (June 1910): 35; Henry S. Williams, "Willful Waste—Willful Want," *World To-Day* 21 (February 1912): 1781; Laughlin, "Increased Cost," pp. 549–50; Mrs. Julian Heath, "How Housewives Waste Money," *Ladies' Home Journal* 30 (February 1913): 73.

23. "The Pinch of Extravagance," *Century* 80 (October 1910): 958; "The High Cost of Living Versus the Cost of High Living," *Woman's Home Companion* 38 (May 1911): 17–18. Daniel Pope, "American Economists and the High Cost of Living: The Late Progressive Era," *Journal of the History of the Behavioral Sciences* 17 (1981): 75–87, astutely analyzes these and other aspects of the response to inflation.

24. "High Cost of Living or Cost of High Living—Which," *Current Literature* 53 (July 1912): 45; Williams, "Willful Waste," p. 1781; George K. Holmes, quoted in "Fallacies as to the High Cost of Living," *Literary Digest* 44 (24 February 1912): 400.

25. Fabian Franklin, *Cost of Living* (Garden City: Doubleday, Page and Co., 1915), pp. v, 30–31, and 158–59.

26. Simon N. Patten, "Crisis in American Home Life," pp. 342–45; Simon N. Patten, "The Standardization of Family Life," American Academy of Political and Social Science, *Annals* 48 (July 1913): 81, 85, and 88.

27. Patten, *Reconstruction*, pp. 61–62 and 66.

28. Ibid., p. 66; Patten, "Crisis in American Home Life," p. 345; Patten, "Standardization," pp. 88–89.

29. Patten, *Reconstruction*, pp. 92 and 94; Patten, "Crisis in American Home Life," pp. 345–46; Patten, "Standardization," p. 88.

30. John L. Payne, "Has the Cost of Living Increased?" *Ladies' Home Journal* 23 (October 1906): 30; "The Cost of Raising a Family," *American Magazine* 65 (April 1908): 652; William Jennings Bryan, "The First Rule for a Husband and a Wife," *Ladies' Home Journal* 24 (October 1907): 13.

31. "The Discouragement of Thrift," *Independent* 68 (30 June 1910): 1456.

32. John M. Osikson, "Boosting the Thrift Idea," *Colliers* 53 (4 April 1914): 22 and 24; Leeds, *Household Budget*, p. 153.

33. Louis A. Lamb, from an article in *Investments*, quoted in "The Root of the Trouble—Going Too Far 'On Tick'" *Literary Digest* 47 (4 October 1913): 603–4.

34. Osikson, "Boosting," p. 22.

35. Ellen H. Richards, "Who Is to Blame for the High Prices? Why Women Are to Blame," *Ladies' Home Journal* 27 (1 December 1910): 23 and 42.

36. For biographical information, see Janet W. James, "Ellen Henrietta Swallow Richards," *Notable American Women 1607–1950: A Biographical Dictionary* (Cambridge: Harvard University Press, 1971), 3:143–46. For evidence that Richards' style of living was not as strict as her advice, see Caroline L. Hunt, *The Life of Ellen H. Richards, 1842–1911* [1912] (Washington, D.C.: American Home Economics Association, 1958), pp. 62–65.

37. Kathryn K. Sklar, *Catharine Beecher: A Study in American Domesticity* (New Haven: Yale University Press, 1973), pp. xi–xii and 151–67.

38. James, "Richards," 145.

39. Ellen H. Richards, *The Cost of Living as Modified by Sanitary Science* [1899], 3rd ed., enlarged (New York: John Wiley and Sons, 1910), pp. iii, 3, and 140.

40. Ibid., pp. iv–v.

41. Ibid., pp. 133–35.

42. Ibid., pp. 13 and 17.

43. Ibid., pp. 34 and 39.

44. Ibid., pp. 38–40.

45. Ibid., pp. 37, 54, 56, 59, and 68.

46. Ibid., pp. 63, 65, 66, 71, 77, and 83–85.

47. Ibid., pp. 97–98.

48. Ibid., pp. 12, 31, and 127.

49. Ibid., pp. 123, 124, and 126.

50. Ibid., pp. 127–29.

51. Ellen Richards, *The Cost of Living as Modified by Sanitary Science* (New York: John Wiley and Sons, 1899), p. 95.

Chapter 6

1. For two strong defenses of comfort by professional women, see Lucy M. Salmon, "The Economics of Spending," *Outlook* 91 (17 April 1909): 884–85; Lucy M. Salmon, "On Economy," *Good Housekeeping* 52 (January 1911): 98 and 100.

2. William F. Dix, "Is the Cost of Living Really Increasing?" *Independent* 73 (31 October 1912): 1009.

3. Ira S. Wile, "Standards of Living," *Journal of Home Economics* 5 (December 1913): 410; Helen L. Johnson, "Family Finances Fully Explained," *Ladies' Home Journal* 33 (January 1916): 40; "The Increase in Household Expenses," *Harper's Bazar* 40 (December 1906): 1161–162.

4. Johnson, "Family Finances," p. 40; Helen Landon, "Where Shall We Economize?" *Harper's Bazar* 41 (March 1907): 289.

5. For biographical information, see Eva E. vom Baur, "Mrs. Bruère—Modern Housekeeper," *Good Housekeeping* 58 (March 1914): 385–86; *New York Times*, 11 August 1953, p. 27; Joanne Shafer to author, 4 March 1983; Ruth Halloran to author, 18 March 1983.

6. Michael B. Miller, *The Bon Marché: Bourgeois Culture and the Department Store, 1869–1920* (Princeton: Princeton University Press, 1981), pp. 4–5, 165, 169, 178–79, and 237.

7. Martha B. Bruère and Robert W. Bruère, *Increasing Home Efficiency* (New York: Macmillan Co., 1912), pp. 3, 7, 8, and 18; Martha B. Bruère, "First Aid to the Home Budget-Maker," *Outlook* 102 (21 September 1912): 122.

8. Bruère, "First Aid," 122; Bruères, *Home Efficiency*, p. 85; Martha B. Bruère, "Utilization of the Family Income," American Academy of Political and Social Science, *Annals* 48 (July 1913): 119–20; Martha B. Bruère, "Experiments in Spending: How Two Families in the Middle West Distributed Their Incomes," *Woman's Home Companion* 38 (October 1911): 6.

9. Martha B. Bruère, "What Is the Home For?" *Outlook* 99 (16 December 1911): 911–12.

10. Ibid., pp. 912–13.

11. Ibid., p. 913.

12. Ibid.

13. Martha B. Bruère, "Experiments in Spending: The Budgets of a California School-Teacher and a Massachusetts Clergyman," *Woman's Home Companion* 38 (November 1911): 14.

14. Ibid.

15. Ibid.

16. Bruères, *Home Efficiency*, pp. 82 and 85–86.

17. Ibid., pp. 86–87.

18. Bruères, *Home Efficiency*, pp. 25–29 and 86–87; Bruère, "Utilization," p. 119.

19. Bruères, *Home Efficiency*, pp. 82, 83, and 88–89.

20. Ibid., pp. 83 and 88–90.

21. Ibid., pp. 90–92.

22. Ibid., pp. 83 and 90.

23. Ibid., pp. 92–93.

24. Bruère, "What Is the Home For?" pp. 911–12.

25. Bruère, "Experiments" (November 1911), pp. 14 and 80.

26. Martha B. Bruère, "Savings or Efficiency?" *Outlook* 100 (27 January

1912): 192; Bruères, *Home Efficiency*, pp. 22, 263, and 284; Bruère, "Utilization," p. 120.

27. Bruères, *Home Efficiency*, p. 4.

28. Ibid., p. 292; Bruère, "Utilization," p. 120.

29. Bruères, *Home Efficiency*, pp. 9, 47, and 88; Bruère, "First Aid," p. 126; Bruère, "What Is The Home For?" p. 912; Bruère, "Utilization," p. 117.

30. Bruères, *Home Efficiency*, pp. 278 and 235; Martha B. Bruère, "The Cost of Children," *Outlook* 100 (10 February 1912): 324.

31. Bruères, *Home Efficiency*, pp. 36–37, 43, and 88.

32. I. M. Rubinow, "Working Women's Extravagance," *Outlook* 84 (1 December 1906): 848. For changes in notions of scientific nutrition, see Naomi Aronson, "Social Definitions of Entitlement: Food Needs, 1885–1920," *Media, Culture and Society* 4 (January 1982): 54–59.

33. Margaret F. Byington, "Some Unconsidered Elements in Household Expenditure," American Academy of Political and Social Science, *Annals* 48 (July 1913): 112, 115, and 116.

34. John A. Fitch, *The Steel Workers* (New York: Charities Publication Committee, 1910), p. 161; Arthur B. Reeve, "The Standard of Decent Living," *Independent* 63 (29 August 1907): 501; Joseph Jacobs, "The Middle American," *American Magazine* 63 (March 1907): 526; Alvin S. Johnson, "Influences Affecting the Development of Thrift," *Political Science Quarterly* 22 (June 1907): 224 and 239–40.

35. Bruère, "Utilization," p. 117.

36. Robert C. Chapin, *The Standard of Living Among Workingmen's Families in New York City* (New York: Charities Publication Committee, 1909), p. 70; Bruères, *Home Efficiency*, p. 83.

37. Chapin, *Standard of Living*, p. 246.

38. "How Other Folks Live," *Ladies' Home Journal* 30 (January 1913): 41 and (February 1913): 74.

39. "The Increase in Household Expenses," *Harper's Bazar* 40 (August 1906): 754–55.

40. Bruère, "Utilization," p. 119.

41. "The Root of the Trouble—Going Too Far 'On Tick' " *Literary Digest* 47 (4 October 1913): 603; "Fallacies as to the High Cost of Living," *Literary Digest* 44 (24 February 1912): 400–402; Simon N. Patten, "The Crisis in American Home Life," *Independent* 68 (17 February 1910): 342–46.

42. For evidence that the middle class of a later period defined itself in terms of occupation, income, and education, but not by "a spirit of unproductive consumerism," see Marcus K. Felson, "Conspicuous Consumption and the Swelling of the Middle Class in America" (Ph.D. dissertation, University of Michigan, 1973), p. 180.

Chapter 7

1. Paul A. David and Peter Solar, "A Bicentenary Contribution to the History of the Cost of Living in America," in *Research in Economic History: An Annual Compilation of Research*, ed. Paul Uselding (Greenwich, Conn.: JAI, 1977), 2:16.
2. Fabian Franklin, "Gains and Losses Caused by Rising Prices," American Academy of Political and Social Science, *Annals* 89 (May 1920): 1–7.
3. Royal Meeker and Dorothea Kittredge, "Analysis of Some Effects of Increased Cost of Living on Family Budgets," *Monthly Labor Review* 11 (July 1920): 1–2.
4. Jeffrey G. Williamson, "American Prices and Urban Inequality Since 1820," *Journal of Economic History* 36 (June 1976): 325–26; Jeffrey G. Williamson and Peter H. Lindert, *American Inequality: A Macroeconomic History* (New York: Academic Press, 1980), pp. 77–79, 81, and 132; Franklin, "Gains and Losses," p. 1. For additional information on incomes in the period, see Frank Stricker, "The Wages of Inflation: Workers' Earnings in the World War I Era," *Mid-America* 63 (April–July 1981): 93–105.
5. Stuart Chase, "Budget Building," *Good Housekeeping* 62 (April 1916): 508–15.
6. Stuart Chase, "A Budget for Three," *Good Housekeeping* 64 (May 1917): 124–26.
7. Stuart Chase, "A War Budget for the Household," *Independent* 91 (4 August 1917): 169–70. Chase eliminated from the 1917 figures expenses for a maid because they were not also incurred for the previous year.
8. Ibid., p. 169.
9. Ibid., pp. 169–70.
10. Ibid., p. 170.
11. For a dramatic example of wartime, voluntary self-restraint, see "Making a 'Splurge' to Impress the Neighbors," *American Magazine* 86 (August 1918): 30–32 and 79.
12. C. W. Taber, *The Business of the Household* (Philadelphia: J.B. Lippincott Co., 1918), p. 96; Senator McCumber, quoted in "Moral Dangers Resulting From Our 'Orgy of Opulence,'" *Current Opinion* 62 (April 1917): 267.
13. Theodore H. Price, "The War-Induced Economy," *Outlook* 110 (25 August 1915): 1003; Christine Frederick, "Economical Housekeeping as a War Measure," *Touchstone* 2 (February 1918): 435–39; E. S. Martin, "The Great World Movie: My Country 'Tis of Thee!" *Good Housekeeping* 65 (July 1917): 40–41; Katharine F. Gerould, "The New Simplicity," *Harper's Monthly Magazine* 138 (December 1918): 24; Christine Frederick, "The

Economic Strike of the American Housewife," *Current Opinion* 70 (June 1921): 751.

14. Bernard M. Baruch, "Just What Is War Time Thrift? The Question All Women Are Asking Authoritatively Answered for Them," *Ladies' Home Journal* 35 (September 1918): 29; J. Ogden Armour, "Unless Women Realize the Task That Confronts Them, Hunger and National Defeat Are Ahead of Us," *Ladies' Home Journal* 34 (July 1917): 27; "A National Thrift Day," *Bankers Magazine* 92 (July 1916): 2; "The Coming Campaign for Individual Economy," *Literary Digest* 57 (1 June 1918): 77; William J. Couse, "Thrift," *Bankers Magazine* 94 (May 1917): 559 and 561; Alfred L. Roe, "Bankers and Thrift in the Age of Affluence," *American Quarterly* 17 (Winter 1965): 619-33.

15. G. C. Selden, " 'Hysterical Economizing'; Fallacy of the Idea That Free Spending Promotes General Prosperity," *Investment Weekly* 19 (12 May 1917): 11; Alvin H. Hansen, "Thrift and Labor," American Academy of Political and Social Science, *Annals* 87 (January 1920): 44 and 48-49; David Friday, "Wealth, Income and Savings," American Academy of Political and Social Science, *Annals* 87 (January 1920): 32-43; John J. Arnold, "An Economic By-Product of the World War," *Bankers Magazine* 97 (October 1918): 382-83.

16. Irving Fisher, "Business as Usual vs. Save and Work," *Independent* 96 (5 October 1918): 14; Selden, " 'Hysterical Economizing,' " p. 11.

17. "Menace of Thrift," *Nation* 112 (16 February 1921): 256; Taber, *Business of the Household*, p. 7.

18. For a list of the taxes, see Ernest L. Bogart, *War Costs and Their Financing; A Study of the Financing of the War and the After-War Problems of Debt and Taxation* (New York: D. Appleton and Co., 1921), pp. 479-88.

19. Bernard Baruch, *American Industry in the War: A Report of the War Industries Board* (Washington, D.C.: GPO, 1921), pp. 58 and 64; "Coming Campaign," p. 74; Lewis A. Browne, "Why Is a Luxury?" *Forum* 61 (June 1919): 672.

20. Thorstein Veblen, "Menial Servants During the Period of the War," *Public* 21 (11 May 1918): 595, 596, and 599. David B. Danborn, " 'For the Period of the War': Thorstein Veblen, Wartime Exigency, and Social Change," *Mid-America* 62 (October 1980): 91-104, covers Veblen's writings in this period.

21. Taber, *Business of the Household*, pp. 7-8. For a similar discussion, see S. Agnes Donham, "Your Income, and How to Spend It," *Ladies' Home Journal* 38 (March 1921): 107.

22. Taber, *Business of the Household*, pp. 61, 318, 366, and 369-72.

23. Ibid., p. 63.

24. Lord, "Getting Your Money's Worth," pp. 9–10; Taber, *Business of the Household*, pp. 46–49 and 318; Donham, "Your Income and How to Spend It," p. 107.

25. Albert A. Atwood, "Are We Extravagant?" *Saturday Evening Post* 192 (3 January 1920): 119; Bruce Barton, "What Is a Luxury?" *Woman's Home Companion* 47 (July 1920): 4.

26. Barton, "What Is a Luxury?" p. 4; Atwood, "Are We Extravagant?" p. 16.

27. H. Gregg Lewis and Paul H. Douglas, "Studies in Consumer Expenditure (1901, 1918–19, 1922–24)," in University of Chicago, *Studies in Business Administration* 17 (October 1947): 1–53, analyze the data from this and other studies.

28. U.S., Department of Labor, Bureau of Labor Statistics, *Cost of Living in the United States*, Bulletin of the Bureau of Labor Statistics, no. 357 (Washington, D.C.: GPO, 1924), p. 5. This report contains full summaries of the data from the 1918–19 study. ICPSR is in the process of making the data of some of these individual budgets available in computer readable form.

29. BLS, *Cost of Living in the United States*, pp. 5 and 447–55. For a summary of changes in the American standard of living in the twentieth century, see Stanley Lebergott, *The American Economy: Income, Wealth, and Want* (Princeton: Princeton University Press, 1976), pp. 248–98.

30. The quote is from the schedule, p. 1. For estimates of the percentage of families at different levels, see U.S., National War Labor Board, *Memorandum on the Minimum Wage and Increased Cost of Living in the United States* (Washington, D.C.: GPO, 1918), pp. 10 and 14; BLS, *Cost of Living in the United States*, p. 4. For figures on income distribution, see National Bureau of Economic Research (Wesley C. Mitchell et al.), *Income in the United States: Its Amount and Distribution, 1909–1919* (New York: Harcourt, Brace and Co., 1921), 1: 132–33.

31. BLS, *Cost of Living in the United States*, pp. 447–55.

32. "Cost of Living in the District of Columbia," *Monthly Labor Review* 5 (October 1917): 4–5; (November 1917): 1, 5, and 6; (December 1917): 2.

33. National War Labor Board, *Memorandum*, p. 9; William F. Ogburn, "Measurement of the Cost of Living and Wages," American Academy of Political and Social Science, *Annals* 81 (January 1919): 118. Valerie J. Conner, *The National War Labor Board: Stability, Social Justice, and the Voluntary State in World War I* (Chapel Hill: University of North Carolina Press, 1983), pp. 50–67 and 169–70, describes fights over the definition of a "living wage."

34. Royal Meeker, "What Is the American Standard of Living?" *Monthly Labor Review* 9 (July 1919): 6, 12, and 13.

35. National War Labor Board, *Memorandum*, pp. 11 and 47. For the history of the effort to draw up a minimum comfort budget, see National Industrial Conference Board, *Family Budgets of American Wage-Earners: A Critical Analysis*, Research Report no. 41 (September 1921), pp. 41–49.

36. Margaret L. Stecker, "Family Budgets and Wages," *American Economic Review* 11 (September 1921): 456; National Industrial Conference Board, *Family Budgets*, pp. 48–50.

37. Dorothy W. Douglas, "Family Budgets," *Encyclopaedia of the Social Sciences* (New York: Macmillan Co., 1931), 6:77; "Tentative Quantity-Cost Budget Necessary to Maintain a Family of Five in Washington, D.C.," *Monthly Labor Review* 9 (December 1919): 23.

38. Naomi Aronson, "Social Definitions of Entitlement: Food Needs, 1885–1920," *Media, Culture and Society* 4 (January 1982): 60; Oscar Ornati, *Poverty Amid Affluence* (New York: Twentieth Century Fund, 1966), pp. 12–13.

39. Mary E. McDowell, "Extravagance or Standards?" *Outlook* 123 (10 December 1919): 474.

40. Gerould, "New Simplicity," pp. 17–18.

41. Atwood, "Are We Extravagant?" pp. 16, 116, and 119.

42. U.S., Department of Labor, Bureau of Labor Statistics, "Cost of Living," pp. 85–86.

43. National Industrial Conference Board, *Family Budgets*, p. 41.

44. "The American Standard," *New York Times*, 29 October 1919, p. 12.

45. U.S., Department of Labor, Bureau of Labor Statistics, *Tentative Quantity and Cost Budget Necessary to Maintain a Family of Five in Washington, D.C., at a Level of Health and Decency* (Washington, D.C.: GPO, 1919), p. 6.

46. Ibid., pp. 11, 18–19, 27, and 41–43.

47. Ibid., pp. 7–10.

48. National War Labor Board, *Memorandum*, p. 14; BLS, *Tentative Quantity and Cost Budget*, pp. 10 and 39–44.

49. Peter N. Stearns, *Lives of Labor: Work in a Maturing Industrial Society* (New York: Holmes and Meier Publishers, 1975), pp. 281–94 and 349.

50. Roy Rosenzweig, *Eight Hours for What We Will: Workers and Leisure in an Industrial City, 1870–1920* (Cambridge: Cambridge University Press, 1983), pp. 199–204.

51. BLS, *Cost of Living in the United States*, pp. 449–51.

52. Henry F. May, *The End of American Innocence: A Study of the First Years of Our Own Time, 1912–1917* [1959] (Chicago: Quadrangle Books, 1964), pp. 333–34, 350, and 361; Robert Sklar, *Movie-Made America: A Cultural History of American Movies* (New York: Random House, 1975), p. 90.

Chapter 8

1. Leo Wolman, "Consumption and the Standard of Living," in *Recent Economic Changes in the United States* (New York: McGraw-Hill Book Co., 1929), 1:13–78; Robert S. Lynd, "The People as Consumers," in *Recent Social Trends in the United States* (New York: McGraw-Hill Book Co., 1933), 2:862 and 871; Frank Stricker, "Affluence for Whom?—Another Look at Prosperity and the Working Classes in the 1920s," *Labor History* 24 (Winter 1983): 5–33; Michael A. Bernstein, "A Reassessment of Investment Failure in the Interwar American Economy," *Journal of Economic History* 44 (June 1984): 479–88.

2. Otis Pease, *The Responsibilities of American Advertising: Private Control and Public Influence, 1920–1940* (New Haven: Yale University Press, 1958), p. 41.

3. Garet Garrett, *The American Omen* (New York: E.P. Dutton and Co., 1928), pp. 80 and 84.

4. James W. Prothro, *The Dollar Decade: Ideas in the 1920s* (Baton Rouge: Louisiana State University Press, 1954), pp. 60–66; Earnest E. Calkins, *Business the Civilizer* (Boston: Little, Brown and Co., 1928), pp. 15, 18, and 29; and Paul M. Mazur, *American Prosperity: Its Causes and Consequences* (New York: Viking Press, 1928), pp. 50–52.

5. Samuel Crowther, "Henry Ford: Why I Favor Five Days' Work With Six Days' Pay," *World's Work* 52 (October 1926): 614. For Ford's attempt to enforce moralism, see Roderick Nash, *From These Beginnings . . . A Biographical Approach to American History* (New York: Harper & Row, 1973), 2:151, 168, 173, and 174, and Stephen Meyer, III, *The Five Dollar Day: Labor Management and Social Control in the Ford Motor Company, 1908–1921* (Albany: State University of New York Press, 1981), pp. 123–47.

6. Edward S. Cowdrick, "The New Economic Gospel of Consumption: Revolutionary Changes Brought About by Our Highly Geared Production Machine," *Industrial Management* 74 (October 1927): 209–11.

7. Prothro, *Dollar Decade*, pp. 6–7 and 17.

8. "The Five-Day-Work Week; Can It Become Universal?" *Pocket Bulletin* 27 (October 1926): 5–6.

9. Edward A. Filene, *The Way Out: A Forecast of Coming Changes in American Business and Industry* (Garden City: Doubleday, Page, and Co., 1924), pp. 201–06 and 225; Edward A. Filene, "Mass Production Makes a Better World," *Atlantic Monthly* 143 (May 1929): 629.

10. T. J. Jackson Lears, "From Salvation to Self-Realization: Advertising and the Therapeutic Roots of the Consumer Culture, 1880–1930," in *The Culture of Consumption: Critical Essays in American History, 1880–1980*, ed.

Richard W. Fox and T. J. Jackson Lears (New York: Pantheon Books, 1983), p. 34.

11. Bruce Barton, "What Is a Luxury?" *Woman's Home Companion* 47 (July 1920): 4; Bruce Barton, *It's A Good Old World: Being a Collection of Little Essays on Various Subjects of Human Interest* (New York: Century Co., 1920), pp. 129, 131, 132, and 153–56; Bruce Barton, *On the Up and Up* (Indianapolis: Bobbs-Merrill Co., 1929), pp. 38–39.

12. The best sources of biographical information are Henry R. Hatfield, "Jessica Blanche Peixotto," in *Essays in Social Economics in Honor of Jessica Blanche Peixotto*, ed. Ewald T. Grether et al. (Berkeley: University of California Press, 1935), pp. 5–14, and Clarke A. Chambers, "Jessica Blance Peixotto," *Notable American Women 1607–1950: A Biographical Dictionary* (Cambridge: Harvard University Press, 1971), 3:42–43.

13. Jessica B. Peixotto, quoted in U.S., National War Labor Board, *Memorandum on the Minimum Wage and Increased Cost of Living* (Washington, D.C.: GPO, 1918), pp. 47–48.

14. Jessica B. Peixotto, "How Workers Spend a Living Wage: A Study of the Incomes and Expenditures of Eighty-two Typographers' Families in San Francisco," in *University of California Publications in Economics* (Berkeley: University of California Press, 1929), 5:163, 169, and 173. For distribution of income figures, see Maurice Leven, Harold G. Moulton, and Clark Warburton, *America's Capacity to Consume* (Washington, D.C.: Brookings Institution, 1934), p. 205.

15. Peixotto, "How Workers Spend," pp. 182, 183, 188, 194, 195, 196, and 198.

16. Ibid., pp. 199–203 and 205.

17. Jessica B. Peixotto, *Getting and Spending at the Professional Standard of Living: A Study of the Costs of Living an Academic Life* (New York: Macmillan Co., 1927), pp. 37–43. The quote from the report of the faculty wives is in ibid., p. 43.

18. Ibid., pp. 62, 78, and 105.

19. Ibid., pp. 122, 123, 126, 177, and 178; Peixotto, "How Workers Spend," pp. 183 and 185.

20. Peixotto, *Getting and Spending*, pp. 127–28, 187n, 201, 225, and 278.

21. Ibid., pp. 143, 190, 263, and 280.

22. Ibid., pp. 5, 38, 41, 196, 228–29, and 280–81.

23. Ibid., pp. 10–11, 15–16, 32–33, and 43–45; Jessica B. Peixotto, "Family Budgets of University Faculty Members," *Science* n.s. 68 (23 November 1928): 496.

24. Peixotto, *Getting and Spending*, pp. 5–6 and 36.

25. Ibid., pp. 13–15.

26. Jessica B. Peixotto et al., "Quantity and Cost Estimate of the Standard of Living of the Professional Class," in *University of California Publications in Economics* (Berkeley: University of California Press, 1928), 5:iii, 133–34, and 153–55.

27. She made such references in other writings on the same subject: Peixotto, "Family Budgets," p. 496; Jessica B. Peixotto, "Campus Standards of Living," *Survey* 62 (15 April 1929): 119.

28. Peixotto, *Getting and Spending*, pp. 32, 36, 120, and 264.

29. "How the American Middle Class Live: By One of Them," *Scribner's Magazine* 86 (December 1929): 696; Helen H. Lamale, "Changes in Concepts of Income Adequacy Over the Last Century," *American Economic Review* 48 (May 1958): 296; Morris E. Leeds and C. Canby Balderston, *Wages: A Means of Testing Their Adequacy* (Philadelphia: University of Pennsylvania Press, 1931), pp. 8 and 10; John E. Hollitz, "The Challenge of Abundance: Reactions to the Development of a Consumer Economy, 1890–1920" (Ph.D. dissertation, University of Wisconsin-Madison, 1981).

30. Peixotto, "Family Budgets," p. 501.

31. Jessica Peixotto, Foreword to Jessica B. Peixotto and Otto A. Jeschien, *The Home Budget: Formerly 'The Economizer'; An Efficient Household Account Book That Does Not Require Any Tedious Bookkeeping* [1915], 15th ed. (Berkeley: Economizer Publishing Co., 1927).

32. *Cost of Living Survey*, Report to the California State Civil Service Committee Relative to the Cost of Living in California for Selected Family Groups (Sacramento: California State Printing Office, 1923), p. 19.

33. One of the best sources on this middle range of households is Christine Frederick, "New Wealth, New Standards of Living, and Changed Family Budgets," American Academy of Political and Social Science, *Annals* 115 (September 1924): 74–82.

34. Among the other important students of consumption who expressed similiar ideas are Warren C. Waite, *Economics of Consumption* (New York: McGraw-Hill Book Co., 1928); Hazel Kyrk, *A Theory of Consumption* (Boston: Houghton Mifflin Co., 1923); Elizabeth E. Hoyt, *The Consumption of Wealth* (New York: Macmillan Co., 1928).

35. Peixotto, *Getting and Spending*, p. 31.

36. Robert S. Lynd and Helen M. Lynd, *Middletown: A Study in American Culture* (New York: Harcourt, Brace and World, 1929). Richard W. Fox, "Epitaph for Middletown: Robert S. Lynd and the Analysis of Consumer Culture," in *Culture of Consumption*, ed. Fox and Lears, is the best point of entry to considerable scholarship on the Lynds.

37. Lynds, *Middletown*, pp. 12, 17, 39, 71, 80, 226, 245, and 471.

38. Ibid., 39, 47, 80, 226, and 260. Theodore Caplow, "The Changing

Middletown Family," *Journal of the History of Sociology* 2 (Fall–Winter 1979–80): 68, notes the parallel analysis of traditional societies and Muncie as communities influenced by outside forces.

39. Lynds, *Middletown*, pp. 225, 312, and 479.

40. Ibid., pp. 21, 52, 73, 80, 82–83, 87, and 225.

41. Ibid., pp. 82n and 84.

42. Ibid., pp. 222, 294, 370, 496–500, and 502.

43. TB [Trevor Bowen], "*Small City Study*: Minutes of Conference held March 19 [1926], on Chapters I–IX of the manuscript submitted by Mr. Lynd," Robert S. Lynd and Helen M. Lynd Papers, Manuscript Division, Library of Congress, Washington, D.C.; Galen M. Fisher to Robert S. Lynd, 30 November 1926, Lynd Papers; "General Comments By S. Went on Section I of Small City Study," 5 May 1927, Lynd Papers; Trevor Bowen, "Notes on First Section, Chapters I to IX, of Lynd's Manuscript," 6 May 1927, Lynd Papers; C. Luther Fry, "Notes on the Lynd Manuscript," 6 May 1927, Lynd Papers.

44. Lynds, *Middletown*, pp. vi, 3–4, and 6.

45. John Frederick Lewis, Jr., review of *Middletown*, source unknown [1929], Lynd Papers; H. L. Mencken, "A City in Moronia," *American Mercury*, 16 (March 1929): 379–81.

46. Comments of Clark Wissler and Arthur L. Swift in "Conference on Mr. Lynd's Manuscript on The Study of a Small Industrial City at Town Hall Club, November 16, 1926," Lynd Papers.

47. For a candid discussion of the problem of objectivity, see Robert S. Lynd, "Prob. of Being Objective in Studying Our Own Culture," manuscript of speech given at Princeton University, 9 December 1938, Lynd Papers.

48. Fox, "Epitaph," p. 107.

49. For evaluations of the Lynds' methods, see Theodore Caplow, "Middletown Fifty Years After," *Contemporary Sociology* 9 (January 1980): 46–48; Richard Jensen, "The Lynds Revisited," *Indiana Magazine of History* 75 (December 1979): 303–08; Fox, "Epitaph," pp. 120–21.

50. On Veblen's importance to Lynd, see Robert S. Lynd to Lewis Corey, 24 November 1950, Lynd Papers; Staughton Lynd, "Robert S. Lynd: The Elk Basin Experience," *Journal of the History of Sociology* 2 (Fall–Winter 1979–80): 14; Fox, "Epitaph," p. 120.

51. Unidentified seven-page essay on *Middletown*, Lynd Papers; R. Clyde White, review of *Middletown*, in Indianapolis *News*, 16 February 1929, p. 12.

52. Winifred D. Wandersee, *Women's Work and Family Values, 1920–1940* (Cambridge: Harvard University Press, 1981), p. 41; Jensen "The Lynds Revisited," pp. 309–10; Joseph Interrante, "The Road to Autopia: The

Automobile and the Spatial Transformation of American Culture," *Michigan Quarterly Review* 19–20 (Fall 1980–Winter 1981): 502–17.

53. Lynds, *Middletown*, pp. 22–24.

54. "Conference on Mr. Lynd's Manuscript . . . November 16, 1926"; Galen M. Fisher to Leon C. Marshall, 19 June 1926, Raymond B. Fosdick files on the ISSR, Rockefeller Archive Center, North Tarrytown, N.Y.; "General Comments by S. Went on Section I of Small City Study," 5 May 1927; Fry, in "Notes"; Bowen, in "Notes"; Faith Williams to Robert S. Lynd, 20 May 1926, Lynd Papers. For his retrospective treatment of the lack of attention to the middle class, see Lynd, "Prob. of Being Objective," pp. 16–17. Irving L. Horowitz, "Robert S. and Helen Merrell Lynd," *International Encyclopedia of the Social Sciences* (New York: Free Press, 1979), 18:472, states that the Lynds were offering an analysis of the middle class.

55. Stuart Chase, "A Very Private Utopia," *Nation* 126 (16 May 1928): 561. For treatments of Chase, see Robert B. Westbrook, "Tribune of the Technostructure: The Popular Economics of Stuart Chase," *American Quarterly* 32 (Fall 1980): 387–408, and R. Alan Lawson, *The Failure of Independent Liberalism, 1930–1941* (New York: Capricorn Books, 1971), pp. 75–84, 87, 226–33, and 267–70. For the works on which I have drawn for these observations, see Margaret and Stuart Chase, *A Honeymoon Experiment* (Boston: Houghton Mifflin Co., 1916), pp. 6–8; Stuart Chase, "My Great-Great-Grandfather and I," *Nation* 123 (1 September 1926): 190–92; Stuart Chase, "Wasting Women," *Survey* 57 (1 December 1926): 268–70; Stuart Chase and F. J. Schlink, *Your Money's Worth: A Study in the Waste of the Consumer's Dollar* (New York: Macmillan Co., 1927), pp. 258–64; Stuart Chase, *The Tragedy of Waste* (New York: Macmillan Co., 1927); Stuart Chase, "Utopia," pp. 559–62; Stuart Chase, "Confessions of a Sun-Worshiper," 128 *Nation* (26 June 1929): 762–65; and Stuart Chase, "Are You Alive?" *Recreation* 22 (May 1928): 68–69. For Chase's contribution to ideas behind Consumers Union, see Norman D. Katz, "Consumers Union: The Movement and the Magazine, 1936–1957" (Ph.D. dissertation, Rutgers University, 1977), pp. 22–24.

56. Waldo Frank, *The Re-Discovery of America: An Introduction to a Philosophy of American Life* (New York: Charles Scribner's Sons, 1929), pp. 107–15; Sinclair Lewis, *Main Street* [1920] (New York: New American Library, 1980); Sinclair Lewis, *Babbitt* [1922] (New York: Harcourt, Brace and Co., 1950); Matthew Josephson, "Mass Civilization and the Individual," *Outlook and Independent* 152 (5 June 1929): 206, 227, and 240; David E. Shi, *Matthew Josephson: Bourgeois Bohemian* (New Haven: Yale University Press, 1981), pp. 118–19; Thomas L. Hartshorne, *The Distorted Image: Changing Conceptions of the American Character Since Turner* (Cleveland: Press of Case

Western Reserve University, 1968), pp. 80–98; Frederick J. Hoffman, "Philistine and Puritan in the 1920s: An Example of the Misuse of the American Past," *American Quarterly* 1 (Fall 1949): 251–54.

57. Laurence Veysey, "A Postmortem on Daniel Bell's Postindustrialism," *American Quarterly* 34 (Spring 1982): 67–68, points out some important continuities between the 1920s and 1930s.

58. Wandersee, *Women's Work*, p. 37.

59. Faith M. Williams, "Changes in Family Expenditures in the Post-War Period," *Monthly Labor Review* 47 (November 1938): 973 and 977.

60. A. F. Hinrichs, Preface to Faith M. Williams and Alice C. Hanson, "Money Disbursements of Wage Earners and Clerical Workers, 1934–36: Summary Volume," U.S., Department of Labor, Bureau of Labor Statistics, *Bulletin*, no. 638 (Washington, D.C.: GPO, 1941), pp. vii–viii; Williams and Hanson, "Money Disbursements," p. 15.

61. Williams and Hanson, "Money Disbursements," pp. 2, 117, 132, and 150.

62. Carle C. Zimmerman, *Consumption and Standards of Living* (New York: D. Van Nostrand Co., 1936), pp. 8, 567, 571, and 577; Carle C. Zimmerman and Merle E. Frampton, *Family and Society: A Study of the Sociology of Reconstruction* (New York: D. Van Nostrand Co., 1935), p. 275. For other evidence of the persistence of traditional patterns and attitudes in the 1930s, see George A. Lundberg, Mirra Komarovsky, and Mary A. McInerny, *Leisure: A Suburban Study* (New York: Columbia University Press, 1934), pp. 123 and 189; Robert S. McElvaine, Introduction, in *Down and Out in the Great Depression: Letters from the "Forgotten Man,"* ed. Robert S. McElvaine (Chapel Hill: University of North Carolina Press, 1983), pp. 15–16.

63. Zimmerman, *Consumption and Standards*, pp. 285, 286, 288, 299, 303, 567, and 575.

64. Margaret L. Stecker, "Intercity Differences in Costs of Living in March 1935, 59 Cities," Works Progress Administration, Division of Social Research, *Research Monograph* no. 12 (Washington, D.C.: GPO, 1937), p. xiii.

65. Ibid., pp. xii–xiv.

66. Ibid., pp. xiv, xvii, and 84.

67. U.S., Department of Labor, Bureau of Labor Statistics, *Tentative Quantity and Cost Budget Necessary to Maintain a Family of Five in Washington, D.C., at a Level of Health and Decency* (Washington, D.C.: GPO, 1919), p. 24; Stecker, "Intercity Differences," p. 83.

68. Stuart Chase, Foreword to Harold Loeb et al., *The Chart of Plenty: A Study of America's Product Capacity Based on the Findings of the National*

Survey of Potential Product Capacity (New York: Viking Press, 1935), p. xiv. Those involved with the study also used a figure of $2500 per year per family as the goal; however, they did not provide a detailed breakdown of the budget components: Mordecai Ezekiel, *$2500 a Year: From Scarcity to Abundance* (New York: Harcourt, Brace and Co., 1936), pp. 120–21.

69. Harold Loeb, Conclusion in *Report of the National Survey of Potential Product Capacity* (New York: New York City Housing Authority, 1935), p. 247; Chase, Foreword, p. xv.

70. Loeb, Conclusion, pp. 246–47; Harold Loeb, "Recreation," in *Report*, pp. 183 and 188; Loeb et al., *Chart of Plenty*, p. 154; Ezekiel, *$2500 a Year*, p. 132.

71. Stuart Chase, review of *Middletown*, in *Nation* 128 (6 February 1929): 164.

72. Stuart Chase, *Mexico: A Study of Two Americas* (New York: Macmillan Co., 1931), pp. 326–27.

73. The quote is from Stuart Chase, "Address," *Consensus* 19 (January 1935): 26. My summary of Chase's position in the 1930s draws on Stuart Chase, "Declaration of Independence," *Harper's* 164 (December 1931): 27–36; Stuart Chase, *—Move the Goods!* (New York: John Day Co., 1934), p. 18; Stuart Chase, *The Economy of Abundance* (New York: Macmillan Co., 1934).

74. Alfred M. Bingham, *Man's Estate; Adventures in Economic Discovery* (New York: W.W. Norton and Co., 1939), pp. 19, 23–24, 27, and 86; Char Miller, *Fathers and Sons: The Bingham Family and the American Mission* (Philadelphia: Temple University Press, 1982), pp. 167–71; Alfred M. Bingham to his parents, 17 April 1927, Alfred Bingham Papers, Yale University Library; Alfred M. Bingham, "Tabloid Civilization," Bingham Papers. For discussions of Bingham, see Miller, *Fathers and Sons*, pp. 159–210; Donald L. Miller, *The New American Radicalism: Alfred M. Bingham and Non-Marxian Insurgency in the New Deal Era* (Port Washington: Kennikat, 1979), especially pp. 7–8, 13, 42–43, 109, and 172; Richard H. Pells, *Radical Visions and American Dreams: Culture and Social Thought in the Depression Years* (New York: Harper & Row, 1973), pp. 74–76 and 94–95; Lawson, *Failure of Independent Liberalism*, pp. 92–93 and 237–41.

75. Alfred M. Bingham, *Insurgent America; Revolt of the Middle-Classes* (New York: Harper and Brothers, 1935), pp. 86–87 and 192; Alfred M. Bingham, "Looking Forward: I. Introduction," *Common Sense* 1 (30 March 1933): 3–5; Alfred M. Bingham, "Looking Forward: VI. Life, Liberty and the Pursuit of Happiness," *Common Sense* 1 (8 June 1933): 14–15.

76. Robert S. Lynd and Helen M. Lynd, *Middletown in Transition: A Study in Cultural Conflicts* (New York: Harcourt, Brace and Co., 1937), p. 203.

77. Ibid., pp. 293–94.

78. Ibid., p. 46.

79. R. S. Lynd, "People as Consumers," pp. 866–67; Robert S. Lynd, "Family Members as Consumers," American Academy of Political and Social Science, Annals 160 (March 1932): 89; Robert S. Lynd, "The Consumers' Advisory Board in the N.R.A.," Publishers' Weekly 125 (28 April 1934): 1607–1608; Robert S. Lynd, Knowledge for What? The Place of Social Science in American Culture (Princeton: Princeton University Press, 1939), pp. 234–35. The two most important treatments of the work of Robert S. Lynd in the 1930s are Fox, "Epitaph," pp. 129–41, and Mark C. Smith, "Robert Lynd and Consumerism in the 1930's," Journal of the History of Sociology 2 (Fall–Winter 1979–80): 99–120.

80. On most points the Lynds' experiences and beliefs confirmed this more general vision. On his assumption of the existence of a natural folk with sharply limited material needs and his preference for the genuineness of the working class before consumer culture tainted it, see Fox, "Epitaph," pp. 109–10; Lynds, Middletown, pp. 12, 39, 76–77, 80, 87, and 226; Robert S. Lynd, "Crude-Oil Religion," Harper's Magazine 145 (September 1922): 431–32; Robert S. Lynd, "Done in Oil," Survey 49 (1 November 1922): 140. On how people seek compensation in consumption and commercial leisure, see Fox, "Epitaph," p. 110; Lynds, Middletown, p. 80. For nonpecuniary, spontaneous activity, see Fox, "Epitaph," p. 124; Lynd, "Done in Oil," p. 146; Lynd, Knowledge for What?, pp. 192–97. For the importance of spiritual as opposed to material values, see Robert S. Lynd, " '—But Why Preach?' " Harper's Monthly Magazine 143 (June 1921): 83 and 85; Horowitz, "Robert S. and Helen Merrell Lynd," p. 474. On the Lynds' "puritanism," see Fox, "Epitaph," p. 106; [Robert S. Lynd], "Miscellaneous items about Robert S. Lynd," memorandum dated 9 March 1954, Lynd Papers; Helen M. Lynd, Possibilities (Youngstown, Ohio: Inkwell Press, 1978), pp. 16, 20, and 32–33. On criticism of the middle-class culture with which he grew up, see Lynd, "Prob. of Being Objective," p. 7. For a later and fuller analysis of consumer society, see Robert S. Lynd, "Princeton Political Science Students Talk," manuscript of speech, [1958], Lynd Papers.

81. This summary relies on Henry F. May, The End of American Innocence: A Study of the First Years of Our Own Time, 1912–1917 [1959] (Chicago: Quadrangle Books, 1964), pp. 333–34, 340, 350, and 361; Robert Sklar, Introduction, in The Plastic Age (1917–1930), ed. Robert Sklar (New York: George Braziller, 1970), pp. 1–8 and 16–24; Christopher Lasch, The New Radicalism in America: [1889–1963]: The Intellectual as a Social Type (New York: Alfred A. Knopf, 1965), pp. x, xiii, and xv; James Hoopes, Van Wyck Brooks: In Search of American Culture (Amherst: University of Massachusetts Press, 1977), pp. xii–xiii, 57, 60, 64, 78, and 119; Van Wyck Brooks, "Our

Awakeners," *Seven Arts* 2 (June 1917): 235–48; Van Wyck Brooks, "The Culture of Industrialism," *Seven Arts* 1 (April 1917): 655–66; Randolph Bourne, "The Heart of the People," *New Republic* 3 (3 July 1915): 233; Randolph Bourne, "The Handicapped" [1911], in *The Radical Will: Randolph Bourne, 1911–1918*, ed. Olaf Hansen (New York: Urizen Books, 1977), pp. 73, 79, 83, and 84; "Youth" [1912], in *Radical Will*, pp. 93 and 96; "The Experimental Life" [1913], in *Radical Will*, pp. 149 and 157; "This Older Generation" [1915], in *Radical Will*, pp. 159–60; Randolph Bourne, "The History of a Literary Radical" [1919], in *War and the Intellectuals: Essays by Randolph S. Bourne, 1915–1919*, ed. Carl Resek (New York: Harper & Row, 1964), pp. 188–89; "Twilight of the Idols" [1917], in *War and the Intellectuals*, p. 59; Randolph Bourne, "Trans-National America" [1916], in *War and the Intellectuals*, pp. 113–14.

82. For the way World War I fostered concerns about mass society and standardization, see David M. Kennedy, *Over Here: The First World War and American Society* (New York: Oxford University Press, 1980), pp. 47, 92, and 113–14.

83. Herbert J. Gans, *The Levittowners: Ways of Life and Politics in a New Suburban Community* (New York: Alfred A. Knopf, 1967), p. vi. Though it is difficult to discover much about Peixotto's life, it is possible she too fits many aspects of these patterns. For her description of the academic notion of the ideal standard of living, see *Getting and Spending*, pp. 5–6.

84. Sheila K. Bennett and Glen H. Elder, Jr., "Women's Work in the Family Economy: A Study of Depression Hardship in Women's Lives," *Journal of Family History* 4 (Summer 1979): 153.

85. Lewis Mumford, *Technics and Civilization* [1934] (New York: Harcourt, Brace and World, 1963), pp. 429 and 432; Lewis Mumford, *Faith for Living* (New York: Harcourt, Brace and Co., 1940), pp. 212, 215, 217, 280, 282, 286, 290, and 313–17. For another example of the hope that the war would purify America of materialism, see May, *End of American Innocence*, p. 365.

Epilogue

1. Richard W. Fox, "Epitaph for Middletown: Robert S. Lynd and the Analysis of Consumer Culture," in *The Culture of Consumption: Critical Essays in American History, 1880–1980*, ed. Richard W. Fox and T. J. Jackson Lears (New York: Pantheon Books, 1983), p. 129, says *Middletown* was like a "secular jeremiad" that listed the evidence of backsliding and called "for conversion to a new, nonpecuniary culture."

2. Henry Nash Smith, *Virgin Land: The American West as Symbol and Myth* [1950] (Cambridge: Harvard University Press, 1970), p. 187.

3. Patrick Brantlinger, *Bread and Circuses: Theories of Mass Culture as Social Decay* (Ithaca: Cornell University Press, 1983), explores some of these continuities.

4. Richard Hoggart, *The Uses of Literacy; Aspects of Working-Class Life with Special Reference to Publications and Entertainments* (London: Chatto and Windus, 1957); Herbert J. Gans, *The Urban Villagers: Group and Class in the Life of Italian-Americans* [1962] (New York: Free Press, 1965), pp. 193–96; Herbert J. Gans, *The Levittowners: Ways of Life and Politics in a New Suburban Community* (New York: Alfred A. Knopf, 1967), pp. 185–96 and 417–20; Herbert J. Gans, *Popular Culture and High Culture; An Analysis and Evaluation of Taste* (New York: Basic Books, 1974); Lee Rainwater, *What Money Buys: Inequality and the Social Meanings of Income* (New York: Basic Books, 1974); James Agee, *Let Us Now Praise Famous Men* (Boston: Houghton Mifflin, 1941), pp. 159–73; Kai T. Erikson, *Everything in Its Path: Destruction of Community in the Buffalo Creek Flood* (New York: Simon and Schuster, 1976), pp. 174–77.

5. James J. Flink, *The Car Culture* (Cambridge: MIT Press, 1975), p. 18.

6. Marshall Sahlins, *Culture and Practical Reason* (Chicago: University of Chicago Press, 1976); Mary Douglas and Baron Isherwood, *The World of Goods* (New York: Basic Books, 1979).

7. David K. Shipler, "Russians Covet Western Affluence but Are Wary of Its Political Setup," *New York Times*, 14 June 1979, p. 1.

8. John Kenneth Galbraith, *The Affluent Society* (Boston: Houghton Mifflin Co., 1958), p. 140. For an important critique of Galbraith's position, see Michael Schudson, "Criticizing the Critics of Advertising: Toward a Sociological View of Marketing," *Media, Culture and Society* 3 (January 1981): 3–12.

9. David Riesman, *The Lonely Crowd: A Study of Changing American Character* (New Haven: Yale University Press, 1950).

10. Herbert Marcuse, *Eros and Civilization: A Philosophical Inquiry into Freud* [1955] (New York: Vintage Books, 1962); Philip E. Slater, *The Pursuit of Loneliness: American Culture at the Breaking Point* (Boston: Beacon, 1970).

11. John Tirman, "Austerity as a Guide," *New York Times*, 9 November 1980, sec. E, p. 19; Roger D. Masters, "Why a Depression Might be Good for Us All," *New York Times*, 31 August 1979, p. A 23.

12. Two other important post-1973 books are Fred Hirsch, *Social Limits to Growth* (Cambridge: Harvard University Press, 1976), and William Leiss, *The Limits to Satisfaction: An Essay on the Problem of Needs and Commodities* (Toronto: University of Toronto Press, 1976).

13. Daniel Yankelovich, *New Rules: Searching for Self-Fulfillment in a World Turned Upside Down* (New York: Random House, 1981). For criticism of *New Rules*, see Christopher Lasch's review in *New York Review of Books*, 3 December 1981, pp. 22–24.

14. See three books by Albert O. Hirschman: *Exit, Voice, and Loyalty: Responses to Decline in Firms, Organizations, and States* (Cambridge: Harvard University Press, 1970); *The Passions and the Interests: Political Arguments for Capitalism before Its Triumph* (Princeton: Princeton University Press, 1977); and *Shifting Involvements: Private Interest and Public Action* (Princeton: Princeton University Press, 1982).

Appendix B

1. BLS, schedules for Fall River, Massachusetts, Industrial and Social Branch, Civil Archives Division, National Archives, Washington, D.C.

2. #8, #17, #24, #25, #39, #84, #119, #120, #125, #149, and #154. The numbers refer to handwritten figures in the upper right-hand corner of the individual manuscript documents.

3. #8 and #120.

4. Those starting families are #84 and 119; the others were #8, #17, #25, #39, #125, #149, and #154.

5. #39.

6. National Bureau of Economic Research (Wesley C. Mitchell et al.), *Income in the United States: Its Amount and Distribution, 1909–1919* (New York: Harcourt, Brace and Co., 1921), 1:132.

7. #133.

8. #75.

9. #124.

10. #109.

11. #14.

12. #57.

13. #87.

14. #8.

15. #33. This family did spend $34.00 for a vacation, $24.96 for telephone, $7.28 for tobacco, and nothing for liquor.

16. The high attending families are #50, #83, #85, #99, and #154. The very high attenders are #25, #39, #95, #111, and #149.

17. These high-income, low attending families are #16, #17, #19, #57, and #125.

18. The manuscripts include the names of family members. Using that information, I have not been able to detect clear ethnic differences.

19. Mirra Komarovsky, *Blue-Collar Marriage* (New York: Random House, 1964) is a classic study of the orientation of working-class life around home and relatives.

20. Massachusetts, Bureau of Statistics of Labor, *Twelfth Annual Report* (Boston: Rand, Avery, and Co., 1881), pp. 449–53.

21. George E. Bevans, *How Workingmen Spend Their Spare Time* (New York: n.p., 1913), pp. 19–21 and 66.

Index

Numbers in italics refer to tables

Index

Bell, Daniel: *The Cultural Contradictions of Capitalism*, xvii, 170
Bellamy, Edward, 30, 32
Benevolence. *See* Charity; Organizations: contributions to; Philanthropy; Religion: contributions to
Bevans, George E.: *How Workingmen Spend Their Spare Time*, 58, 182
Biases and assumptions of budget studies. *See* Budget studies, analysis, and methodology of
Bingham, Alfred M., xxxi, 135, 158, 159–60, 164
BLS. *See* Bureau of Labor Statistics
Books, as budget item. *See* Education and reading materials
Bosworth, Louise M.: *The Living Wage of Women Workers*, 65–66
Bruère, Martha B. and Robert, xxx, 87–99
—Allison family (case study), 91–93, 92
—and Chapin, contrasted, 103–4, 104
—*Increasing Home Efficiency*, 87, 93
—Parnell family (case study), 89–91, 91
—and Progressive investigators, 102–3
—and Richards, contrasted, 87, 88, 98, 100–102, 102
—Wells family (case study), 89, 90
Bryan, William Jennings, 78
Budgets. *See also names of specific budget items*
—balanced, 56
—compared: 1875–1981, 174–75;1907–19, 128, 129; of Bruères and Chapin, 103–4, 104; of Bruères and Richards, 102; of Chapin and *Ladies' Home Journal*, 104–5, 105
—middle class: 1912, 90–92; 1913, 105; 1915, 111; 1916–17, 113; 1922, 142; 1927, 145; 1935, 158
—standardization of, 37, 76
—of workers: 1875, 15; 1918–19, 178; 1921, 139; 1935, 156–57
Budget studies, analysis and methodology of, xix–xxi, xxix–xxx

—assumptions and biases of, xix–xx, 131, 173; of Bruères, 103–4; of MBSL, 16–17, 18–19, 22–29; of Peixotto, 142–44; of Progressives, 58–66
—conservative moralism as framework for, 16–17, 18, 29, 50, 155–56
—critical and censorious aspect of: early 20th century, 131; in MBSL survey (1875), 13, 15–16, 17–19; Progressive, 50, 51, 60–66; reduction of (20th century), xxxi, 29, 50, 66, 131, 140, 146, 156, 169
—ethnicity in. *See* Ethnicity
—methodological problems of, 23–24, 57–58, 121
—value of, 169–70
Budget studies, individual
—of BLS: *Family Expenditures . . . 1935–36*, 153–54; survey (1918–19), 120–23, 177, 178, 179–82; *Tentative Quantity and Cost Budget* (1919), 127–32
—Bruères', 87–104
—Chapin survey (1909), 51–58
—MBSL survey (1875), 13–29; compared with later studies, 121, 131–32, 156
—National Survey of Potential Product Capacity (1935), 157–58, 158
—NWLB (1918), 123–24, 125, 128–29
—Peixotto's: 1917, 138; 1921, 138–40, 139; 1922, 141–44, 142, 1927, 144–45, 145
—Zimmerman's, 154–55
Bureau of Labor Statistics (BLS) (U.S.)
—*Family Expenditures in Selected Cities, 1935–36*, 153–54
—household budget survey (1918–1919), 120–23, 177, 178, 179–82
—on standard of living (1919), 125
—*Tentative Quantity and Cost Budget . . .* (1919), 127–32
Burial Expenses, 53, 55, 129
Bushnell, Horace, 5
Byington, Margaret F., 64, 99–100

Individualism. *See also* Conformity
—*vs.* communal life (Zimmerman),
154–55
—Gunton on, 44, 46
Indulgence. *See* Self-indulgence
Inflation (early 20th century), xxx, 67–68
—impact of, on middle class, 68, 71–73,
75, 76, 80, 85, 86, 99, 109–10, 119–20;
and sympathy for workers, 98–100
—undermines family, 69–70
Installment buying, 148, 162
Insurance
—life, 15, 87, 121
—for middle class, 87, 95, 96, 97, 142
—for workers, 53, 129, 130
Intemperance. *See* Alcohol
Isherwood, Baron, 171

Jacobs, Joseph, 100
Johnson, Alvin S., 100
Jones, Alice H., xxiv
Josephson, Matthew, 153
Journalism. *See* Magazines
Judgment and criticism of spending
patterns
—early 20th century, 131
—in MBSL survey (1875), 13, 15–16,
17–19
—Patten's, 32–33
—Progressive, 50, 51, 60–66
—reduction of (20th century), xxxi, 29,
50, 66, 131, 140, 146, 156, 169
—Thoreau's, 3–4
—Wayland's, 1–2

Kyrk, Hazel, 147

Laborers. *See* Workers and working
class
Labor statistics, bureaus of. *See also*
Bureau of Labor Statistics; Massachusetts Bureau of Statistics of Labor
—decreasing bias of, 29

—federal, 120
—impersonal data emphasized by, 50
—reluctance of, to study rich, 28
Ladies' Home Journal, family budget in
(1913), 104–5, *105*
Landon, Helen, 87
Lasch, Christopher: *The Culture of
Narcissism,* xvii, 170
Laughlin, J. Laurence, 74
Leisure. *See also* Organizations; Play;
Recreation; Street life; Vacation
—commercial, xxii–xxiii, xxvii; Lynds
on, 148; middle class and, 106–7, 142,
144; Patten on, 35; Progressives on,
62–63; workers and, 122, 129, 130–31. *See also* Amusement parks; Movies; Saloons
—communal. *See* Communal forms of
leisure
—and work, 136, 154; as inseparable,
xxii; as separate, 33, 34–36, 46, 69,
132
—of working class and immigrants. *See*
Workers and working class: leisure
activities of
—and workweek, reduction of, xxvi,
136
Leisure class. *See* Wealthy
Lewis, John Frederick, Jr., 150
Lewis, Sinclair, 152–53
Life insurance, 15, 87, 121
Liquor. *See* Alcohol
Living standards. *See* Standard of living
Lodgers, income from, 52, 56
Loeb, Harold, 157–58
Lord, Isabel E., 118
Luxuries. *See also* Comfort(s); Self-indulgence
—changing definition of, xxiv
—Chase opposes, 112, 113
—Filene on, 137
—Gerould on, 126
—for middle class, 78
—*vs.* necessities, 116, 136, 139–40, 154
—for skilled workers, 20

Index

Index